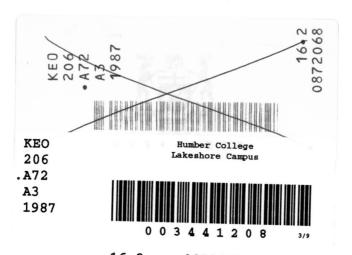
You've Got a Friend

A Review of Advocacy in Ontario

162926867

Report of the Review of Advocacy for Vulnerable Adults

1987

Published by the Ontario Ministry
of the Attorney General

© Queen's Printer for Ontario, 1987

ISBN O-7729-2854-1

Additional copies of this and other Ontario Government
Publications are available from:

The Ontario Government Bookstore, 880 Bay Street, Toronto, Ontario
for personal shopping. Out-of-town customers write to: Publications
Services Section, 5th floor, 880 Bay Street, Toronto, Ontario, M7A
1N8. Telephone (416) 965-6015 or toll free in Ontario
1-800-268-7540. In area code 807, dial 0-Zenith 67200. Hearing
impaired call: (416) 965-5130 or toll free in Ontario, 1-800-268-7095.
Master Card and Visa accepted. Cheques and money orders payable to
the Treasurer of Ontario. Prepayment required.

Rev.
Sean O'Sullivan, C.M., LL.D.
Chairman

Brian P. Bellmore, LL.M.
Counsel

Abbé
Sean O'Sullivan, C.M., LL.D.
Président

Brian P. Bellmore, LL.M.
Avocat

Review of Advocacy
for Vulnerable Adults

Examen des mesures d'intervention
en faveur des adultes vulnérables

180 Dundas Street West
22nd Floor
Toronto, Ontario
M5G 1Z8

180, rue Dundas ouest
22e étage
Toronto (Ontario)
M5G 1Z8

416/965-6335

August 1, 1987

Dear Mr. Attorney:

I am pleased to submit to you the Report of the Review of
Advocacy for Vulnerable Adults.

Yours sincerely,

Chairman

The Hon. Ian G. Scott, MPP
Attorney General
18 King Street East
Toronto, Ontario
M5C 1C5

TABLE OF CONTENTS

Foreword...(i)

Text Notes..(v)

Glossary ....(vi)

Executive Summary 1

Sommaire 15

Chapter 1   **Introduction and Background to the   Review of
             Advocacy**   32

             1. Introduction 32
             2 Background 33
                 (a) Impetus for the Review......................33
                 (b) Terms of Reference...........................34
                 (c) Time   Frame...................................35
                 (d) Process 36
                     (i)   Consultation 36
                     (ii) Advisory Committee 37
                     (iii) Visits to Institutions 37
                     (iv) Evaluation of the Psychiatric Patient Advocate
                           Program 37
                     (v)   Principles of Advocacy Prepared by the
                           Advisory Committee on Substitute Decision
                           Making for Mentally Incapable Persons 38

Chapter 2   **What is Advocacy?**   39

             1. Introduction 39
             2. The Concept of Advocacy 40
                 (a) Legal and Social Advocacy Distringuished 40
                 (b) Individual and Systemic Advocacy 42
                 (c) Informal and Formal Advocacy 43
             3. Basic Principles of Advocacy 43
                 (a) Advocacy must be Client Directed 44
                 (b) Advocacy should be Independent 45
                 (c) Advocacy should be Accessible 45
                 (d) Advocacy : Neither Adversarial nor Passive 46
             4. Objectives of Advocacy 47
             5. Advocacy and Case Management/Service Co-ordination .. 48

1. Introduction..52
2. Is there a Need?...52
   (a) The Number of Vulnerable Adults........................52
      (i)   Physically Disabled Persons......................53
      (ii)   Frail Elderly Persons................................ 53
      (iii) Psychiatrically Disabled Persons.................54
      (iv) Developmentally Handicapped....................55
   (b) The Concept of Vulnerability..............................55
   (c) Existing Advocacy Programs and Services and
       their Drawbacks..58
      (i)   Formal Advocacy Programs.......................58
          a. Psychiatric Patient Advocate Office
              (PPAO).. 58
          b. Office of Child and Family Service
              Advocacy....................................... 60
          c. Advocacy Centre for the Elderly (ACE).... 62
          d. Advocacy Resource Centre for the
              Handicapped (ARCH)......................... 63
      (ii)   Formal Programs with an Advocacy
          Component.. 64
          a. Adult Protective Services Program.......... 64
          b. Tri-Ministry Service Co-ordinators.......... 65
      (iii) Informal Advocacy..................................66
          a. Volunteer Advocacy Services.................66
             1. Self-help Groups........................ 67
             2. Voluntary Associations formed
                by Relatives, Friends and Concerned
                Citizens..................................... 68
                Citizen Advocacy..........................69
             3. Volunteer Associations that provide
                Services.....................................70
             4. Coalitions..................................72
          b. Advocacy of Others.......................... 72
      (iv) Shortcomings of Existing Advocacy Services... 73
          a. Gaps in the System............................73
          b. Conflict of Interest.............................76
          c. Other Shortcomings...........................78
   (d) The Need for Advocates in the Proposed Substitute
      Decisions Authority Act......................................80
      (i)   Background.. 80
      (ii)   Role of the Advocate.............................81
          a. Application to Appoint Conservators and
              Guardians...................................... 81
          b. Termination of Conservatorship or
              Guardianship..................................81
          c. Order for Assessment and its Enforcement..82
          d. Assessment of Capacity for Personal
              Power of Attorney............................82
          e. Annual Visit....................................83
3. Conclusions... 83

Chapter 4   **Options for the Delivery of Advocacy Services in Ontario**   **85**

1. The Ombudsman Model.. 86
   (a) Introduction.. 86
   (b) Massachusetts Ombudsman Program.................... 88
2. The Citizen Advocacy Model................................. 93
   (a) Introduction.. 93
   (b) The Georgia Advocacy Office........................... 95
3. The Advocacy Ontario Model................................. 99
4. The Mixed Advocacy Model................................. 102
   (a) Introduction.. 102
   (b) Informal Advocacy.. 103
   (c) Internal Advocacy... 103
   (d) Independent Advocacy.................................... 103
5. The Shared Advocacy Model................................ 104
   (a) Introduction.. 104
   (b) The Advocacy Commission............................. 107
   (c) Commission Staff... 108
   (d) Regional Offices and Community-Based Boards of
       Directors.. 110
   (e) Regional Advocacy Co-ordinators..................... 113
   (f) Volunteers.. 115
   (g) Local Programs.. 117

Chapter 5   **Recommendations**   **121**

1. Introduction... 121
2. Advantages and Shortcomings of the Ombudsman
   Model... 122
   (a) Advantages.. 122
   (b) Shortcomings.. 123
3. Advantages and Shortcomings of the Citizen Advocacy
   Model... 124
   (a) Advantages.. 124
   (b) Shortcomings.. 124
4. Advantages and Shortcomings of the Advocacy Ontario
   Model... 125
   (a) Advantages.. 125
   (b) Shortcomings.. 125
5. Advantages and Shortcomings of the Mixed Advocacy
   Model... 126
   (a) Advantages.. 126
   (b) Shortcomings.. 126
6. Advantages and Shortcomings of the Shared Advocacy
   Model... 127
   (a) Advantages.. 127
   (b) Shortcomings.. 128

7. Recommendations..128
    (a) The Recommended Model - "Shared Advocacy"......128
    (b) Accountability of the Shared Advocacy Model.........130
        (i)   Attorney General....................................131
        (ii)   Standing Committee of the Ombudsman........132
    (c) Funding the Shared Advocacy Program.................133
    (d) Federal-Provincial Cost Sharing.........................134
    (e) Implementation of the Shared Advocacy Program--
        The Need for Legislation...............................135
    (f) Need for Clear Standards and Procedures to be Set by
        Advocacy Commission....................................137
    (g) Problems Associated with Instruction-Based
        Advocacy...138
    (h) Who Will Be Advocates?................................140
    (i) Data Collection and Analysis...........................141
    (j) Legal Component...142
    (k) Research Component....................................142
    (l) Public Education and Outreach.........................143
    (m) Trusteeship...143
    (n) Regional Board of Directors............................144
    (o) Psychiatric Patient Advocate Office.....................145
    (p) Case Managers/Service Co-ordinators and
        Advocacy...147
    (q) Legislative Protection of Vulnerable Adults............149
    (r) Cost of the Shared Advocacy Program.................153

Closing...156

Endnotes...159

Appendices...161

Bibliography..231

FOREWORD

The reader of this report will find large parts written in the first person plural. This reflects the fact that while this has been an *independent* Review of Advocacy, it has not been an *individual* one.

While no claim is made to speak for others, it is my hope that this report accurately reflects what any objective individual might conclude and recommend on the basis of the information provided. The Review got underway in January and that first month was given to the myriad of administrative details that accompany such studies. During the ensuing months I was greatly assisted by Counsel Brian Bellmore and co-Counsel Ann Merritt who rearranged their busy schedules to collaborate in this project, and who persevered with tremendous dedication, wisdom and commitment. For them this Review became a cause rather than another case -- and it is that personal dimension for which I am most grateful.

The advisory committees were deliberately kept to a minimum to let them flourish as working committees. This they did, in helping evaluate the over 1,450 pages of written submissions as well as offering their individual recommendations and points of view.

It was not easy to choose from among many qualified nominees for these volunteer committees, but anyone who observed our several meetings would have seen that a wide spectrum of views was represented -- and forcefully expressed. I am greatly indebted to all Committee members for giving so generously of their time, valuable insights and sound advice.

Since the committees were advisory, I do not represent the views of this report as being theirs. In some cases, I know quite the opposite. However, I have tried to adjudicate fairly, concurrent with everyone's wish for a more just and caring society.

Along the way we were also helped by the painstaking research so ably conducted by Robin Cox and Susan Milder. It is to their great credit, and that of their respective Ministers -- the Hon. John Sweeney and the Hon. Murray Elston -- that they were freed from other responsibilities to work with this Review with independence and such enthusiasm.

Similarly, I wish to express my appreciation to Cardinal Carter for permission to undertake this Review, and to the staff of *The Catholic Register,* especially Mr. James Meldrum, whose extra efforts allowed me the time and flexibility to do so.

We all had a lot of learning to do; people to see; and territory to cover within a comparatively short period of time. This was made possible by the day-to-day efforts and back-up of a dedicated office staff -- notably Inge Sardy (administrative officer), staff assistants Paul Podesta and Brian O'Hearn, and our secretaries, Norma Lumsden and Linda McClenaghan. Mr. Roland d'Abadie from the Ministry of the Attorney General graciously steered us through the sometimes bewildering requirements commonly called bureaucracy.

Numerous others made a personal contribution to this Review. I am indebted to those who met with us (Appendix 5) and those who prepared written submissions (Appendix 4). These submissions, together with the Review's working papers, will be transferred to the Library of Brock University and provide a wealth of information. I also wish to particularly acknowledge the assistance of Dr. Fred Jervis and Janis Williams of the Center for Constructive Change; Professor Allan Manson, Mary Beth Valentine and Dr. Ty Turner with respect to the Psychiatric Patient Advocate Office and Review; and those officials who opened so many doors and generally assisted this Review: Sue Crawford (Premier's Office); Douglas Ewart and Patrick Monahan (Ministry of the Attorney General); David Corder and Liz Stirling (Ministry of Health); Wayne Davies (Ministry of Community and Social Services); Greg Walker (Senior Citizens' Affairs); Carla Rubio (Office Responsible for Disabled Persons).

It has been a true privilege to be associated with such an important undertaking. Here I confidently speak for all my colleagues and associates in this Review of Advocacy...

So, foremost, *we* would like to thank the vulnerable adults of Ontario, their families and friends, for sharing so much of themselves with us. Their hopes and fears, joys and disappointments, their views on advocacy, its potential and limits -- all these have been at the heart of this Review. May this report be worthy of them.

If any citizen were asked to oversee the design of a new airplane to serve Ontario he or she would certainly call in the experts -- the engineers, scientists and suppliers. But a really good design would also ask for input from those who would work on the plane (the pilots and flight crew) and those passengers for whom the plane was being built.

When all that consultation had taken place, the designer would have lots of ideas for the ideal Ontario airplane: some good ideas, and others that just wouldn't "fly."

But most of all, he/she would conclude at the starting point: we all want the best possible model... because we're all part of the same journey, heading for the same destination.

With thanks to the countless people who brought this lesson home, it's time to move on to a model of advocacy for all Ontario.

S.O'S.

Toronto
August 1, 1987

CONSUMERS ADVISORY COMMITTEE

Mrs. Anne Coy
Toronto

Ms. Patricia Spindel
Toronto

Dr. Dorothea Crittenden
Toronto

Ms. Pat Woode
Georgetown

Ms. Carla McKague
Toronto

Mr. Patrick Worth
Toronto

Ms. Ivy St. Lawrence
Toronto

MINISTERIAL ADVISORY COMMITTEE

Ms. Arna Banack
Office Responsible for Disabled Persons

Mr. Alan McLaughlin
Senior Citizens Affairs

Mr. Stephen Fram
Ministry of the Attorney General

Mr. John Wilson
Community and Social
   Services

Ms. Debi Mauro
Ministry of Health

Mr. Michael Irvine
Ministry of Correctional
   Services

PROVIDERS ADVISORY COMMITTEE

Mr. David Baker
Toronto

Mr. David Mitchell
Pembroke

Ms. Lea Caragata
Toronto

Ms. Judith A. Wahl
Toronto

Dr. W. B. Dalziel
Ottawa

Ms. Kay Wigle
London

Mr. Stephen Lurie
Toronto

TEXT NOTES

- Try as we might, we have inevitably had to employ some of the terms or "labels" that we came to find objectionable in themselves. Thus, the use of such terms as "handicapped" and "disabled", which are used interchangeably in the Report, is not intended to classify any individuals or groups. We yearn for the day when people will simply be regarded as such, without any labelling or stigmatization.

- A printed report is not the most suitable means of communication for a number of individuals who have the most interest in advocacy services. Accordingly, a summary of this report's findings and recommendations is being prepared in alternate forms:

  -- on audio cassette, as a community service of Brock University, St. Catharines, with particular thanks to Dr. W. A. Matheson, Vice-President, and to Marc Giacomelli, on behalf of Creative Interchange/Sound Interchange, Toronto.

  -- on videotape, as a community service of Vickers & Benson Advertising Ltd., Toronto, with particular thanks to Mr. Terrence J. O'Malley, President and Executive Creative Director, and Rawi, Schulz & Company Inc.

GLOSSARY

Adult Protective Service Worker (APSW): a service co-ordinator employed by
an agency to co-ordinate services for developmentally handicapped people living in the
community. The APSW program, which is funded by the Ministry of Community and
Social Services, has as its aim to help developmentally handicapped people live as
independently as possible.

**Advisory Committee on Substitute Decision Making for Mentally
Incapable Persons (Fram Committee):** committee established in 1985 by the
Ministries of Health, Community and Social Services and the Attorney General, under
the chairmanship of Steven Fram, to review all aspects of the law governing and related
to substitute decision making for mentally incapable persons, including personal
guardianship and conservatorship, and to make recommendations concerning the
revision of this law where appropriate.

Advocacy : activity which involves taking up the cause of an individual or group of
individuals and speaking on their behalf to ensure that their rights are respected and their
needs are met.

Case management/service co-ordination: a process or method for ensuring that
consumers are provided with whatever services they need in a co-ordinated, effective
and efficient manner.   Basic functions of case management/service co-ordination include
assessment of client need, development of a comprehensive service plan, arranging for
services to be delivered, monitoring and assessing the services delivered and evaluation
and follow-up. Additional functions may include outreach, direct service provision and
advocacy.

Citizen advocacy: an advocacy approach in which citizen volunteers form one-to-one
ongoing relationships with vulnerable individuals and provide those individuals with
help and friendship.

Conservatorship: a legal process whereby a person is lawfully invested with the
power and charged with the duty to make property decisions on behalf of and for the
benefit of an individual who is mentally incapable of managing property, subject to
statutory restrictions or a court order.

Consumers: a term used in this Review to mean people who receive social and health
services.

Developmental handicap: means a condition of mental impairment present or
occurring during a person's formulative years, that is associated with limitations in
adaptive behaviour.

External advocacy: advocacy that is administratively and fiscally independent of the
human service delivery system.

Formal advocacy: refers to advocacy programs that are organized with special goals, leadership, membership and some type of financial support.

Guardianship: a legal process whereby a person is lawfully invested with the power and charged with the duty to make some or all personal care decisions on behalf of and for the benefit of an individual who is mentally incapable of caring for him or herself subject to statutory restrictions or a court order.

Home for the aged: a home established under the Ministry of Community and Social Services' *Homes for the Aged and Rest Homes Act* or *Charitable Institutions Act* to provide supportive care to elderly persons who can no longer live independently.

Home for Special Care: means a home for the care of persons requiring nursing, residential or sheltered care.

Individual advocacy: refers to advocacy on behalf of a particular individual, as opposed to a group, and assisting that person in realizing his or her wishes.

Informal advocacy: refers to the type of advocacy that occurs on a voluntary and relatively unstructured basis. For example, by a family member or friend.

Internal advocacy: advocacy that is not administratively and fiscally independent of the human service delivery system.

Nursing home: a home established under the Ministry of Health's *Nursing Homes Act* to provide regular nursing care to persons who cannot receive the care they need in their own homes and whose condition does not warrant intensive hospital care.

Power of attorney: legal authority under which someone is empowered to act for another in business or legal matters.

Providers: a term used in this Review to mean the individuals or organizations who directly provide social and health services.

Psychiatric Patient Advocate Office (PPAO): a program established in 1981 by the Ministry of Health, whereby advocates are located in each of the province's 10 psychiatric hospitals to advise patients and staff of patients' rights and to act on the instructions of patients to resolve concerns, queries and complaints.

Psychiatric Patient Advocate Office Evaluation Committee (the Manson Committee): a committee established in 1986 under the chairmanship of Professor Allan Manson, to evaluate the Psychiatric Patient Advocate Office and to make recommendations in regard to the future of the program.

Service co-ordination: see case management/service co-ordination.

Social/Non-legal advocacy: activity which involves speaking or pleading on behalf of another by using non-legalistic measures.

Systemic advocacy: advocacy which influences social and political systems to bring about changes in laws, rules, regulations, policies and practices for the benefit of groups of people.

Tri-ministry Service Co-ordinator: a service co-ordinator employed by a nursing home, residential home for special care, or an agency to assess the needs of developmentally handicapped children and adults in those institutions and to co-ordinate services and activities that will allow them to develop to their fullest potential.

Vulnerable adults: a term used in this Review to include the following groups of adults: frail elderly; physically handicapped; psychiatrically disabled; and developmentally handicapped.

Executive Summary

1. Introduction and Background to the Review

Ontario needs advocacy.

More particularly, we as Ontarians need to be advocates.

Most of us already are. We can do more.

If we are to improve our society, we must.

Primary responsibility for advocacy must remain with us as individual citizens, as families, as friends and as neighbours of Ontario's vulnerable population.

Primary responsibility for advocacy education, and the development and support of advocacy services is the proper role of government.

Therefore, this Review of Advocacy, having considered Ontario's needs and options, recommends a Shared Advocacy Model for this Province.

While recognizing the need for equally dedicated, professionally trained, and suitably paid advocates, this Review has concluded that the heart and soul of advocacy services will depend upon caring volunteers.

(a) Impetus

- the Attorney General of Ontario announced the initiation of a Review of Advocacy for Vulnerable Adults in Ontario to address "an unmet need for non-legal advocacy for vulnerable adults living in institutional care settings and in the community."

- the impetus for the Review came largely from the many organizations and agencies that represent and assist vulnerable adults, which have repeatedly and strongly expressed the need for better non-legal advocacy services in Ontario.

- the general issue of advocacy was inititally referred for consideration to the Advisory Committee on Substitute Decision Making for Mentally Incapable Persons, which had been established in 1985 by the Ministries of Health, Community and Social Services and the Attorney General, to review the current guardianship and conservatorship legislation in this Province.

- as the Substitute Decision Making Committee could not reach a consensus on the appropriate mandate and form of advocacy services, it was decided to refer this issue to an independent review.

(b) Terms of Reference

- the general Terms of Reference for the Review are as follows:

    1. To consider the need for advocacy for adults in institutional care settings as well as those adults that may require such services and are living in the community.

    2. To analyze thoroughly the concept of advocacy in relation to disadvantaged adult populations in Ontario, e.g. frail elderly, physically handicapped, psychiatrically disabled, developmentally handicapped.

    3. To develop options concerning the establishment of advocacy services, including organizational structure and accountability for each option.

    4. The consideration of need will include a detailed review relating to the co-ordination of advocacy with:

        a) existing case management and other delivery systems; and

        b) existing legal and volunteer advocacy services.

(c) Process

- in attempting to meet the Terms of Reference, the Review engaged in extensive consultation which included over 185 written submissions; informal and formal meetings; visits to representative institutions and consideration of existing advocacy programs.

2. The Concept of Advocacy

- for the purpose of the Review, "advocacy" means "non-legal" or "social" advocacy, as opposed to "legal" advocacy.

- "social" advocacy entails speaking or pleading on behalf of others with vigour, vehemence and commitment by using non-legalistic resources: a social advocate, unlike a legal advocate, does not directly invoke or participate in the legal process to obtain the desired result.

- in the context of this Review, advocacy entails speaking on behalf of "vulnerable adults" who are living in institutional care settings, as well as in the community.

- social advocacy includes advocacy on both an individual and systemic basis, and may be either formal or informal.

- social advocacy includes the following four basic principles:

    -- advocacy must be client directed or "instruction based";

    -- advocacy must be administratively and fiscally independent of the human service delivery system;

    -- advocacy must be accessible;

    -- advocacy is not necessarily adversarial.

- the following objectives of social advocacy, as identified by the Advisory Committee on Substitute Decision Making for Mentally Incapable Persons, are endorsed by the Review:

  -- to promote respect for the rights, freedoms and dignity of the persons advocates serve, both individually and collectively;

  -- to ensure that their clients' legal and human rights are recognized and protected;

  -- to assist their clients to receive the health care and social services to which they are entitled and which they wish to receive;

  -- to enhance the autonomy of their clients by advocating on their behalf, both individually and collectively;

  -- to assist their clients to lead lives that are as independent as possible, and in the least restrictive environment possible;

  -- to help protect disadvantaged persons from financial, physical and psychological abuse;

  -- to fully explain the implications of and provide advice with respect to guardianship and conservatorship under the *Substitute Decisions Authority Act* (or the current legislation it is intended to replace).

3. Major Findings

- The evidence presented to the Review identified a clear need for a co-ordinated and effective advocacy system in Ontario.

- Statistics indicate that there are potentially 1 million or more vulnerable adults, as defined by the Terms of Reference, living in Ontario at the present time who could have need of advocacy. So long as individuals advocate for themselves and caring family, friends and volunteers do so on behalf of others, the actual needs for supplementary advocacy services will be significantly less.

- The concept of "vulnerability" can create a need for advocacy as the vulnerable are often dependent on others which can leave them susceptible to abuse, neglect or abandonment.

- Institutionalization creates vulnerability by eroding a patient/resident's rights to self-determination and independence.

- Ontario has a mixture of fragmented advocacy services which are only available to a limited number of vulnerable adults. These services are provided largely by internal advocates employed by service providers, families and volunteer groups. In the case of internal advocates there is the perception that they are limited by conflicts of interest which may undermine the confidence of the vulnerable adults in the service.

- The present system lacks a clear mandate to provide advocacy services as there are no uniform standards of service or training programs for advocates and those who advocate are hampered by the lack of a clear right of access to care facilities, clients and clients' records.

- The gaps in the present system produce inequities and discrimination. Vulnerable adults in some care facilities receive advocacy services from dedicated volunteers and others may receive quality advocacy if they are fortunate to be assigned care providers who are committed to advocating on behalf of their clients. Regrettably, the majority of our vulnerable adults and particularly those residing in smaller communities do not have access to any advocacy programs.

- Other shortcomings of a number of current advocacy services include: underfunding; lack of resources; excessive workloads; lack of direction and support of advocates; lack of supervision of advocates; and limited accountability.

- There are alarming numbers of vulnerable adults who have been abandoned by family and friends in long-term care facilities and in the community.

- Over 5,000 developmentally handicapped persons reside in provincial institutions. Most have lived in institutional settings their entire lives and do not have access to an advocacy program. In contrast, psychiatric patients who reside in psychiatric institutions for an average of two months at a stay are provided with the services of a full-time staff advocate and rights advisor in each institution. Similarly, residents of nursing homes and homes for the aged and the physically handicapped have no access to effective advocacy services other than those that may be provided on an *ad hoc* basis by volunteer organizations.

- The lack of co-ordinated advocacy services accessible to all vulnerable adults requiring assistance is a profound injustice.

MAJOR RECOMMENDATIONS

- After reviewing a multitude of internal and external advocacy programs five options are evaluated in this Report, viz:

  (1) Advocacy Ombudsman;

  (2) Citizen Advocacy;

  (3) Advocacy Ontario;

  (4) Mixed Advocacy Model;

  (5) Shared Advocacy.

- Each of these programs has its individual strengths and weaknesses which are evaluated utilizing the following criteria and goals of an ideal advocacy system developed jointly by the Review's three Advisory Committees:

1. Safeguards against unnecessary guardianship;

2. Independent (from Ministries affected, funding sources, providers);

3. Encourages self-advocacy where possible (self-sufficiency, self-determination);

4. Enhances role of families and volunteers;

5. Educates (families, volunteers, community) - delabels, destigmatizes, identifies gaps in services,and promotes awareness that advocacy is everybody's business;

6. Flexible (special needs, geographic requirements, multilingual);

7. Responsive (personal concern, carries forward complaints, endeavours to resolve them);

8. Promotes co-operation with Providers and Ministries;

9. Accessible;

10. Seeks improvements in programs (reformative);

11. Has clout;

12. Accountable.

- Measuring the five models against these criteria, **the Review recommends the Shared Advocacy Model** as the most appropriate and effective method of delivering advocacy services to Ontario's vulnerable adults.

Shared Advocacy Model

- this model is based upon a sharing of responsibility for the delivery of advocacy services among government, volunteers and community groups.

- it is an evolutionary/slow growth model which draws upon the successful experience of the Ontario Legal Aid Clinic Funding Program by encouraging community groups to develop advocacy service programs to meet the particular needs of their community and to apply for funding these programs.

- implementation of Shared Advocacy will occur over a period of two to three years. The first step is the establishment of a provincial Advocacy Commission with a clear mandate to provide non-legal advocacy services to vulnerable adults residing in all institutions and care facilities and in the community.

- responsibility for the provincial program is vested in an independent Advocacy Commission which is to be appointed by the Lieutenant Governor-in-Council.

- the Commission will report to the Legislature through the Attorney General or a redesignated Standing Committee on the Ombudsman and Advocacy.

- legislation should be developed which also contains clear statutory authority for trained and certified advocates to have access to institutions and care facilities where vulnerable adults reside, and, in the case of those living in the community, the right to meet in private.

- the legislation should also provide authority for certified advocates to have access, with the consent of the patient, to the patient's medical and treatment records.

- the Commission would maintain a small central office with staff experienced in the following areas: training and education; the needs and concerns of frail elderly, developmentally disabled, psychiatrically disabled and physically handicapped persons; and relevant legal issues.

- direct advocacy services would be provided through regional offices covering the province and through local advocacy programs.

Advocacy Commission

- Commission members should be citizens with a demonstrated commitment to the interests of the vulnerable and should not be employed by a service provider, ministry or agency.

- the Commission through its central office staff would have overall responsibility for the advocacy system in the province, including:

  -- developing policies and standard practices and procedures for the regional offices and the local programs;

  -- funding and terminating funding of regional offices and local programs;

  -- providing expertise and support to the regional offices and local programs;

  -- establishing training and certification programs to be given to all advocacy co-ordinators, volunteers and advocates in local programs through the regional offices;

  -- monitoring the regional offices and local programs;

  -- conducting education and awareness conferences for vulnerable adults, their families, volunteers, providers and the general public and aggressively publicizing advocacy services through a variety of media and its own public education/awareness campaign;

  -- establishing a province-wide reporting system to collect and analyze data concerning complaints, problems and responses for the purpose of identifying and promoting the resolution of systemic issues;

  -- providing information to service providers and government regarding the problems of vulnerable adults and the needs for legislative or internal changes to the service delivery system;

  -- promoting the interests of the vulnerable through education and representation.

Regional Offices

- individual advocacy will be delivered through seven regional offices located throughout the province whose mandate is to provide vulnerable adults with advocacy services within 24 hours of a request for assistance. Regional advocacy co-ordinators will also engage in outreach programs through volunteers and local community groups to ensure the needs of the vulnerable in the region are met.

- the mandate of each regional office is to provide vulnerable adults with non-legal advocacy services within twenty-four hours of a request for assistance and to engage in an aggressive outreach program through volunteers and local community groups to meet the needs of the vulnerable adults in the region.

- each regional office is to be operated and managed by a community-elected Board of Directors accountable to the Commission for the provision of advocacy services in the region. The majority of these community-based Boards is to consist of consumer representatives.

- the regional Board of Directors would carry out its responsibilities through a regional office comprised of three full-time staff advocacy co-ordinators: one co-ordinator responsible for vulnerable adults residing in the community, and one co-ordinator responsible for vulnerable adults residing in institutions; with a Regional Director responsible for overseeing the regional office and assisting the other co-ordinators.

- the advocacy co-ordinator's responsibilities will include:

  -- implementing advocacy services by vigorously making known in the community the needs for and potential of advocacy services on behalf of vulnerable adults;

  -- implementing and maintaining advocacy services for vulnerable adults residing in institutions and communities within the region;

  -- safeguarding vulnerable adults from inappropriate guardianship by advocating on behalf of any individual who is the subject of guardianship related preceedings under the contemplated substitute decision making legislation;

  -- assisting local groups to develop programs for the provision of advocacy services in the area and to assist them to apply to the Commission for funding;

  -- recruiting and training volunteers in sufficient numbers to serve as advocates to the vulnerable adults residing in care facilities and private residences within the region where no local programs are serving these individuals;

  -- ensuring that advocates visit all care facilities designated for vulnerable adults within the region on a regular basis;

-- providing support and assistance to volunteer advocates when required in resolving problems or complaints;

-- receiving, investigating and resolving complaints or problems which volunteer advocates or advocates in local programs are unable to resolve themselves;

-- ensuring that all advocates comply with the applicable procedures and policies of the Advocacy Commission;

-- stimulating local groups to establish citizen advocacy programs in their communities based upon the principles and practices of Citizen Advocacy as established in consultation with the Advocacy Commission;

-- maintaining records of complaints and problems received, actions taken, findings, responses and recommendations;

-- filing quarterly reports with the Commission regarding the activities of the regional office and local programs

Local Programs

• the needs of the vulnerable adults throughout our province vary substantially due to such factors as the nature of the disability, their residence (at home or in a care facility), the size and location of the community, and the resources, both volunteer and professional, available in that locale.

• it is imperative that the Shared Advocacy Model be flexible and adaptable in order to respond to the particular needs and resources of each community. Regional advocacy co-ordinators will assist communities to define their particular needs, devise appropriate programs and apply for necessary funding of the programs to the Regional Board of Directors and to the Advocacy Commission.

• all applications for funding local programs should contain a description not only of the group of vulnerable adults to be served but also the groups which will not be served by the proposed program and to provide justification for this. If the applicants are unable to justify the omission, funding would be denied. In this way, the Regional Board would be reminded that there are groups who are not being served by the local programs and the Board will ensure that these groups are not forgotten in subsequent applications for funding.

Volunteer Advocates

- where no local programs exist to meet the needs of the vulnerable, the advocacy co-ordinators in the regional office will be responsible for advocacy services until such time as a local program has evolved.

- in order for the advocacy co-ordinators to provide these services within a 24 hour period, it will be necessary for the co-ordinators to recruit and train a small corps of volunteers throughout the region.

- the volunteers will receive training and certification according to standards developed by the central office and their responsibilities will include:

  -- visiting vulnerable adults in care facilities and in the community on a regular basis;

  -- receiving and investigating problems or complaints of vulnerable adults and working to resolve them through consultation and negotiation;

  -- reporting problems, complaints and actions taken to the regional office.

Additional Recommendations

- it is recommended that the program be funded by the provincial government through an annual funding application process.

- after reviewing the annual budget requests of each of the 7 Regional Boards, the Commission would determine the appropriate level of funding to recommend to government.

- the Commission's request for funding should be submitted together with an annual report to the Standing Committee on the Ombudsman or the Attorney General. If the former route is chosen, that Committee should be re-structured and re-designated the Standing Committee on the Ombudsman and Advocacy.

Psychiatric Patient Advocate Office

- the existing advocacy program being provided to residents of provincial psychiatric institutions, through the Psychiatric Patient Advocate Program, should be integrated into the Shared Advocacy Model as a mutual strengthening of both programs.

- in the interests of specialized advocacy services for psychiatric patients, the Psychiatric Patient Advocate Co-ordinator should be appointed to the staff of the central office and assigned responsibility for the provision of advocacy services to psychiatric patients in institutions and in the community, and the psychiatric patient advocates should continue to report to and be supervised by their co-ordinator.

Case Managers/Service Co-ordinators and Advocacy

- advocacy should be distinguished from case management/service co-ordination. While advocacy is often an important component of service co-ordination, the converse is not necessarily so: true advocacy does not include a service co-ordination function.

- thus, case managers/service co-ordinators should not be included in an independent provincial advocacy program.

- however, it is also recommended that advocacy should continue to be an important component of the service co-ordinator's functions within the limits of that individual's position with the service provider. In the event that the service co-ordinator's advocacy efforts reach the point where they are compromised by his or her position, he or she should refer the matter to the Advocacy Commission.

Legislative Protection of Vulnerable Adults

- it is recommended that Ontario enact protective legislation for vulnerable adults requiring any person having knowledge of the abuse or neglect of a vulnerable adult to inform the appropriate authorities.

- it is further recommended that where there is reasonable proof that there has been abuse or neglect, and the vulnerable adult has by reason of choice or otherwise remained in the residence where the neglect or abuse occurred, an advocate be assigned by the regional office to develop a relationship with the vulnerable adult which would provide an ongoing monitoring of the situation and facilitate the reporting of subsequent abuse should it occur.

Cost of the Shared Advocacy Program

- because of the evolutionary nature of the proposed Shared Advocacy Model, contemplating slow growth of the program over a period of several years, it is impossible to project a specific cost.

- whatever those projected costs, government must consider the implementation of advocacy services in the light of what it will cost, in human terms, if nothing is done to address the pressing needs of Ontario's vulnerable adults for advocacy services.

- there is nothing in this Report that cannot be implemented if there is the political will to do so.

Sommaire

1. Introduction et renseignements généraux sur l'examen

L'intervention est nécessaire en Ontario.

Plus particulièrement, nous devons, comme Ontariens et Ontariennes, être des intervenants.

Nous le sommes déjà, pour la plupart. Mais nous pouvons faire davantage.

Nous le devons, si nous voulons améliorer notre société.

C'est principalement à nous qu'il incombe d'intervenir, comme citoyens, comme familles, comme amis et comme voisins de la population vulnérable de l'Ontario.

C'est principalement au gouvernement qu'il incombe de faire l'éducation à l'intervention et d'assurer la création et le soutien de services d'intervention.

Le Groupe d'examen des mesures d'intervention en faveur des adultes vulnérables recommande donc, après avoir examiné les besoins de l'Ontario et les solutions possibles, un modèle d'intervention partagée pour la province.

Tout en reconnaissant la nécessité d'avoir des intervenants totalement engagés, professionnellement formés et suffisamment rémunérés, le groupe d'examen a conclu que les services d'intervention vont dépendre essentiellement du travail de bénévoles.

a) Impulsion

- Le Procureur général de l'Ontario a annoncé un examen des mesures d'intervention en faveur des adultes vulnérables de l'Ontario en vue de répondre à un besoin non satisfait de services d'intervention non juridiques pour les adultes vulnérables qui vivent dans des établissements ou les collectivités.

- L'impulsion à l'examen a été donnée en grande partie
par les nombreux organismes qui représentent et aident
les adultes vulnérables, et qui ont exprimé à maintes
reprises et avec force la nécessité d'avoir de
meilleurs services d'intervention non juridiques en
Ontario.

- La question générale de l'intervention a d'abord été
soumise au Comité consultatif sur la substitution de la
prise de décision pour les personnes ne jouissant pas
de toutes leurs facultés mentales; ce comité avait été
constitué en 1985 par le ministère de la Santé, le
ministère des Services sociaux et communautaires et le
Procureur général en vue d'examiner la législation
actuelle de l'Ontario en matière de tutelle.

- Les membres du comité n'ayant pu s'entendre sur le
mandat et la forme des services d'intervention, on a
décidé de renvoyer la question à un groupe d'examen
indépendant.

b) **Mandat**

- Le mandat du groupe était le suivant :

   1. Examiner la nécessité d'avoir des services
   d'intervention pour les adultes qui résident
   dans des établissements ainsi que pour les
   adultes qui vivent dans les collectivités et
   qui peuvent avoir besoin de tels services.

   2. Analyser à fond la notion d'intervention par
   rapport aux adultes défavorisés de l'Ontario
   (personnes âgées de santé délicate, handicapés
   physiques, malades mentaux, déficients mentaux,
   etc.).

   3. Trouver des solutions possibles concernant
   l'établissement de services d'intervention, en
   précisant dans chaque cas la structure
   organisationnelle et l'imputabilité.

4. Procéder à une étude approfondie de la coordination des services d'intervention avec

    a) les systèmes actuels de gestion des dossiers et autres systèmes de prestation, et

    b) les services d'intervention juridiques et volontaires qui existent actuellement.

c)   Processus

. Afin de s'acquitter de son mandat, le groupe d'examen a mené des consultations approfondies, qui ont comporté plus de 185 mémoires; a tenu des rencontres formelles et informelles; a visité des établissements représentatifs; et a étudié les programmes d'intervention existants.

2.   Notion d'intervention

. Aux fins de l'examen, on entend par "intervention" une intervention "non juridique" ou "sociale", par opposition à l'intervention "juridique".

. L'intervention "sociale" consiste à parler ou à intercéder avec force et détermination au nom d'autres personnes en utilisant des ressources non juridiques; contrairement à un intervenant juridique, un intervenant social ne recourt pas directement à la procédure judiciaire pour obtenir le résultat désiré.

. Dans le cadre de l'examen, l'intervention consiste à parler au nom d'adultes vulnérables, qui vivent dans des établissements ou les collectivités.

. L'intervention sociale peut s'exercer sur le plan individuel ou collectif et elle peut être formelle ou informelle.

. L'intervention sociale s'appuie sur les quatre principes
suivants :

- l'intervention doit être axée sur le client ou
  fondée sur l'éducation;

- l'intervention doit être, sur les plans
  administratif et financier, indépendante du
  système de prestation des services aux
  personnes;

- l'intervention doit être accessible;

- l'intervention n'est pas nécessairement
  hostile.

. Le groupe d'examen appuie les objectifs suivants de
l'intervention sociale, qui ont été identifiés par le Comité
consultatif sur la substitution de la prise de décision pour
les personnes qui ne jouissent pas de toutes leurs facultés
mentales :

- promouvoir le respect des droits, des libertés
  et de la dignité des personnes que les
  intervenants desservent, sur les plans
  individuel et collectif;

- faire en sorte que les droits reconnus par la
  loi et les droits de la personne sont protégés;

- aider les clients à recevoir les services
  médicaux et sociaux auxquels ils ont droit et
  qu'ils désirent obtenir;

- accroître l'autonomie des clients, en
  intervenant en leur nom, sur les plans
  individuel et collectif;

- aider les clients à vivre de façon aussi
  indépendante que possible et dans un milieu qui
  est le moins restrictif possible;

- aider à protéger les personnes défavorisées
  contre les abus financiers, physiques et
  psychologiques;

- expliquer à fond les répercussions de la
  Substitute Decisions Authority Act (ou la loi

qu'elle doit remplacer) en ce qui concerne la
tutelle et donner des conseils à ce sujet.

3. **Principales constatations**

D'après les faits dont a été saisi le groupe d'examen,
l'Ontario a nettement besoin d'un système d'intervention
coordonné et efficace.

Selon les statistiques, il existe peut-être un million ou
plus d'adultes vulnérables, au sens où l'entend le mandat,
qui vivent actuellement en Ontario et qui pourraient avoir
besoin de services d'intervention. Tant que les personnes
se défendront elles-mêmes et que les familles, les amis et
les bénévoles le feront au nom d'autres personnes, les
besoins réels en services d'intervention supplémentaires
seront sensiblement moins grands.

La notion de "vulnérabilité" peut créer le besoin de mesures
d'intervention, car les personnes vulnérables sont souvent
dépendantes d'autres personnes, ce qui peut les exposer à
l'abus, à la négligence ou à l'abandon.

L'institutionnalisation crée la vulnérabilité en minant les
droits d'un patient-résident à l'autonomie et à
l'indépendance.

L'Ontario compte un assortiment de services d'intervention
fragmentés qui ne sont offerts qu'à un nombre limité
d'adultes vulnérables. Ces services sont fournis en grande
partie par des intervenants internes qui sont employés par
des fournisseurs de services, des familles et des groupes de
bénévoles. En ce qui concerne les intervenants internes, on
semble croire que leur travail est limité par la possibilité
de conflits d'intérêts, qui pourraient miner la confiance
des adultes vulnérables à l'égard des services.

- Le système actuel n'a pas de mandat clair pour fournir des services d'intervention, car il n'existe pas de normes de service uniformes ou de programme de formation pour les intervenants, et ces derniers sont gênés par l'absence d'un droit d'accès incontestable aux établissements, aux clients et aux dossiers des clients.

- Les lacunes du système actuel donnent lieu à des injustices et des actes discriminatoires. Les adultes vulnérables qui séjournent dans certains établissements de santé reçoivent des services d'intervention de bénévoles dévoués, tandis que d'autres ne recevront des services de qualité que s'ils ont la chance d'être confiés à des personnes qui sont déterminés à intervenir au nom de leurs clients. Malheureusement, la majorité de nos adultes vulnérables, et en particulier ceux qui vivent dans les collectivités plus petites, n'ont accès à aucun programme d'intervention.

- Un certain nombre des services d'intervention actuels présentent également d'autres lacunes : insuffisance des fonds, manque de ressources, charge de travail excessive, absence d'orientation et d'appui pour les intervenants, manque de supervision des intervenants et imputabilité limitée.

- Il existe un nombre alarmant d'adultes vulnérables qui ont été abandonnés par leurs familles et leurs amis dans des établissements de santé de longue durée et dans la collectivités.

- Plus de 8 000 déficients mentaux résident dans des établissements provinciaux. La plupart d'entre eux ont vécu toute leur vie dans des établissements et n'ont pas accès à un programme d'intervention. Par contre, les malades mentaux qui séjournent dans des établissements

psychiatriques pour des périodes moyennes de deux mois
bénéficient des services d'un intervenant à plein temps et
d'un conseiller en matière de droits. De même, les
résidents de maisons de soins infirmiers et de foyers pour
personnes âgées et les handicapés physiques n'ont pas accès
à des services d'intervention efficaces autres que ceux qui
peuvent être fournis dans des cas spéciaux par des
organismes bénévoles.

. Le manque de services d'intervention coordonnés et
accessibles à tous les adultes vulnérables qui ont besoin
d'aide constitue une grave injustice.

PRINCIPALES RECOMMANDATIONS

. Après avoir analysé une multitude de programmes
d'intervention internes et externes, le groupe d'examen a
évalué cinq solutions possibles :

       (1) ombudsman de l'intervention

       (2) intervention par des citoyens

       (3) intervention partagée

       (4) "Advocacy Ontario"

       (5) modèle d'intervention mixte

. Chacun de ces programmes a ses points forts et ses points
faibles, qui ont été évalués à l'aide des critères suivants
et des objectifs d'un système d'intervention idéal mis au
point conjointement par les trois comités consultatifs du
groupe d'examen :

1.   offrir une protection contre la tutelle inutile;

2.   être indépendant (des ministères concernés, des sources de financement, des fournisseurs);

3.   encourager l'auto-intervention dans toute la mesure du possible (autosuffisance, autodétermination);

4.   mettre en valeur le rôle des familles et des bénévoles;

5.   éduquer (les familles, les bénévoles, la collectivité) : désétiqueter et déstigmatiser les groupes, identifier les lacunes des services et faire savoir que l'intervention est l'affaire de tous;

6.   être souple (besoins particuliers, exigences géographiques, multilinguisme);

7.   répondre aux besoins (préoccupations personnelles, traitement des plaintes, règlement des problèmes);

8.   promouvoir la collaboration avec les fournisseurs et les ministères;

9.   être accessible;

10. viser à améliorer les programmes (réforme);

11. exercer de l'influence;

12. exiger la responsabilité des actes.

.   Ayant évalué les cinq modèles en fonction de ces critères, **le groupe d'examen recommande le modèle d'intervention partagée,** comme la façon la plus appropriée et la plus efficace de fournir des services d'intervention aux adultes vulnérables de l'Ontario.

Modèle d'intervention partagée

.   Ce modèle préconise le partage des responsabilités entre le gouvernement, les bénévoles et les groupes communautaires pour ce qui est de fournir les services d'intervention.

. Il s'agit d'un modèle fondé sur une évolution et une croissance lentes, qui s'inspire de l'expérience du programme de financement des cliniques d'aide juridique de l'Ontario, en encourageant les groupes communautaires à mettre au point des programmes d'intervention qui répondent aux besoins particuliers de leur collectivité et à demander des fonds pour ces programmes.

. Le modèle d'intervention partagée sera mis en oeuvre sur une période de deux à trois ans. La première étape consiste à créer une Commission des mesures d'intervention en Ontario et à lui confier un mandat clair pour fournir des services d'intervention non juridiques aux adultes vulnérables dans tous les établissements de santé et les collectivités.

. La responsabilité du programme provincial est confiée à une Commission des mesures d'intervention, qui est indépendante et qui est nommée par le lieutenant-gouverneur en conseil.

. La commission rend compte à la législature par l'intermédiaire du Procureur général ou du nouveau Comité permanent de l'ombudsman et de l'intervention.

. On devrait adopter une loi qui prévoit un droit légal clair permettant aux intervenants formés et accrédités d'avoir accès aux institutions et aux établissements de santé dans lesquels résident des adultes vulnérables et, dans le cas de ceux qui vivent dans les collectivités, de les rencontrer en privé.

. La loi devrait également permettre aux intervenants accrédités d'avoir accès, avec le consentement du patient, au dossier médical du patient.

. La commission gérerait un petit bureau central doté d'employés expérimentés dans les domaines suivants : formation et éducation; besoins et préoccupations des personnes âgées de santé délicate, des déficients mentaux, des malades mentaux et des handicapés physiques; et toutes les questions légales pertinentes.

. Des services d'intervention directs seraient offerts par l'intermédiaire de bureaux régionaux qui desserviraient toute la province et favoriseraient des programmes d'intervention locaux.

Commission des mesures d'intervention

. Les membres de la commission seraient d'éminents citoyens qui se sont engagés à défendre les intérêts des personnes vulnérables et qui ne sont pas employés par un fournisseur de services, un ministère ou un organisme.

. La commission assumerait, par l'intermédiaire du personnel de son bureau central, la responsabilité globale du système d'intervention dans la province, et exercerait notamment les fonctions suivantes :

- élaborer des politiques et des pratiques et procédures normalisées pour les bureaux régionaux et les programmes locaux;

- assurer le financement des bureaux régionaux et des programmes locaux;

- conseiller et appuyer les bureaux régionaux et les programmes locaux;

- créer des programmes de formation et d'accréditation qui seraient offerts, par l'entremise des bureaux régionaux, à tous les coordonnateurs des mesures d'intervention, les bénévoles et les intervenants dans les programmes locaux;

- surveiller les bureaux régionaux et les programmes locaux;

- organiser des conférences d'éducation et de
sensibilisation à l'intention des adultes vulnérables,
de leurs familles, des bénévoles, des fournisseurs de
services et du grand public, et assurer une publicité
dynamique des services d'intervention par divers médias
et sa propre campagne publique d'éducation et de
sensibilisation;

- mettre sur pied un système provincial visant à
recueillir et à analyser les données sur les plaintes,
les problèmes et les réponses, en vue d'identifier et
de régler les problèmes systémiques;

- fournir des renseignements aux fournisseurs de services
et au gouvernement en ce qui concerne les problèmes des
adultes vulnérables et la nécessité d'apporter des
modifications législatives ou internes au système de
prestation des services;

- promouvoir les intérêts des personnes vulnérables grâce
à l'éducation et à la représentation.

Bureaux régionaux

. L'intervention individuelle sera assurée par l'intermédiaire
de bureaux régionaux répartis dans la province, qui ont pour
mandat de fournir des services d'intervention aux adultes
vulnérables dans les 24 heures qui suivent une demande
d'assistance. Des coordonnateurs régionaux des mesures
d'intervention organiseront également, avec l'aide de
bénévoles et de groupes communautaires locaux, des
programmes d'action directe en vue de répondre aux besoins
des personnes vulnérables dans la région.

. Chaque bureau régional a pour mandat de fournir aux adultes
vulnérables des services d'intervention non juridiques dans
les 24 heures qui suivent une demande d'assistance et
d'organiser, avec l'aide de bénévoles et de groupes
communautaires locaux, un programme d'action directe en vue
de répondre aux besoins des adultes vulnérables dans la
région.

- Chaque bureau régional sera géré par un conseil d'administration élu par les membres de la collectivité et responsable devant la commission de la prestation de services d'intervention dans la région. Ces conseils d'administration doivent se composer en bonne partie de représentants des consommateurs.

- Le conseil d'administration régional s'acquitterait de ses responsabilités par le biais d'un bureau régional composé de trois coordonnateurs à plein temps : un coordonnateur responsable des adultes vulnérables qui vivent dans les collectivités et un coordonnateur responsable des adultes vulnérables qui résident dans des établissements; un directeur régional chargé de superviser le bureau régional et d'aider les coordonnateurs.

- Chaque coordonnateur exercerait notamment les fonctions suivantes :

  - mettre en oeuvre les services d'intervention en faisant connaître de façon dynamique, au sein de la collectivité, le besoin et le potentiel des services d'intervention au nom des adultes vulnérables;

  - offrir des services d'intervention aux adultes vulnérables qui vivent dans les établissements et les collectivités de la région;

  - protéger les adultes vulnérables contre la tutelle inappropriée en intervenant au nom de toute personne qui fait l'objet d'une instance relative à la tutelle en vertu de la législation qui est envisagée concernant la substitution de la prise de décision;

  - aider les groupes locaux à créer des programmes pour fournir des services d'intervention dans la région et à s'adresser à la commission pour obtenir des fonds;

  - recruter et former un nombre suffisant de bénévoles pour agir en qualité d'intervenants auprès des adultes vulnérables qui résident dans des établissements de santé et des résidences privées de la région, lorsqu'il n'y a aucun programme local à leur intention;

- s'assurer que les intervenants visitent régulièrement tous les établissements de santé pour adultes vulnérables dans la région;

- fournir un soutien aux intervenants bénévoles qui ont besoin d'aide pour régler des problèmes ou des plaintes;

- recevoir, analyser et résoudre les plaintes ou les problèmes que les intervenants bénévoles ou les intervenants des programmes locaux ne peuvent régler eux-mêmes;

- veiller à ce que tous les intervenants se conforment aux procédures et politiques applicables de la Commission des mesures d'intervention;

- inciter les groupes locaux à instaurer des programmes d'intervention par les citoyens au sein de leur collectivité, selon les principes et les pratiques de l'intervention par les citoyens, qui ont été établis de concert avec la Commission des mesures d'intervention;

- tenir des dossiers concernant les plaintes et les problèmes reçus, les mesures prises, les constatations, les réponses et les recommandations;

- soumettre des rapports trimestriels à la commission concernant les activités du bureau régional et des problèmes locaux.

Programme locaux

. Les besoins des adultes vulnérables dans la province varient considérablement, selon la nature de leur handicap, leur résidence (à la maison ou dans un établissement), la taille et l'emplacement de la collectivité et les ressources des bénévoles et des professionnels qui sont disponibles.

. Il est essentiel que le modèle d'intervention partagée soit souple et adaptable, afin de pouvoir tenir compte des besoins et des ressources de chaque collectivité. Les coordonnateurs régionaux des mesures d'intervention aideront les collectivités à déterminer leurs besoins particuliers, à mettre au point des programmes appropriés et à demander les fonds nécessaires au conseil d'administration régional et à la Commission des mesures d'intervention.

. Toutes les demandes de financement des programmes locaux devraient contenir une description non seulement du groupe d'adultes vulnérables qui seront desservis, mais également des groupes qui ne seront pas desservis par le programme proposé, et fournir une justification de cet état de choses. Si les requérants ne sont pas en mesure de justifier l'omission, des fonds ne seraient pas fournis. De cette façon, le conseil d'administration régional serait conscient que certains groupes ne sont pas desservis par les programmes locaux et s'assurerait que ces groupes ne sont pas négligés dans les demandes de financement subséquentes.

Intervenants bénévoles

. Lorsqu'il n'existe aucun programme local pour répondre aux besoins des personnes vulnérables, les coordonnateurs du bureau régional seront responsables des services d'intervention jusqu'à ce qu'un programme local puisse être établi.

. Pour que les coordonnateurs soient en mesure de fournir ces services dans un délai de 24 heures, ils devront recruter et former un petit groupe de bénévoles dans toute la région.

. Les bénévoles seront formés et accrédités selon les normes élaborées par le bureau central; ils devront notamment s'acquitter des responsabilités suivantes :

-   visiter régulièrement les adultes vulnérables dans les établissements de santé et les collectivités;

-   recevoir et analyser les problèmes ou plaintes des adultes vulnérables et chercher des solutions par la consultation et la négociation;

- rendre compte au bureau régional des problèmes, des plaintes et des mesures prises.

Recommandations supplémentaires

. Il est recommandé que le programme soit financé par le gouvernement provincial par le biais de demandes de fonds annuelles.

. Après avoir examiné les demandes budgétaires de chacun des sept conseils d'administration régionaux, la commission déciderait du niveau de financement à recommander au gouvernement.

. La demande de fonds de la commission, accompagnée d'un rapport annuel, serait adressée au Comité permanent de l'ombudsman ou au Procureur général. Dans le premier cas, ce comité serait restructuré et deviendrait le Comité permanent de l'ombudsman et de l'intervention.

Bureau du programme de défense des droits des malades mentaux

. Le programme d'intervention qui est offert actuellement aux résidents des établissements psychiatriques provinciaux, par le biais du programme de défense des droits des malades mentaux, serait intégré au modèle d'intervention partagée de manière à renforcer les deux programmes.

. Dans l'intérêt des services d'intervention spécialisés offerts aux malades mentaux, le coordonnateur du programme de défense des droits des malades mentaux devrait être inclus dans le personnel du bureau central et être chargé de fournir des services d'intervention aux malades mentaux dans les établissements et les collectivités, et les intervenants auprès des malades mentaux devraient continuer de relever de leur coordonnateur et d'être supervisé par lui.

Responsables des dossiers/coordonnateurs des services et intervention

- Il faudrait établir une distinction entre l'intervention et la gestion des dossiers ou la coordination des services. L'intervention représente souvent un élément important de la coordination des services mais l'inverse n'est pas forcément vrai : la véritable intervention ne comporte pas une fonction de coordination des services.

- Par conséquent, on ne devrait pas inclure les responsables des dossiers et les coordonnateurs des services dans un programme d'intervention provincial indépendant.

- Cependant, on recommande aussi que l'intervention continue de représenter un élément important des fonctions du coordonnateur des services internes, dans les limites de son travail avec le fournisseur de services. Si les efforts du coordonnateur en matière d'intervention en viennent à être compromis par sa position, il devrait soumettre la question à la Commission des mesures d'intervention.

Protection législative des adultes vulnérables

- On recommande que l'Ontario adopte, en faveur des adultes vulnérables, des mesures législatives de protection qui exigent que toute personne ayant connaissance de l'abus ou de la négligence d'un adulte vulnérable en informe les autorités compétentes.

- On recommande également que, s'il existe des preuves raisonnables de l'abus ou de la négligence et que l'adulte vulnérable est, par choix ou autrement, demeuré dans la résidence où s'est produit l'abus ou la négligence, le bureau régional confie à un intervenant la tâche d'établir des rapports avec l'adulte vulnérable en vue d'assurer une surveillance permanente de la situation et de faciliter le signalement de tout abus subséquent.

Coûts du programme d'intervention partagée

- En raison de la nature évolutive du modèle d'intervention partagée, qui prévoit une croissance lente du programme sur une période de plusieurs années, il est impossible de projeter des coûts précis.

- Quels que soient les coûts prévus, le gouvernement doit envisager la mise en oeuvre des services d'intervention en tenant compte de ce qu'il en coûtera, sur le plan humain, si rien n'est fait pour répondre aux besoins pressants des adultes vulnérables de l'Ontario en matière de services d'intervention.

- Si la volonté politique y est, tout ce que propose le rapport peut être mis en oeuvre.

CHAPTER 1

Introduction and Background to the Review of Advocacy

1. Introduction

It is often stated that the measure of any society is the way in which it cares for its most vulnerable. In our society, there is general agreement that the most vulnerable have a right to the basic necessities of life -- food, shelter and medical care. Indeed, in Ontario we have one of the best social service and health care systems in the world. In addition, we have the Ontario Human Rights Code and the Canadian Charter of Rights and Freedoms to ensure and protect the human rights of our vulnerable citizens.

Yet, despite these important measures, there are still many whose rights are not being fully recognized and who are not receiving the assistance they deserve. We are all familiar with the disturbing sight of "street people" -- bag ladies and vent men -- who live and sleep and may die on the streets of our cities. We are also well aware of those in long-term care facilities and other institutions who have been forgotten or have no one who truly cares. And there are others: the many who live in isolation in the community, victims of neglect or abandonment; and the abused who, trapped by their caregivers and their own vulnerability, are unable to reach out and ask for help.

Requiring assistance, notwithstanding one's circumstances, is nothing to be ashamed of. We all need assistance throughout our lives -- from simply asking someone for directions, to asking someone to look after us when we are sick and unable to care for ourselves. Indeed, the adage "no man is an island" is what "society", "community-living" is based upon -- people living together and helping each other.

However, it is important to acknowledge that there are times in our lives when we don't know how to ask for assistance; or who to ask; or times when we are simply unable to ask. Such difficulties in reaching out are exacerbated if one is vulnerable because of a mental or physical disability or frailty. It is in situations such as these that we need someone to speak for us on our behalf. This is what advocacy is all about.

2.   Background

On December 16, 1986, the Attorney General of Ontario, The Honourable Ian Scott, announced the initiation of a Review of Advocacy for Vulnerable Adults (see Appendix 2). In his Statement to the Legislature, he spoke of his "conviction that there is an unmet need for non-legal advocacy for vulnerable adults living in institutional care settings and in the community", and noted that he and his colleagues, the Minister of Health, the Minister of Community and Social Services, the Minister Responsible for Senior Citizens' Affairs and the Minister Responsible for Disabled Persons "share the conviction that vulnerable adults must be heard and that health and social services must respond to their needs."

The Attorney General further stated that while there was a generally agreed upon need "for more and better non-legal advocacy", careful consideration must be given to ascertaining the best method or methods to deliver advocacy services to ensure that such services would "respond to the real needs of vulnerable adults" and "be effective and meaningful". It was for these reasons that the Review was initiated.

(a)   Impetus for the Review

It would appear that the impetus for the Review came largely from the many organizations and agencies that represent and assist vulnerable adults. These groups repeatedly and strongly expressed the need for better non-legal advocacy services in this province. One particular organization, Concerned Friends of Ontario Residents in Care Facilities, undertook the significant task of designing a model for the establishment of independent advocacy services in Ontario. This model is described in a submission, entitled "Advocacy Ontario", which was presented to the Attorney General in June, 1986.

Initially this proposal and the general issue of advocacy was referred to the Advisory Committee on Substitute Decision Making for Mentally Incapable Persons (the Fram Committee) for consideration. The purpose of this Committee, which was established in 1985 by the Ministries of Health, Community and Social Services and the Attorney General, is to review all aspects of the law governing and related to substitute decision making for mentally incapable persons, including personal guardianship and conservatorship, and to make recommendations concerning the revision of this law where appropriate. Over a number of months, the Fram Committee engaged in extensive discussions concerning the appropriate mandate and form of advocacy services, but had difficulty in reaching a consensus. As a result of these discussions, the progress of the Fram Committee's work on its original mandate was delayed. At this point, it was decided to refer the issue of advocacy to an independent review.

(b)   Terms of Reference

The general Terms of Reference for the Review are set out as follows:

1.   To consider the need for advocacy for adults in institutional care settings as well as those adults that may require such services and are living in the community.

2.   To analyze thoroughly the concept of advocacy in relation to disadvantaged adult populations in Ontario, e.g. frail elderly, physically handicapped, psychiatrically disabled, developmentally handicapped.

3.   To develop options concerning the establishment of advocacy services, including organizational structure and accountability for each option.

4.   The consideration of need will include a detailed review relating to the co-ordination of advocacy with:

a) existing case management and other delivery systems; and

b) existing legal and volunteer advocacy services.

In addition, the Terms of Reference required that the Review "consult existing advocacy programs, both volunteer and established publicly funded programs... and seek oral and written submissions from relevant organizations as part of the consultation process." The Review was also asked to "consider the principles of advocacy services developed by the Advisory Committee on Substitute Decision Making for Mentally Incapable Persons" and to "take into consideration the pending evaluation of the Psychiatric Patient Advocate Program," this latter evaluation known as the Manson Committee.

(c) Time Frame

The Review was originally scheduled to report on July 1, 1987. However, this deadline was subsequently extended at the Attorney General's request to August 1, 1987 in order to take into account the work of the Psychiatric Patient Advocate Program Evaluation Committee.

Notwithstanding the extension, the Manson Committee was regrettably but understandably unable to provide us with any formal research material or a draft report. At the outset, we wish to acknowledge the additional time for research and analysis required by the researchers and the Manson Committee conducting the evaluation of the Psychiatric Patient Advocate Program. As well, its Chairman, Professor Allan Manson, has made a number of trips to Toronto specifically to ensure ongoing consultation and liaison between our two studies. We are most grateful to Professor Manson and his Committee members for their openness and co-operation -- and now hope that this Advocacy Report will assist them as they complete their own important work.

(d)   Process

In attempting to fulfill its Terms of Reference, the following process was followed by the Review.

(i)   Consultation

Shortly after the Attorney General's announcement of the Review, arrangements were made to run a newspaper advertisement in major provincial dailies describing the Review and inviting the receipt of written submissions (see Appendix 3). In addition, over 300 letters were sent to relevant organizations, groups and individuals, as well as all MPP's. Mailing lists were obtained from concerned ministries, for example, the Ministry of Community and Social Services, the Ministry of Health, the Office for Senior Citizens' Affairs and the Office Responsible for Disabled Persons, and we were advised of others who should be notified by interested organizations, groups and individuals. In response, the Review received 185 written submissions from the individuals, groups and organizations listed in Appendix 4.

In addition to soliciting written submissions, the Review encouraged informal consultation and discussion and, in this regard, held over 90 informal meetings with concerned and knowledgeable groups and individuals. The names of those with whom we met are set out in Appendix 5 of the Report. While the Review welcomed the broadest possible consultation, it was not possible, given our restricted seven month time frame, to engage in formal, public hearings throughout the province.

As part of the consultation process, the Review also consulted with officials in various states in the United States that have implemented notable advocacy programs.

(ii) Advisory Committees

In the Terms of Reference of the Review, it was required that the chairperson be "supported by three advisory committees representing consumers, providers, and affected Ministries." In attempting to meet this requirement, we first solicited advice from a number of groups, individuals and government ministries concerning appropriate appointments to the Committees and then engaged in the formidable task of selecting from the list of very well qualified and respected nominees. It was decided that, in order to better facilitate the consultation process, the size of each Committee should be limited to seven members. Committee members were not chosen as representatives of the groups or organizations with which they were or had been affiliated, but were selected on the basis of their own individual merit and broad experience. A list of the Committee members is set out in Appendix 6. Their work was invaluable to the Review.

(iii) Visits to Institutions

In addition, a number of representative types of institutions and care facilities were visited by members of the Review staff. In this regard, the Minister of Health appointed staff members as inspectors under section 15 of the *Public Hospitals Act* and section 16 of the *Nursing Homes Act*. The decision of which facilities to visit was aided by suggestions that were solicited from relevant Ministries, organizations and individuals. Unfortunately, because of our limited time frame, and commitments to committee meetings and individual consultations, we were restricted in the number of facilities that could be visited.

(iv) Evaluation of the Psychiatric Patient Advocate Program

As noted earlier, the Terms of Reference required that the Review take into consideration the pending evaluation of the Psychiatric Patient Advocate Program. In this regard, we engaged in a continued liaison with Professor Allan Manson, the Chairman of the Psychiatric Patient Advocate Program Evaluation Committee, and met with him on several occasions.

(v) Principles of Advocacy Prepared by the Advisory Committee on Substitute Decision Making for Mentally Incapable Persons

The Review was also required by its Terms of Reference to consider the principles of advocacy services developed by the Fram Committee. Although this Committee discontinued its consideration of the specific operational proposals for advocacy services, it continued to engage in discussions concerning the appropriate principles of advocacy services in order to assist the work of the Review. This statement of principles, which is included as Appendix 7, was of considerable value to the Review and was carefully considered when preparing the Report.

We are certainly indebted to that Committee, and its Chairman, Mr. Stephen Fram, for making so readily available to us the detailed work and recommendations which followed their months of study.

"Ruby is an 82 year old woman with a medical history of senile dementia and strokes... Ruby resided with her daughter, who although not officially named guardian, exercised control over her mother's care. Community police records indicated a history of beatings. Ruby stated that she feared for her life, home and possessions. The police noted a considerable deterioration in Ruby since she had first come to their attention. The public health nurse had observed the daughter inebriated and being verbally abusive. Ruby had been seen at a local hospital's emergency department with injuries she claimed were caused by her daughter. The daughter denied the accusations. Having been found to be a mentally incompetent person, any testimony which Ruby might give in court could not be considered sufficient to form the basis of charges. Ruby's condition continued to deteriorate. She became incontinent in bowel and bladder. At the time of her last admission to a nursing home, she was found to be dehydrated and malnourished with bruises..."

From a brief submitted by the Toronto Mayor's Committee on Aging.

CHAPTER 2

WHAT IS ADVOCACY

1. Introduction

Over recent years, the term "advocacy" has become increasingly popular and is now widely and variously used by different individuals in different contexts. Indeed, it has clearly transcended the narrowly defined function of members of the legal profession to include an activity claimed by a number of others -- including service providers, family members, health care and social service professionals, and volunteers.

Prior to 1970, the word "advocacy" could rarely be found in human services literature. However, as is often the case, certain circumstances, including the nature of the times in which we live, can propel a concept to the forefront of public attention in a relatively short period of time. The recent concern with advocacy reflects, perhaps, the increasing proliferation and complexity of our society's laws, policies, and procedures, as well as the recent rapid expansion of human service programs. Further, the current interest in advocacy no doubt has been fostered by our society's growing awareness of human and legal rights as reflected in the Canadian Charter of Rights and Freedom and the Ontario Human Rights Code.

However, when any new concept emerges, it is usually accompanied by confusion concerning its exact nature and the principles that it encompasses. After being exposed to a new term, people will often include it within their vocabulary without a clear understanding of what it means exactly, or what it entails. Similarly, with respect to advocacy, there is a certain amount of confusion surrounding the proper use of the term. Indeed, in one study in the United States in which the concept of advocacy was examined on a nationwide basis, it was reported that many people used the word "to denote all the good things they did for others."[1]

Accordingly, it is important at this preliminary stage to examine this term and to clarify its meaning in the context of the Review and for the purpose of this Report. In this regard, the general concept of advocacy will be considered and the different types of advocacy discussed. In addition, certain important principles and objectives of advocacy will be identified. Further, consideration will be given to the concept of case management and how it differs from the concept of advocacy.

2.   The Concept of Advocacy
(a) Legal and Social Advocacy Distinguished

In attempting to define "advocacy", it is useful first to consider a dictionary definition. The Concise Oxford Dictionary defines " advocacy" as "the function of an advocate; pleading in support of" and the noun "advocate" as "one who pleads for another; one who speaks in favour of (proposal) etc.; professional pleader in courts of justice, barrister." As suggested by this dictionary definition, the most well-known and best understood type of advocacy is "legal advocacy" -- where a lawyer is retained by a client to plead a legal case on his or her behalf before an administrative tribunal or court of law.

It is important to note, however, that the type of advocacy that the Review is required to consider is not advocacy of a legal nature. Rather, as suggested by our Terms of Reference and explicitly stated in the Attorney General's Statement to the Legislature, the purpose of the Review is to make recommendations concerning the delivery of "non-legal" advocacy services, also referred to as "social advocacy".

Similar to legal advocacy, social advocacy means speaking or pleading on behalf of others and entails many of the same professional responsibilities: for example, an assessment of the situation; advising the client and assisting him or her to decide upon the best course of action; and using one's skills and best efforts to pursue the client's wishes through all lawful, ethical and reasonable means. The basic difference, however, is that a social advocate speaks or pleads on behalf of another by using non-legalistic measures: he or she, unlike a lawyer, does not directly invoke or participate in the legal process to obtain the desired result. This distinction was noted in the following excerpt from the submission that was received from the Ontario Office of the Official Guardian:

> Any program for the delivery of social advocacy services must make a careful distinction between those services and legal advocacy. Present law [*Law Society Act*, R.S.O. 1980, c.233, s.50; *Solicitors' Act*, R.S.O. 1980, c.478, s.1] requires, with some exceptions, that only a qualified barrister and solicitor may give legal advice for a fee, or represent persons before the courts. A person providing social advocacy services who is not a qualified barrister and solicitor should therefore not provide legal advisory services to a client or represent a client in court, although social advocacy may include accessing legal advocacy either directly from the private bar, from a legal aid referral service or from an agency such as the Advocacy Resource Centre for the Handicapped that specializes in legal services to the disabled.

In further attempting to define social advocacy, many commentators have suggested that merely speaking or pleading on behalf of someone is not enough -- that the essence of social advocacy incorporates speaking on behalf of an individual with vigor, vehemence and commitment. This aspect of social advocacy is described as follows: "advocacy implies fervor and depth of feeling in advancing a cause, or the interest of another person; it calls for doing more than what is done routinely, and what would be found routinely acceptable; in this sense, the advocate acts at least as vigorously for another person or group as for him/herself."[2]

In the context of this Review, advocacy entails speaking with vigor, vehemence and commitment on behalf of "vulnerable adults", also referred to in our Terms of Reference as "disadvantaged adults", who are living in institutional care settings, as well as in the community. Four examples of vulnerable adults are specified in our Terms of Reference: frail elderly, physically handicapped, psychiatrically disabled, and developmentally handicapped persons. Accordingly, for the purpose of this Report, the concept of advocacy has been restricted to these particular groups. It has become clear during the course of this Review, however, that the need for advocacy cuts across barriers such as age or any specific definition of "vulnerable".

Before turning to consider some of the important principles inherent in social advocacy, it is important to describe and distinguish briefly the following different types of advocacy: individual and systemic, as well as formal and informal.

(b) Individual and Systemic Advocacy

Individual advocacy refers to advocacy on behalf of a particular individual, as opposed to a group, and assisting that person to realize his or her wishes. In this type of advocacy, the client is an active participant who articulates the problem and defines the action to be taken. In addition to helping vulnerable adults to present and resolve their problems and complaints, individual advocacy also involves developing a caring personal relationship that typically includes friendly visiting and monitoring their care.

Systemic advocacy, on the other hand, involves influencing social and political systems to bring about changes in laws, rules, regulations, policies and practices for the benefit of groups of people. Rather than dealing with an individual need, this type of advocacy focuses on changing the broader features of an overall system. For example, an advocate may repeatedly be confronted with an injustice that affects a number of vulnerable adults and see a need to redress the injustice on a broader scale by improving the existing system. This could involve activities designed to influence legislative change or, on a narrower level, could involve effecting a policy change within an institution, such as the revocation of an inequitable rule, procedure or institutional guideline that negatively affected many of the patients/residents.

Individual and systemic advocacy are usually compatible and frequently practised together. Many advocates whose primary function is individual advocacy will supplement this activity with some systemic advocacy in those cases where the need for this type of advocacy has been identified.

(c) Informal and Formal Advocacy

"Informal advocacy" connotes the type of advocacy that occurs on a voluntary and relatively unstructured basis by, for example, a family member or other relative, friends, neighbours and volunteers. Informal advocacy also includes self-advocacy which involves acting on one's own behalf.

"Formal advocacy", on the other hand, refers to advocacy programs that are organized with special goals, leadership, membership and some type of financial support. Advocacy becomes more formal to the extent that the individuals performing it are paid for providing advocacy services, perform the function exclusively, and may be mandated by legislation.

In between informal and formal advocacy fall those advocacy activities provided by, for example, social service and health care professionals whose primary role is not one of advocacy, but "who are engaged in these activities as a component of fulfilling their professional roles and in whose roles inhere a special moral obligation and a natural inclination to advocate."[3]

3. Basic Principles of Advocacy

In attempting to define non-legal or social advocacy, it is helpful to examine certain basic principles that appear to underlie this concept. In identifying these principles, the Review was greatly assisted by the "Statement of Principles Regarding the Provision of Advocacy Services to Mentally Disadvantaged Persons" prepared by the

Fram Committee, set out in Appendix 7 to this Report, as well as by the submissions that were received and the discussions held with the Advisory Committees and other individuals. In the following sections, four basic principles of advocacy are discussed.

(a) Advocacy must be Client Directed

One of the basic principles of advocacy is that it be client directed or "instruction-based": the actions of an advocate must be guided by the instructions of a client and the advocate must serve the client on a voluntary and consensual basis. An advocate should not substitute for a client's instructions his or her own personal or professional view of what course of action is in the "best interests" of the client. This principle of advocacy was discussed as follows in the submission received from the Psychiatric Patient Advocate Office:

> Central to advocacy is the determination of the interest of the client and the servicing of those interests. Generally, an advocate becomes fully acquainted with the client's problem, and canvasses options and strategies for dealing with that problem. An advocate then discusses these options and strategies with the client, advises the client, and then takes instructions from the client. Advocacy thus implies what may be called "client sovereignty" virtually as a matter of definition.

However, the obligation to take instructions is not synonymous with blindly or inappropriately following a client's directions. Obviously, an advocate will not act on instructions that are illegal or impossible to carry out. In addition, the authority of an advocate in a given situation cannot be any greater than that of his or her client: if, for example, the client has been found to be financially incompetent, an advocate cannot assist that individual to enter into a contract.

(b) Advocacy should be Independent

Another principle that clearly emerged during the course of the Review was that advocacy must be as independent as possible. In order to avoid any potential or perceived problems with conflict of interest, advocates should be administratively and fiscally independent of the human service delivery system.

Advocates should not, for example, be employees of health care facilities or other agencies that provide services to vulnerable adults. Independence is necessary since the interests of a client, as expressed in his or her instructions, may at times be inconsistent with the interests of a service provider. Indeed, it has been suggested that "internal" advocacy or "in-house" advocacy which is part of, or directly accountable to, the same authority as the service delivery system is not true advocacy, but merely an adjunct of the service delivery system itself. Further, the "mere fact that genuine advocacy may take place in some such arrangements at some point in time does not mean that the function itself is set up to be advocacy as it ought to be conceptualized and structured."[4]

(c) Advocacy should be Accessible

A third basic principle of advocacy is that it must be accessible. In order for an advocate to be able to assist vulnerable adults, he or she must be readily accessible to them whether they are in institutions or in the community. It is essential that advocates must be assured of the opportunity to communicate with vulnerable adults without interference from others. Accordingly, advocates must be free to establish a physical presence in care facilities and encouraged to engage in outreach activities to ensure that persons in need of their services are aware of them. In addition to ensuring physical access to clients and potential clients, the principle of accessibility includes the right, with a client's consent, to access clinical records and members of a treatment team where a vulnerable adult is in an institutional setting.

Further, in order to ensure that advocacy will be genuinely accessible, it is important that the confidentiality of advocate/client communications be protected. It is extremely difficult for clients to feel free to seek assistance from an advocate unless confidentiality is assured. The nature of advocacy is to deal with very sensitive and personal information and clients must be confident that this information will not be divulged without their knowledge and permission. It has been suggested, however, that there must be certain limited exceptions to this right of confidentiality, for example: "where access is required to ascertain whether or not the advocate has acted negligently, and where a client dies in circumstances in which it would be in the public interest for the advocate to testify at an inquest."[5]

(d) Advocacy: Neither Adversarial nor Passive

As a concept, open to several interpretations, advocacy has sometimes created resistance and negativity among certain individuals and groups. Social advocacy is often equated with adversarial activity -- with legal advocacy and litigation and with intrusive and disruptive behaviour. It has sometimes been perceived as a threat to the traditional interpersonal and professional relationships that exist in the health care and social service system.

This present-day connotation of conflict and antagonism is not inherent in the basic concept of advocacy and has arisen, perhaps, as a result of a lack of understanding of the concept and because of the manner in which some advocates may have pursued their duties. In addition, in the absence of advocacy services, vulnerable people in Ontario have had to resort to litigation to enforce their rights.

However, advocacy should not be primarily adversarial in nature. Indeed, little is to be gained through an overzealous and abrasive approach and the costs can be high: overt or covert sanctions against residents and patients; stress; undue expenditures of time and money; increased resistance to subsequent requests; and alienation of those upon whom the vulnerable person must rely.

Advocacy should not have the effect of polarizing relationships. Rather, it should be seen as a way to achieve co-operation -- where all parties work together, instead of in opposition, to advance the rights of all vulnerable adults and to improve health care and service delivery. Such co-operation is best achieved through conciliation, mediation and reasoned discussion rather than through adversarial tactics and court orders.

The correct perception of any new role is key to its efficacy, as Ontario's first Ombudsman, the late Arthur Maloney, Q.C., noted in his *Blueprint for the Office of the Ombudsman in Ontario* (1979) prepared after the initial three years of that Office's service. For many of the same reasons, an advocate should be viewed and should function in a way that Mr. Maloney recommended for the Ombudsman's staff: more as a diplomat than as a police officer.

Nonetheless, one should not confuse advocacy that is primarily non-adversarial with passive compliance. A non-adversarial approach should not be at the expense of avoiding sensitive, difficult or unpopular issues. While it is believed that the greater the degree of understanding and acceptance of advocacy, the less frequent the need for adversarial measures, it is still important that formal, legal advocacy services or other more adversarial measures be available *as a last resort* to respond to extreme failures in the system.

4.   Objectives of Advocacy

In attempting to define the concept of social advocacy, it is helpful to consider what the primary objectives of such services should be. In this regard, the objectives that were identified for the Review by the Fram Committee in its "Statement of Principles Regarding the Provision of Advocacy Services to Mentally Disadvantaged Persons" are set out as follows:

> •   to promote respect for the rights, freedoms and dignity of the persons... [advocates] serve, both individually and collectively;

- to ensure that their clients' legal and human rights are recognized and protected;

- to assist their clients to receive the health care and social services to which they are entitled and which they wish to receive;

- to enhance the autonomy of their clients by advocating on their behalf, both individually and collectively;

- to assist their clients to lead lives that are as independent as possible, and in the least restrictive environment possible;

- to help protect.... disadvantaged persons from financial, physical and psychological abuse;

- to fully explain the implications of and provide advice with respect to guardianship and conservatorship under the *Substitute Decisions Authority Act* (or the current legislation it is intended to replace).

Those objectives, defined for the more limited advocacy on behalf of mentally disadvantaged persons, are endorsed.

The work of this Review, with a broader mandate, has elaborated upon them with goals of advocacy as developed at a plenary session of our three advisory committees. They are outlined in chapter 5 and, consistent with the foregoing Fram recommendations, propose worthy and practical objectives for comprehensive advocacy services.

5.   Advocacy and Case Management/Service Co-ordination

As discussed in the introduction to the Report, one of the objectives of the Review is to consider the co-ordination of advocacy with existing case management systems. However, before one can do so, it is important first to understand the concept of "case management", which hereinafter will also be referred to as "service co-ordination", and how it is related to advocacy.

Service co-ordination has been defined as the "process or method for ensuring that consumers are provided with whatever services they need in a co-ordinated, effective and efficient manner."[6] The need for service co-ordination arose primarily as a result of two factors.   First, throughout the 1960s and 1970s, a rapid expansion of human service programs occurred which resulted in a network of services that was very complex, confusing and difficult to access.   Accordingly, a need was created for a body of specialists who had the expertise to co-ordinate the provision of such services.

The second factor that contributed to the need for service co-ordination was the government policy of deinstitutionalization -- the release of persons from long-term care institutions and their integration in the community.   While in institutions, all basic physical needs of the residents were met; indeed, the institutional model provided a continuity of care.   However, once these persons were released into the community the responsibility for their care and support became diffused among a number of different agencies and levels of government.

Five basic functions of service co-ordination have been identified:[7]

- assessment of client need;

- development of a comprehensive service plan;

- arranging for services to be delivered;

- monitoring and assessing the services delivered;

- evaluation and follow-up.

These five functions will appear in almost every description of a service co-ordination system, regardless of its context.   There are, however, additional functions that may be associated with a particular service co-ordination program. Those that appear most frequently are outreach, direct service provision, and advocacy.[8]

The difficulty of determining the exact nature of a service co-ordinator's responsibilities is discussed as follows:[9]

> Specifying the particular functions performed by case managers is not a simple task. Although great care is often taken to define the scope of activities that case managers engage in, the reality is that substantial differences typically exist between officially mandated patterns of case manager activity and actual patterns of service ... The reason for this is that someone thrust into the case manager role must function essentially as a trouble-shooter, confronting and resolving a wide range of problems, many of which are unpredictable. More specifically, case managers have the unenviable task of assuring that clients receive appropriate, coordinated and continuous care from service systems whose design provides for none of these features. As a result, persons acting as case managers must be ready to play whatever role the situation may require -- outreach worker, broker, advocate, counselor, teacher, community organizer, planner, or administrator.

As discussed above, advocacy may well constitute an important part of a service co-ordinator's job. In attempting to access services for their clients, opposition may be encountered; accordingly, it may be necessary for a service co-ordinator to assume the role of advocate in order to fulfill his or her responsibilities to a client. Service co-ordinators may also engage in systemic advocacy. In trying to co-ordinate services for their client, it is inevitable that they will identify gaps in the service system, which many may attempt to rectify.

While advocacy is often an important component of service co-ordination, it would appear that the converse is not necessarily so. The primary function of an advocate is to advocate. In engaging in this activity, however, limited service co-ordination activities may be necessary in order to meet a client's needs.

Much discussion, and often lively debate, has taken place over the similarities and differences between advocacy and case management/service co-ordination. Having listened attentively to these many points of view, we have concluded that an important distinction exists -- and needs to be borne in mind as one considers this Review of Advocacy. That is: *while case management often includes advocacy as a component, true advocacy does not include a case management function.*

"A 20 year old physically handicapped man was working in a sheltered workshop. He had a severe speech impediment which could only be improved through constant practice in conversation. Unfortunately, his co-worker was not inclined to converse. Through the intervention of a citizen advocate, he was assigned a different work-mate. Although there is at times more conversation than work, it is obvious to everyone that the young man's speech is rapidly improving."

From a brief submitted by Citizen Advocacy for Ottawa-Carleton.

CHAPTER 3

THE NEED FOR ADVOCACY

1.   Introduction

Having defined for the purpose of this Review what advocacy is and its
objectives, it is imperative to ask whether there is, in fact, a need for some type of
advocacy system or systems in this province.   In this chapter of the Report, we will
attempt to answer that question.

The first section of the chapter will provide information concerning the number of
"vulnerable adults" as defined by our Terms of Reference, currently residing in Ontario.
The concept of vulnerability will then be analyzed in order to understand its relationship
to the need for advocacy.   The formal advocacy programs currently operating will also
be considered, as well as the informal advocacy activities of volunteers and others, in
order to determine whether such programs and activities are sufficient to meet the
advocacy needs of our vulnerable adults.   In addition, a section will be included
outlining the specific advocacy role that will be created should the new guardianship
legislation be enacted as proposed by the Fram Committee.

2. Is there a Need?

(a) The Number of Vulnerable Adults

It is impossible to obtain completely accurate or up-to-date statistics on the number
of "vulnerable adults" that reside in Ontario at the present time.   It is even more difficult
to determine who of such individuals would require the assistance of an advocate.
Futhermore, while many of us are not "vulnerable" at this particular moment in time,
there are no guarantees that tomorrow, or next month, or next year, or 20 years from
now, we will not find ourselves in such a position and in need of an advocate.   In order
to provide us with some guidance, however, we did attempt to obtain some general

statistics concerning the different vulnerable adult populations specified in our Terms of Reference.

(i) Physically Disabled Persons

According to the *Report of the Canadian Health and Disability Survey* (1983-84), (Statistics Canada), 13.6% of the Ontario adult population, or approximately 937,000 people, reported a mild, moderate or severe physical disability in 1983-84. From a low of 4.0% among those aged 15-24, the rate of disability rose significantly with age with 38.4% of those over 65 years of age reporting some degree of physical disability.

(ii) Frail Elderly Persons

With regard to our elderly population, it would appear that Ontario is progressing through an extended period of major demographic change. Between 1960 and 1980, the number of senior citizens (65+) increased from 8% to 10% of the population. At present , the senior population in Ontario is about one million -- approximately 11% of the population.[1] By 2030, when the last of the baby boom reaches 65, seniors will represent 23% of the population.[2]

That is not to suggest, however, that persons over the age of 65 automatically become "frail" or "vulnerable". Indeed, it is estimated that the majority of seniors between the ages of 65 and 85 are healthy, independent and self-sufficient. Statistics show, however, that in the "older/elder" category -- those over 85 years of age -- the incidence of ill health and frailty is high. For example, it has been reported that one older/elderly person in five suffers from some form of dementia or brain disease.[3] Statistics also indicate that the elderly are living longer and, that by 2001, the number of older/elderly persons will have doubled.[4]

In 1985, the percentage of elderly who were in nursing homes and homes for the aged was estimated at 7.3%.[5] There are currently 331 nursing homes operating in the province with 29,991 residents[6] and 182 homes for the aged with between 28,000 and 29,000 residents.[7] In addition, there are also a large number of other long-term care facilities for the elderly, including chronic care institutions, rest homes and retirement homes.

(iii) Psychiatrically Disabled Persons

With respect to psychiatrically disabled persons, the following statistics were obtained from the Ministry of Health.[8] During 1985 to 1986, there were 11,025 admissions to the 10 provincial psychiatric hospitals; 34,910 admissions to psychiatric units in public hospitals; and 5,777 admissions to other psychiatric facilities. As of March 31, 1986, there were 4,293 patients in the ten provincial psychiatric hospitals, 1,927 patients in the psychiatric units of public hospitals and 816 patients in other psychiatric hospitals.

As well, there are currently 252 residential homes for special care with approximately 1,963 residents, most of whom are former psychiatric patients. In addition, 3,259 former psychiatric patients currently reside in nursing homes.[9]

It is estimated that, in any one year, 8% or more of the residents in Ontario will receive medical services for a psychiatric diagnosis.[10] Further, between 1 in 4 and 1 in 7 people will seek assistance for a mental health problem sometime during their life.[11]

Statistics received from the Office Responsible for Disabled Persons indicate that, between 1964-1979, there was a 75% drop in Ontario of psychiatric patients in institutions and that the province has shifted from custodial, institutional type care to community-based support and rehabilitation programs. The Office commented, however, that currently the needs of these individuals for affordable and accessible housing, rehabilitation programs, and community services are not being adequately addressed. Indeed, it is estimated that, in 1986, there were approximately 12,000 homeless former psychiatric patients.[12]

(iv) Developmentally Handicapped

It would appear that, at present, there are approximately 78,000 people with developmental disabilities, the large majority of whom are adults.[13] The largest number of such persons are between the ages of 15 and 34. Approximately 10% of all developmentally handicapped persons reside in some type of institution.[14]

(b) The Concept of Vulnerability

In the previous section, the statistics illustrate that there exists a significant number of people in our province who can be identified as "vulnerable adults". It is important at this juncture to consider why these adults are vulnerable and how their vulnerablility contributes to the need for advocacy.

For the purpose of this Review, vulnerable adults have been defined as people with some type of physical, emotional or cognitive impairment. In many cases, people with disabilities have special needs and are often reliant upon others to meet those special needs: such dependency can create vulnerability. Many vulnerable adults are dependent upon the health care and social service system in our province, which can be complex, confusing and difficult to access without assistance -- particularly if one is disabled. Vulnerable adults are also often dependent upon their caregivers, whether family members, friends or institutional staff, and this dependency can leave them susceptible to abuse, neglect or abandonment.

Further, certain vulnerable adults often have difficulty in communicating. This may be due to the disability itself -- for example, a problem with speaking, or hearing -- or may result from isolation, lack of opportunity or an inability to speak English or French. With respect to the latter communication barrier, it would appear that one out of every five persons in Ontario over 65 years of age speaks a mother tongue other than English or French.[15] According to the 1981 census, 20% of this group are unable to hold a conversation in either of Canada's official languages.[16] Problems with communication clearly increase people's vulnerability because of the difficulty involved in making their wishes known.

Furthermore, in many cases, vulnerable adults are not encouraged to communicate their wishes. Indeed, our society often tends to see a vulnerable person's disability first, rather than his or her abilities, with the result that our disadvantaged citizens can be treated in a very paternalistic way. The views and desires of vulnerable adults are often discounted and those of others -- caregivers, social service and health care professionals -- substituted in their place. The motive for this behaviour is, in most cases, benign and charitable: the decision-makers are simply acting "in the best interests" of the individuals. However, such treatment detracts from people's rights to self-determination and, as a result, makes them more vulnerable and reliant on others. Furthermore, emphasis on a person's incapacity often becomes a self-fulfilling prophecy, encouraging vulnerable adults to depreciate themselves and remain dependent.

There is a compounding effect. In addition to having to cope with a handicap or disability, the vulnerable adult may feel undervalued by others and may also incur the further handicap of lowered self esteem and its ensuing emotional/psychological problem.

As noted in the previous section, there are a significant number of vulnerable adults resident in institutions. *Institutionalization, of its very nature, creates vulnerability.* An institutional setting deprives people of a substantial degree of control over their lives and of many of their rights. Residents of institutions cease to make basic decisions and are required to live by rules and regulations that affect every aspect of their daily lives. For example, they are told when to go to bed, when to get up, what they can eat and often what to wear. Control over finances may be taken away, privacy is eroded or non-existent, and they can no longer come and go as they please. For these patients and residents, this lack of power, this lack of personal autonomy, can lead to a sense of isolation, frustration, panic, and depression and a loss of sense of purpose and self-worth.

People who reside in institutions often become stereotyped. Indeed, institutionalization fosters a number of common assumptions about the residents of long term care facilities, including "the notion that their lives started when they entered the institution, that bed rest is good for them, that they are in an institution for their own good, and because one thing is wrong with them, all their capacities are reduced."[17]

Unfortunately, patients and residents in institutions are often unaware of their rights or, if aware, are afraid to exercise them. These individuals are generally restricted in the wishes and complaints that may be voiced because of a fear of reprisal. They become conditioned to demonstrate behaviour patterns that conform to and suppport the need for institutional order.

In addition, many in institutions are unable to seek assistance on their own because of their physical, mental or emotional disability or illness. In many cases, no one except family members monitor their living conditions. However, most families are uneducated about health care and, accordingly, lack the knowledge and expertise to detect and identify serious problems related to the patient's or resident's care. In other cases, there is no one -- no family or friends to assist them or to speak on their behalf.

In the above paragraphs, we have identified certain aspects of the vulnerabilities shared by many of the disadvantaged adults identified in our Terms of Reference. It is clear that because such vulnerabilities can leave these individuals open to abuse, neglect and abandonment, there is a need for advocacy on their behalf. Indeed, advocacy is needed, to:

- promote respect for the rights, freedoms and dignity of these persons;

- ensure that the legal and human rights of vulnerable adults are understood, recognized and protected;

- assist disadvantaged adults to receive the health care and social services to which they are entitled and which they wish to receive;

- assist vulnerable adults to speak for themselves in order to maximize their right to self-determination;

- enhance the autonomy of vulnerable adults by advocating on their behalf -- *as they wish* -- both individually and collectively;

- protect them from financial, physical and psychological abuse; and

- assist them to lead lives that are as independent as possible and in the least restrictive environment as possible.

(c) Existing Advocacy Programs and Services and their Drawbacks

While a clear need for advocacy for vulnerable adults has been identified in the previous sections, it is important to acknowledge that, at present, there exists in Ontario both formal and informal advocacy services for these individuals. Accordingly, in analyzing whether an additional advocacy system or systems is needed, the adequacy of the current advocacy programs and services must be considered.

In this section of the Report, the existing formal advocacy programs and formal programs that have an advocacy component are described, as well as the informal advocacy services that are provided by volunteer groups and others. The section concludes with an analysis of a number of the limitations of these programs and services.

(i) Formal Advocacy Programs

a. Psychiatric Patient Advocate Office (PPAO)

The Psychiatric Patient Advocate Office (hereinafter referrred to as the PPAO) was established by the Ministry of Health in 1982. Currently, there are 12 psychiatric patient advocates (hereinafter referred to as PPA's) in the program with offices in the 10 provincial psychiatric hospitals. There is a single advocate in each of the following eight provincial psychiatric hospitals: Brockville, Hamilton, Kingston, Lakehead, London, North Bay, St. Thomas and Whitby. Queen Street Mental Health Centre and Penetanguishene Mental Health Centre each have two advocates.

All advocates are independent of hospital administration and report to a Provincial Co-ordinator who, in turn, reports directly to the Minister of Health, sometimes through the Deputy Minister. The program is also supported by an Advisory Committee which includes mental health consumers and providers, and lay and legally trained advocates. The responsibilities of the Committee include advising the Provincial Co-ordinator, reporting regularly to the Minister and the Deputy on the progress of the program and making recommendations on appropriate changes to the program's designated concept.

The basic duties of patient advocates are to investigate concerns, inquiries and complaints; to link patients with legal counsel or community resources; and to recommend to the Ministry ways to improve mental health care. The specific mandate of the PPAO is set out as follows:

- to advance the legal and civil rights of psychiatric patients in all provincial psychiatric hospitals;

- to inform the patient, family, hospital staff and the community about patients' legal and civil rights;

- to assist, facilitate and help resolve the complaints made by psychiatric patients by providing an avenue for resolution through negotiation according to the patient's instructions;

- to investigate alleged incidents and assess institutional and systemic responses to them; and

- to refer patients, when necessary, to outside community advocacy resources such as community organizations, lawyers, or physicians who may offer a second psychiatric opinion.

In fulfilling its mandate, the program has assumed two primary functions: individual casework and systemic advocacy. With respect to the former, the program is restricted to in-patients of provincial psychiatric hospitals and is mainly reactive in nature. Hospital patients and staff are advised about the duties of the patient advocates through posters, brochures and word of mouth, and referrals are accepted from family, friends, staff and other patients. The work is largely initiated by the clients and the patient advocates must act in response to the instructions of these clients.

According to the brief submitted to the Review by the PPAO, over the first four years of operation, the program served approximately 12,000 in-patients who sought assistance concerning approximately 30,000 problems that involved a variety of legal, therapeutic and social issues. Each year, approximately 20% of those admitted to provincial psychiatric hospitals have asked a patient advocate for help. Consistently, over the past four years, legal concerns have represented 40-50% of the issues raised;

therapeutic or treatment issues 20%; and social issues approximately 30%. Psychiatric patient advocates do not undertake formal legal representation of their clients in courts and tribunals.

The broader role of the program is to engage in systemic advocacy which involves issues of hospital-wide or system-wide concern. This objective, which includes an educational component, is pursued in a number of ways and has resulted in both administrative, policy and legislative change.

In July 1986, after three years of operation, an external evaluation of the Psychiatric Patient Advocate Office was initiated by the Ministry of Health. An Evaluation Committee, chaired by Professor Allan Manson, was constituted to oversee the conduct and management of a comprehensive evaluation of the PPAO. The Manson Committee's Terms of Reference are as follows:

- to examine the structure, mandate and processes of the Psychiatric Patient Advocate Office;

- to evaluate the quality and extent of services provided and their impact on patient/clients and their families;

- to assess the consequential impact on the mental health care delivery system and other relevant systems in Ontario; and

- to consider the future of the Psychiatric Patient Advocate Office and psychiatric patient advocacy in Ontario.

As noted in Chapter 1, the Terms of Reference required that the Review take into consideration the pending evaluation of the PPA Program. In this regard, we engaged in a continued liaison with Professor Manson and met with him on several occasions.

b. Office of Child and Family Service Advocacy

In 1978, the Ministry of Community and Social Services established an Advocacy Unit within the Children's Services Division in order to assist service co-ordinators to find appropriate help for their "hard to serve" juvenile corrections or child welfare cases. The Advocacy Unit was formally established as the Office of Child and Family Service Advocacy in November, 1985, pursuant to the newly enacted *Child and Family Services Act.*. Its mandate, which is prescribed by section 98 of the legislation, is set out as follows:

- to co-ordinate and administer a system of advocacy, except for advocacy before a court, on behalf of children and families who receive or seek approved services or services purchased by approved agencies;

- to advise the Minister on matters and issues concerning the interest of those children and families; and

- to perform any similar functions given to it by this Act or the regulations or another Act or the regulations made under another Act.

The Office has a staff of three: a Co-ordinator who reports directly to the Assistant Deputy Minister of Operations, an administrative assistant, and a secretary.

The main function of the Office of Child and Family Services Advocacy is to intercede and speak on behalf of children and their families who, without assistance, may not be able to obtain needed services or to resolve problems that have arisen in attempting to access the service system. Although the majority of cases dealt with concern children and their families, the Office does handle cases involving adults and increasingly more such cases are being referred.

Among the adult cases most frequently dealt with are head injured adults; adults with multiple handicaps; sex offenders; severely physically disabled adults needing attendant care; autistic adults; and handicapped adults living in the community who are being abused by relatives or caregivers. In many instances, these cases are referred to the Office because the adult involved does not fit easily into any service category or is having difficulty accessing the services that are available. According to a recent report on the Advocacy Office, entitled *Planning for the Office of Child and Family Service Advocacy*, it remains undecided whether the Office should continue to provide services to handicapped adults. It is reported therein that dealing with adult cases is considerably more time consuming than dealing with cases involving children and that, if it were decided to extend the Advocacy Unit's mandate officially to include adults, the Office would require considerably more resources and probably a different organization.

c. Advocacy Centre for the Elderly (ACE)

The Advocacy Centre for the Elderly (hereinafter referred to as ACE) was established in 1984 and is a specialized legal aid clinic designed to serve the legal needs of elderly people of low income who reside in Metropolitan Toronto. In addition, ACE serves as a resource centre for other legal aid clinics in Ontario and lawyers with respect to legal issues that concern elderly people.

ACE, which is funded by the Ministry of the Attorney General through the Ontario Legal Aid Plan, currently has a staff of six: three lawyers, one community legal worker, and two support staff. The Centre provides the following services:

- advice, referral, and legal casework;
- representation of clients before courts and tribunals;
- research towards law reform;
- public legal education and outreach; and
- advocacy services for institutionalized elderly.

With respect to the provision of the latter services, in 1986 the Board of Directors of ACE requested and received monies from the Clinic Funding Committee of the Ontario Legal Aid Plan to employ an "institutional advocate". It was felt "that a lawyer who devoted most of his/her time to legal needs that might arise among residents of long-term care facilities, would not only strengthen ... [ACE's] ability to serve [its] constituency but, by affecting the behaviour of the institutional care providers, benefit residents and their families generally".[18]

In the past year, the institutional advocate has had dealings with residents in approximately 35 institutions. Most of the casework focuses on complaints or concerns of residents and/or their families. Issues concerning quality of care, lack of services, transfers within and between facilities, and discharges constitute the majority of the institutional advocate's caseload.

During 1985-86, ACE provided summary advice to over 2,000 individuals and referred nearly 1,500 inquiries to other agencies or professionals, mostly to the private Bar or to other legal clinics that were more closely situated to the client. During this period, ACE received approximately the same number of referrals, mostly from social agencies and other clients. Currently, ACE lawyers carry about 200 open files.

d. Advocacy Resource Centre for the Handicapped (ARCH)

The Advocacy Resource Centre for the Handicapped (hereinafter referred to as ARCH) was founded in 1979 and is a legal clinic run by and for handicapped persons. ARCH is a non-profit organization governed by a Board of Directors that represents more than 35 organizations which advocate on behalf of disabled persons. The Board comprises primarily disabled persons.

ARCH's mandate is to meet the legal needs of individuals with a broad range of mental or physical handicaps. More specifically, its mandate includes the following objectives:

- to provide direct legal services emphasizing those clients who are not adequately served, with a view to identifying barriers to accessing the legal system;

- to engage in legal education activities with respect to the legal rights and needs of handicapped people;

- to carry out legal research with the objective of expanding the rights of handicapped people;

- to work to establish legal precedents that will benefit handicapped people.

Approximately one-half of ARCH's funding comes from the Clinic Funding Program of the Ontario Legal Aid Plan. The balance comes from its member organizations, foundations, various levels of government and private donations. ARCH has five full-time lawyers and an outreach worker and handled 96 cases during 1986.

(ii) Formal Programs with an Advocacy Component

a. Adult Protective Services Program

The Adult Protective Services Program (hereinafter referred to as the APS Program) was initiated in 1974 by the Ministry of Community and Social Services in conjunction with its program to deinstitutionalize developmentally handicapped persons. The goals of the APS Program are to enable developmentally disabled adults living within a community setting to lead lives as normal and independent as possible within that setting and to ensure the provision of social support services to meet an individual's needs.

There are currently 132 Adult Protective Service Workers (hereinafter referred to as APSWs) in Ontario. All APSWs are employed and supervised by local generic or specialized agencies which are funded for this service by the Ministry of Community and Social Services. There are 63 different agencies across the province that sponsor this program including, for example, community colleges, YWCA/YMCA, health units, hospitals, family service agencies, counselling agencies and associations for the developmentally handicapped.

The overall responsibility of APSWs is to facilitate their clients' adaptation to community life so that the clients may gain the maximum degree of independence possible in each area of their life. The specific mandate of an APSW "is to serve clients primarily by finding services, preferably generic, (case management role), and by advocating on behalf of their clients, as well as on behalf of developmentally handicapped adults in general (advocacy role)."[19]

While the primary responsibilities of an APSW are service co-ordination and advocacy, other functions include the following:
- assisting the client with locating and retaining accommodation;
- outreach;
- medical/dental care co-ordination;
- assisting the client with problem-solving and the acquisition of living skills;

- providing emotional support to the client;
- primary trusteeship;
- liaising with family members and others as appropriate; and
- public education.

The relationship between an APSW and his or her client is entirely voluntary: the APSW does not have guardianship or legislative custodial authority. In addition, the active participation of the client in decision-making is encouraged to the fullest extent possible. During 1986-87, it is estimated that 7,500 developmentally handicapped adults were served by APSWs in Ontario.[20]

It should be noted that there is a similar program funded by the Ministry of Community and Social Services for children with developmental handicaps. The Family Support Workers Program provides service co-ordination, counselling and advocacy services to families with developmentally handicapped children. These programs are usually housed in associations for the developmentally handicapped, while others are housed in generic community agencies such as the Catholic Family Services Bureau or a family support agency.

b. Tri-Ministry Service Co-ordinators

In 1982, the Ministries of Community and Social Services, Health, and Education established the Tri-Ministry Program to address the needs of approximately 3,000 developmentally handicapped people living in nursing homes and residential homes for special care. Pursuant to this program, the Ministry of Community and Social Services provided funding to hire Tri-Ministry Service Co-ordinators whose primary responsibility was to assess the needs of developmentally handicapped children and young adults living in nursing homes and residential homes for special care, and to co-ordinate services and activities for them that would enable them to develop to their fullest potential. Currently, there are 27 service co-ordinators in the province.

Some service co-ordinators are employed directly by nursing homes or residential homes for special care, while others are employed by community agencies such as community colleges, hospitals, family service agencies and counselling agencies. Activities carried out by service co-ordinators include the following:

- interviewing clients to identify needs or monitor progress;

- providing emotional counselling to clients;

- meeting with other individuals and service providers to discuss the client's problems; and

- locating support services for the client such as transportation, sheltered workshop programs, activity and recreation programs.

In addition, an important component of these largely service co-ordination functions is to advocate on a client's behalf.

In April, 1987, the Ministry of Community and Social Services announced plans to develop community living alternatives over the next year for some 130 developmentally handicapped people living in nursing homes as a first step in creating community placements for all developmentally handicapped residents of nursing homes. Service co-ordinators will be playing an active role in assisting these clients in making the transition from institutional to community living.

(iii) Informal Advocacy

a. Volunteer Advocacy Services

Among the most vigorous advocates for vulnerable adults in Ontario are the numerous voluntary associations that have been formed to protect the rights and improve the quality of life of the members of specific vulnerable groups. Voluntary associations in the province generally fall into four basic categories: self-help organizations; associations formed by family members and friends of vulnerable persons; associations that also provide services; and coalitions. Although each individual association has its own unique characteristics, certain generalizations can be made about the structure and organization of associations in each category and about the approach they take towards advocacy on behalf of their constituency groups.

1. Self-help Groups

There are a number of self-help groups that have been organized in Ontario -- for example, People First of Ontario, PUSH Ontario (People United for Self-Help), On Our Own, BOOST (Blind Organization of Ontario with Self-help Tactics) and Action Awareness. All such groups, including but not only those mentioned, should be commended for their important work and for the invaluable assistance they have provided for others.

These groups, which have been formed primarily to promote the well-being of their members, are non-profit, charitable organizations. These organizations can be relatively small, localized associations, as well as province or country-wide with a network of local branches or affiliated local associations. Most operate on funds received from charitable donations with some assistance, often in the form of project grants, from various levels of government.

Activities carried out by self-help groups range from publishing newsletters and organizing workshops and seminars for members to informal service activities such as providing peer counselling and organizing peer support groups. In addition, discussions with members of different self-help groups, as well as the submissions that were received, revealed that one of the most important functions of these groups is to advocate on behalf of their members. The advocacy role of these organizations includes both individual and systemic advocacy activities -- from advising members about their rights to pressuring government for reform to programs and legislation.

An equally important goal of these self-help groups is to encourage vulnerable people to advocate for themselves and, as a result, to help these individuals develop a sense of their own strengths and abilities. In their advocacy activities, self-help groups operate with a unique credibility: because their membership consists of people with similar vulnerabilities, they are particularly able to understand and express the concerns and problems of those on whose behalf they are advocating.

2. Voluntary Associations formed by Relatives, Friends and Concerned Citizens

Voluntary associations formed on behalf of particular vulnerable groups by relatives, friends or concerned citizens share many of the same characteristics of self-help groups. These associations, which include, for example, Concerned Friends of Ontario Citizens in Care Facilities, Patients' Rights Association, Ontario Friends of Schizophrenics, the Ontario Association for Children and Adults with Learning Disabilities, and Citizen Advocacy groups, are also non-profit, charitable organizations that may be small and localized or province-wide with a network of local branches. As well, funding generally comes from charitable donations with some receiving project funding from various levels of government.

Voluntary organizations of this type also consider advocacy to be one of their primary roles. As the members of these organizations are often personally involved with an individual in the represented disability group, they feel that they are in a special position to understand the needs of those being advocated for. As well, these organizations generally engage in both individual and systemic advocacy.

Within this category of volunteer associations, there are a number of groups throughout the province that engage in a distinct form of advocacy, known as "citizen advocacy". The nature of this type of advocacy is discussed below.

Citizen Advocacy

Wolf Wolfensberger, with whom this concept is generally associated, has described citizen advocacy in the following way: "An unpaid competent citizen advocate volunteer, with the support of an independent citizen advocacy agency, represents -- as if they were his/her own -- the interests of one or two impaired persons by means of one or several advocacy roles, some of which may last for life".[21] The idea of citizen advocacy was formulated by Wolfensberger in the mid 1960's and grew out of a project in Nebraska to deinstitutionalize developmentally handicapped individuals. The first citizen advocacy office was opened in 1970 in Lincoln, Nebraska.

In Canada, the Canadian Association for Community Living hosted a national citizen advocacy workshop in 1971 to introduce the concept to this country and to provide encouragement for the initiation of such programs in major Canadian cities. Today, citizen advocacy programs are operating in most provinces and throughout the United States.

In Ontario, there are currently nine citizen advocacy groups which operate in the following areas: Toronto, Etobicoke, Oshawa, Welland, St. Mary's, Windsor-Essex, Sudbury, Ottawa-Carleton and Brockville. These groups are non-profit, voluntary organizations that recruit citizen volunteers ("advocates") to work, usually on a one-to-one basis, with persons who have certain disabilities ("protégés" or "partners"). The general objectives of citizen advocacy are expressed, as follows, in the objectives of the Citizen Advocacy Corporation of Ottawa-Carleton:

> To encourage and assist handicapped, impaired or disadvantaged individuals in realizing their potential by:
>
> (a) matching the disadvantaged person "protégé" with a competent volunteer "citizen advocate" who agrees to protect the protégé's interests and rights as if they were his or her own;
>
> (b) providing support, and access to resources required by protégé-advocate pairs;
>
> (c) operating an agency that is independent and autonomous to assure the advocate of freedom from conflict of interest while acting on the protégé's behalf.

Citizen Advocates perform a number of functions with respect to their protégés. Certain of these are discussed in the following excerpt from the submission received from the Ottawa-Carelton Citizen Advocacy Office:

> Advocates provide assistance in those areas where need has been established between the protégé and staff member. Some of the general activities with which advocates become involved are: sharing time with a protégé, offering companionship and support, encouraging involvement in the community and recreational outings. In addition, advocates may also engage in more specific

activities such as helping to develop independent living skills such as shopping, budgeting and banking, sharing experiences to develop problem-solving skills for daily living, and assist in obtaining medical, social, education, or legal services. All protégés are matched with the intent that the advocate will ensure that all protégés' rights are understood and protected and their personal lives are enriched.

For each citizen advocacy office, an elected volunteer board of directors (i.e. interested members of the community) hires and supervises a small number of co-ordinators whose responsibility is to attract, select and train suitable volunteer citizen advocates and match them with protégés. The co-ordinators do not carry out advocacy functions directly; they do, however, provide support and back-up to the citizen advocate. Co-ordinators may also recruit volunteer "associate advocates", such as doctors and lawyers, who are available to provide professional advice and assistance to the citizen advocate, as well as volunteer "crisis advocates", whose role is to assist with the resolution of specific short-term problems facing citizen advocates and their protégés.

The number of matches that an office is able to make varies and depends, for instance, upon the number of co-ordinators that an office can afford to hire and the number of suitable citizen advocates that can be found. We have been advised that, at the present time, the Windsor-Essex office has 26 active matches, Toronto has between 40-50, and the Ottawa-Carleton Citizen Advocate Office has 98. Funding for citizen advocacy programs is often difficult to find and sustain. Some citizen advocacy organizations, for example, believe that funding from government sources interferes with the independence of the program and, as a result, will accept only private donations.

3. Volunteer Associations that provide Services

Another type of non-profit volunteer association is one that provides services to certain types of vulnerable adults either directly or through local chapters or affiliated associations. These associations, which often originated as self-help groups or as volunteer associations formed by relatives and friends, include, for example, the Canadian Mental Health Association, the Canadian Hearing Society, the Alzheimer Association of Ontario, the Handicapped Action Group, the Multiple Sclerosis Society of Canada, the Canadian Paraplegic Association and the Ontario Association for Community Living.

These associations are organized in a number of different ways. In many cases, the provincial organization with a volunteer board of directors oversees a network of local chapter or regional offices; in other cases, the provincial association acts as a federating body for a network of affiliated, autonomous local associations. While these organizations often have paid staff who assist with the administration of the organization and the delivery of services, they also continue to rely heavily on the participation of volunteer members in most aspects of their operation. Funding for these associations is received from charitable sources, as well as from government -- including ongoing provincial monies to local chapters or associations for the provision of services.

Many of these associations also engage in advocacy-related activities. One example is the Ombudsman Office for Windsor and Essex County, which is an independent program sponsored by the Canadian Mental Health Association and funded by United Way.

The Windsor Ombudsman Office, which was started in 1975, is available to persons resident in the region who have received or are receiving in-patient or out-patient psychiatric care. The role of the Ombudsman is to inform and advise such individuals about their rights and to advocate on their behalf.

Another example is the Northumberland Advocacy Office which is funded by the Port Hope-Cobourg and District Association for the Mentally Retarded. This office was created in 1984 to provide advocacy services for children and adults in Northumberland County with a developmental handicap.

In addition to directly advocating on behalf of certain vulnerable groups or individuals, these associations often support other voluntary associations in their advocacy efforts by providing resources and consultation.

4. Coalitions

A number of volunteer organizations also engage in systemic advocacy and, in order to further this objective, have formed coalitions. Such coalitions may be created solely for the purpose of advocating with respect to one particular issue of common concern or their duration may be of a longer nature. The Ontario Coalition of Senior Citizens' Organizations and the Ontario Coalition for Nursing Home Reform (soon to be known as the Ontario Coalition for Long-Term Care Reform), for example, fall within the latter category. While their constituent organizations originally coalesced to address one particular issue, they subsequently chose to remain together in order to address other issues of common concern.

b. Advocacy of Others

In addition to the advocacy efforts of different volunteer organizations, it is important to acknowledge the informal advocacy that is practised by others. Indeed, for most persons, informal advocates, such as family members and friends, will be their natural and primary advocates.

There can be many benefits to this type of advocacy relationship. As the advocates in this case are likely to know the vulnerable adult very well, including his or her personal history, special needs and circumstances, they are particularly able to understand the vulnerable adult's needs and desires. Further, the relationship between these individuals is likely to be ongoing, which lends stability to the advocacy relationship. In addition, it is difficult to replace the bonds of love and trust that normally exist in family relationships and friendships which foster well intentioned and zealous advocacy.

In addition to family and friends, informal advocacy is also widely practised by doctors, nurses and other health care professionals, social workers, service co-ordinators, and the clergy both in the community and in institutional settings. For example, since 1972, the Ministries of Health, Community and Social Services, and Correctional Services have engaged the services of chaplains to ensure the delivery of pastoral care within certain government owned and operated institutions. One of the important components of chaplaincy services has been to advocate on behalf of vulnerable persons within such institutions in a non-adversarial and non-legal way.

(iv) Shortcomings of Existing Advocacy Services

As discussed in the previous section, there are a number of different advocacy programs and services in our province. However, it would appear that, notwithstanding their existence, current advocacy services in Ontario have a number of drawbacks. Many of the submissions that were received, for example, described current advocacy services in Ontario as "fragmented and inadequate" or as "a fragmented patchwork which requires rationalization". In addition, these briefs, together with the discussions that were held with members of the Advisory Committees and other knowledgeable parties, identified certain shortcomings of the current situation, which are discussed in the following sections of this chapter.

a. Gaps in the System

Consideration of the formal advocacy programs in Ontario indicates that there are many vulnerable adults, both in institutions and in the community, who do not have access, or, at best, very limited access, to non-legal advocacy services.

For example, the Psychiatric Patient Advocate Program is limited to in-patients of the 10 provincial psychiatric hospitals. It is not mandated to provide advocacy services for the significant number of persons receiving psychiatric care in the psychiatric units of general and private hospitals, or in programs under the auspices of the hospitals, such as, approved homes, homes for special care and outpatient programs. Neither does it have the jurisdiction nor resources to meet the advocacy needs of former psychiatric patients who are living in the community.

As discussed in an earlier section of the chapter, out of 52,000 annual admissions to some form of psychiatric facility, there are approximately 35,000 people who are admitted to psychiatric units of general hospitals and about 5,000 to community and private hospitals. According to certain submissions that were received, a significant number of requests for advocacy services have been made by these individuals to the PPAO, thereby indicating an unmet advocacy need.

It would appear that there is also a need for advocacy for former psychiatric patients living in the community. Many such individuals move from psychiatric hospitals to a semi-institutional environment in the community, such as residential homes for special care. As discussed in the previous section, there are, for example, approximately 5,220 people residing in residential homes for special care and nursing homes and many do not have the benefit of therapeutic, rehabilitation programs or other supports. Many other former psychiatric patients live in privately operated lodging and boarding homes where the conditions and quality of care vary greatly.

Various estimates have been made concerning the number of psychiatrically disabled persons living in the community without proper support and community services. One unfortunate indication of this dilemma is the very significant number of re-admissions to psychiatric facilities. Referred to as the "revolving door syndrome", discharged psychiatric patients who are unable to find the support and assistance that they need in the community repeatedly find themselves back in an institution. Further, it was suggested in a number of submissions that the needs of former psychiatric patients living in the community, such as housing, social services, employment, medical treatment, crisis intervention, and recreation, will not be met even minimally without some form of advocacy.

In addition to certain psychiatrically disabled persons, there are other groups of vulnerable adults who currently have limited access to advocacy services. For example, frail elderly persons living in institutional settings, as well as in the community, do not have the protection of a formal advocacy program.

In an earlier section, it was noted that persons who are institutionalized are particularly vulnerable and often in need of someone to speak on their behalf. While volunteer groups, such as Concerned Friends of Ontario Citizens in Care Facilities, play an extremely important role in the development of advocacy services, they are limited by their resources in what they can accomplish. These groups readily admit that they alone cannot hope to address the needs of all vulnerable adults residing in care facilities.

It would also appear that vulnerable elderly people living in the community would benefit from the availability of more formalized advocacy services. Indeed, we have all heard disturbing media reports of the neglect, abandonment, and abuse of the elderly in our communities. The Federal Government's National Clearing House on Family Violence, for example, estimates that between 2-4% of senior citizens in our country are victims of elder abuse.

This need for advocacy for the frail elderly, living in institutions and in the community, was discussed as follows by the Advocacy Centre for the Elderly in its submission to the Review:

> While we have no special competence to judge the extent of the unmet "need" for advocacy across the Province, we can report that client contacts at the Advocacy Centre for the Elderly have risen quite rapidly as awareness of our service has expanded. These contacts are such as to lead us to believe that there is a large unsatisfied need for both legal and non-legal advocates. Every indication is that our in-take will continue to grow. In that connection, we have requested monies from the Clinic Funding Committee to expand our staff. The need for representation for the non-institutionalized elderly plus the special needs of elderly people in long-term care facilities, both individually and in relation to the institutions where they are residents, have outstripped the assistance that can be provided by a staff of six.
>
> Our experience confirms a concern that a substantial fraction of elderly people are at risk in regard to enjoying and exercising their basic human and legal rights. While in some cases this is attributable to reduced physical or mental capabilities or by the restrictions imposed by an institutional environment, poverty is often the problem, exacerbated by a concurrent lack of readily available information and support.
> ....
> ACE also receives many requests for assistance in handling related "non-legal" problems. These requests are referred to a variety of health and social services. Many of the requests for assistance do not appear to have an appropriate referral or the appropriate services do not have the capacity to handle all the referrals.

Other gaps in the provision of formal advocacy services in our province include physically handicapped persons. Although advocacy may be provided on an informal basis by family, friends or other concerned citizens, these individuals do not have access to paid advocates, similar to the Psychiatric Patient Advocates. Further, while developmentally handicapped persons living in the community, in nursing homes, and in some residential homes for special care may have access to APSWs and service co-ordinators paid to pursue advocacy, the over 5,000 developmentally disabled persons living in other institutions do not have similar services.[22] This is incongruous and unfair.

b. Conflict of Interest

Although psychiatric patients in provincial psychiatric hospitals have access to PPAs, and a number of developmentally handicapped persons have APSWs and service co-ordinators to act as their advocates, the advocacy potential of these professionals has been sometimes viewed as not being sufficiently independent of government and, accordingly, susceptible to conflict of interest.

It has been suggested, for example, that because the PPAO is situated within the Ministry of Health which funds both the PPAO and the province's psychiatric hospitals, the ability of the PPAs to advocate independently on behalf of their clients is impeded. It is argued that, because PPAs are employed by Health, they will find it difficult to criticize certain actions or policies of the Ministry or its psychiatric institutions or to recommend, for example, that litigation be initiated against the Ministry in appropriate cases. Similar concerns have also been expressed with regard to APSWs and service co-ordinators. As they are hired by agencies that receive funding from the Ministry of Community and Social Services and which often provide services for developmentally handicapped persons, there could exist, or be perceived to exist, a conflict of interest and a limit to their independence and efficacy .

The potential problem of conflict of interest is also relevant to advocates who are operating within other service delivery organizations: for example, health care professionals and staff who are employed by hospitals, or advocates who work in volunteer organizations that also provide services for vulnerable adults. As they are operating within a service delivery organization, they could be subject to pressure or control by that organization and may not be able to offer a client an unbiased perspective or to advocate freely and vigorously on their behalf. Indeed, there is usually a point at which even the most dedicated and generous staff member will no longer risk disapproval, job security or a good working relationship.

This danger of conflict of interest, which was identified by many of those with whom we met and in the submissions that we received, is summarized in the following excerpt from the Advocacy Ontario brief (June, 1986) prepared by Concerned Friends of Ontario Citizens in Care Facilities:

> The structure of the current advocacy system .... has created serious conflicts of interest for many of its workers. It is difficult, if not impossible, to effectively advocate for a client with one's own employer. That is the situation facing service co-ordinators employed by nursing homes and homes for special care, and by adult protective service workers employed by institutions or by Associations for the Mentally Retarded.
>
> It is similarly difficult for advocates sponsored by agencies funded by a Ministry which also funds direct services to their clients.
> ....
> All APSWs, service co-ordinators, and psychiatric patient advocates find themselves in this position. They lack the independence to take whatever action is necessary on behalf of their clients when these actions bring them into conflict with the Ministry which pays their salaries. This has resulted in some workers wishing to emphasize the "social work" aspects of their roles, rather than stressing the human rights aspects of their work through advocacy.
>
> The only advocate currently functioning in a conflict-free position is the institutional advocate housed within the Advocacy Centre for the Elderly. Funded, at arm's length, by the Ministry of the Attorney General, through the Ontario Legal Aid Plan administered by the Law Society of Upper Canada, the institutional advocate for elderly residents of long-term care facilities is free to act independently.

An additional problem associated with conflict of interest concerns lack of trust. It has been suggested that a vulnerable adult may be reluctant to accept assistance from advocates who are in a potential conflict of interest position. They may question, for example, whether the advocate will be able to work sincerely on their behalf and to vigorously pursue their wishes. Moreover, they may feel an understandable reluctance to share in confidence their experiences or criticisms regarding the Ministry or officials who also employ that advocate.

c. Other Shortcomings

In addition to the real or perceived problem of conflict of interest, existing advocacy services have been criticized for other reasons. For example, it has been suggested that the formal advocacy programs currently operating are underfunded and, as a result, are unable to meet the advocacy needs of the vulnerable population. It would appear that many APSWs and service co-ordinators carry caseloads that are excessive with the result that they have difficulty in fulfilling their mandates.

Lack of resources is also a problem facing volunteer organizations that engage in advocacy activities. Most of these organizations struggle to obtain adequate funding -- sometimes without success. For example, the Citizen Advocacy Office in Windsor-Essex was forced to close its doors for a four-year period until sufficient funding was found. Indeed, all of the volunteer organizations that had input in the Review expressed the need for stable, ongoing funding.

Other problems facing existing advocacy services in Ontario concern a lack of direction and support in certain programs. For example, it was suggested that there is often inappropriate placement of APSW programs within agencies that provide little or no direction or support with respect to the advocacy role to be played by individual workers. Further, as the program apparently differs from agency to agency, there are inconsistencies throughout the province with respect to the nature of an APSW's responsibilities. We were advised that this lack of direction in the program, together with the lack of support on the part of certain agencies, has deterred some APSWs from the advocacy component of the job.

This problem of lack of support is also particularly relevant to informal advocates, such as family and friends. In many cases, these individuals will be on their own in advocating for a vulnerable adult, with no formal organization or government agency to provide support or back-up.

Other drawbacks of existing advocacy services are the lack of training and supervision of informal advocates, as well as limited accountability. Many advocates who operate outside of formal advocacy programs do not receive any initial training or any on-going training and upgrading of their advocacy skills. As a result, a particular advocate may lack the knowledge or expertise to obtain the desired result. Further, without adequate supervision or accountability, there is no way to ensure that an advocate is doing a proper job -- that their efforts are effective, that they are not exploiting the client, and that they are truly respecting the wishes of the vulnerable person. Without a proper means of evaluation and a formal accountability mechanism, a bad advocate is difficult to detect and remove.

At this juncture, it is important to add that there are a number of government programs and initiatives that clearly indicate this province's continued commitment to meeting the needs and aspirations of our vulnerable citizens. Some of these which are especially worthy of note have been listed in Appendix 8.

It is neither the purpose nor the intent of this Review to evaluate or critique these initiatives individually. Rather, we welcome them as evidence of a pattern which expresses a genuine sense of caring and an openness to social reform.

The provision of more cohesive and effective advocacy services is the logical next step if Ontario is to maintain its tradition of innovative leadership in social services. Advocacy is consistent with the goal and direction of these other initiatives to help ensure full participation in the daily life of our communities by all those who so desire.

From the evidence presented to this Review, these initiatives, while deserving of commendation, would be more effective if accompanied by an advocacy system which helped ensure their availability to those very citizens most in need of assistance.

(d) The Need for Advocates in the proposed Substitute Decisions Authority Act

(i) Background

As discussed in the introduction to the Report, in 1985, the Ministries of Health, Community and Social Services and the Attorney General established the Advisory Committee on Substitute Decision Making for Mentally Incapable Persons, which is chaired by Mr. Stephen Fram, Counsel, Policy Development Division, Ministry of the Attorney General. The purpose of this Committee is to review all aspects of the law governing and related to substitute decision making for mentally incapable persons, including personal guardianship, and to make recommendations concerning the revision of this law where appropriate. The Fram Committee, which is broadly representative of the community and government, has produced two interim reports and is in the process of preparing its final report which, it is anticipated, will be completed in the Fall of 1987.

In the report, which will include a proposed *Substitute Decisions Authority Act*, the Committee will be recommending that an advocate be involved whenever use of the proposed legislation could remove the legal right of an individual to make an important decision. *It is the view of a significant majority of Committee members that the role to be played by these advocates is so vital that this legislation, if enacted by the government, should not come into force until a formal advocacy system is in place to perform this function.*

The Fram Committee is concerned that, without adequate safeguards, the possibility exists that guardianship or conservatorship might be used inappropriately or indiscriminately. Persons with diminished mental capacity could be victimized by those who wish to benefit from such arrangements or by those who, although well-intentioned, are overprotective. Further, the Fram Committee is concerned that, as a result of the acknowledged shortage of adequate supportive services, guardianship or conservatorship might be used unnecessarily in circumstances where the provision of supportive services would suffice.

(ii) Role of the Advocate

Under the proposed *Substitute Decisions Authority Act,* an advocate would play a number of important roles which are discussed in the following sections. Basically, the function of an advocate would be to advise people of their rights in order to prevent excessive and inappropriate use of guardianship and conservatorship.

a. Application to Appoint Conservators and Guardians

The proposed legislation requires that, whenever an application is brought for the appointment of a conservator or guardian, an advocate would be required to explain the implications to the person who is the subject of the application. It would be the responsibility of the advocate to visit the person and explain to him or her the nature of the application and the process that will be followed to ensure that the person understands, to the extent possible, what is occurring.

As a result of this visit, the advocate may find that the person is competent to manage his or her financial affairs or to take care of his or herself and is being exploited by a family member or friend. On the other hand, the individual may be content that the application is being brought, but unhappy with the proposed guardian or conservator. If the person wished to oppose the application, it would be the responsibility of the advocate to ensure that the person receives legal assistance.

b. Termination of Conservatorship or Guardianship

Where an application is brought to terminate a conservatorship or guardianship by someone other than the person under conservatorship or guardianship, the draft legislation also proposes that an advocate meet with this person to explain the consequences of the application -- that, for example, the individual will become responsible for the managment of his or her property or for his or her own personal care.

In some situations, the advocate might find that the person does not want the conservatorship or guardianship terminated where, for example, the person or persons bringing the application are seeking to exploit the individual.

c. Order for Assessment and its Enforcement

Under the proposed *Substitute Decisions Authority Act*, an assessment of a person's mental capacity can be ordered pursuant to applications for the appointment or termination of conservators or guardians. Where entry by professionals to a person's residence for the purpose of such an assessment is refused, or where an order to appear in a designated place for an examination is not complied with, the court may issue an enforcement order. The enforcement order will empower certain officials to enter a person's residence with the use of force, if necessary, in order to carry out the assessment order.

The proposed legislation provides, however, that, before the court will make an enforcement order, an advocate must first visit or attempt to visit the person who has been ordered to be assessed in order to explain the significance of the assessment order. It is anticipated that, in the majority of cases, an assessment would be ordered where abuse, neglect or exploitation of an incapable person by family members is suspected. The Fram Committee is of the view that non-compliance with the order, in such instances, would likely be instigated by those who are harming the incapable person. The purpose of the advocate's visit would be to attempt to arrange voluntary compliance with the assessment without the need for an enforcement order.

d. Assessment of Capacity for Personal Power of Attorney

Pursuant to the proposed *Substitute Decisions Authority Act*, a power of attorney for personal care may be granted. By using this type of power of attorney, individuals would be able to designate a particular person to make personal care and medical treatment decisions for them should they become incapacitated. However, before such a power of attorney may be invoked, the Act provides for certain safeguards.

It is provided, for example, that a power of attorney for personal care will not take effect unless the grantor's mental capacity has been assessed by at least two independent assessors. In addition, the power of attorney will not be invoked until copies of the assessors' reports have been served on the person by an advocate who is required to ensure that the person is informed of the significance of the reports, as well as of the right to oppose the process.

As in the other instances where an advocate is to be called upon, that individual's primary function is to ensure that the allegedly incapable person is as aware as possible of what is happening and what his or her rights are in the circumstances.

e. Annual Visit

Lastly, the proposed *Substitute Decisions Authority Act* requires that advocates must annually visit those persons incapable of personal care who have guardians or personal attorneys. The visit of the advocate is to provide some assurance that these individuals are not being neglected or abused by their substitute decision makers. In addition, the visit is to ensure that the personal attorney or guardian is aware of the programs that are available to assist the incapable person.

3. Conclusion

In our view, the foregoing sections of this chapter clearly indicate the need for some type of cohesive and effective advocacy system or systems in this province. As noted earlier, the statistics indicate that there are a substantial number of persons in our province who suffer from some type of physical, emotional, or cognitive impairment and are potentially vulnerable. It was also discussed how "vulnerability" can create a need for advocacy -- for someone to be there to ensure that the needs and wishes of vulnerable adults are respected.

Further, both the formal and informal advocacy programs and services currently operating in the province were examined and it was seen how these programs and services, however well intentioned and worthwhile, cannot adequately meet the needs of Ontario's vulnerable adults. The need for an advocacy system was highlighted by the proposed recommendations of the Fram Committee. Should these proposals be enacted, advocates will be essential to fulfill certain important and specific roles in safeguarding our civil liberties.

In addition, the submissions that were received and discussions that were held further convinced us of the need for advocacy. We were moved by the stories of those who so desperately needed the assistance of someone to act as their advocate -- the many troubling stories of those who "fell through the cracks" because there was no one there for them. At the same time, we rejoiced at the experiences of those who have been so greatly assisted and continue to be assisted by the efforts of an advocate -- leading us to conclude that advocacy does, indeed, make a difference.

In conclusion, perhaps the need for advocacy can best be illustrated by the following excerpt from a training manual for the citizen advocacy program in Georgia:[23]

Think you for coming & Betsy when I need

This note was written by a man considered, labelled, and treated 'vegetable'. It says, "Thank you for coming by Betsy when I needed."

Betsy is his volunteer advocate.

CHAPTER 4

Options for the Delivery of Advocacy Services in Ontario

The manifest needs of Ontario's vulnerable adults for advocacy services, as outlined in chapter 3, present the difficult challenge of establishing an effective, responsive and efficient system for the delivery of advocacy to the over 1 million vulnerable adults residing in large and small communities and institutions throughout the province.

The written submissions and research have identified a multitude of internal and external advocacy programs currently in existence in a number of jurisdictions. As well, and as discussed earlier, Concerned Friends of Ontario Residents in Care Facilities have presented a comprehensive advocacy model entitled "Advocacy Ontario". On the basis of our review of all of these programs, we have identified the following models for consideration:

(1)   Advocacy Ombudsman;
(2)   Citizen Advocacy;
(3)   Advocacy Ontario;
(4)   Mixed Advocacy;
(5)   Shared Advocacy.

Each of these models is described in the following sections of this chapter.

1. THE OMBUDSMAN MODEL

(a) Introduction

In the United States, Ombudsman programs have been established in a number of states for the purpose of delivering advocacy services to vulnerable adults. These were established independently of the service delivery system and were designed to replace the internal programs which some states had established voluntarily.

The genesis of these programs occurred in the late 1960's and early 1970's when the U.S. experienced unparalleled social unrest on the part of its underprivileged citizens, including many elderly and other vulnerable adults. Led mostly by the physically disabled, this period of advocacy for people with disabilities resulted in dramatic reforms, including the philosophy and practice of independent living, and legislative reforms recognizing the civil rights of persons with disabilities. Congress produced four major enactments which provided incentives for the development of advocacy for the disabled:

- *Rehabilitation Act*, 1973

- *Developmentally Disabled Assistance and Bill of Rights Act*, 1975

- *Mental Health Systems Act*, 1980

- *Older Americans Act*, 1965

Also important to the development of advocacy was the proliferation of voluntary advocacy associations concerned with the welfare of the disabled. The parent-sponsored National Association of Parents and Friends of Retarded Children, formed in 1950 (renamed the National Association for Retarded Citizens in 1983), pressed for legislative and other reforms necessary to ensure that developmentally handicapped persons shared fully in all human rights and services. This organization has a membership of over

250,000. In the 1970's the American Coalition of Citizens with Disabilities was formed. This is an umbrella coalition of over 85 self-advocacy organizations representing 36 million disabled Americans including mentally handicapped, physically disabled, developmentally handicapped and psychiatrically disabled.

More recently, Congress enacted the *Protection and Advocacy for Mentally Ill Individuals Act* which requires states which accept federal block grants for mental health care services to create independent advocacy programs for psychiatrically disabled persons. The Act mandates that state advocacy systems pursue administrative, legal and other appropriate remedies to ensure the protection of psychiatrically disabled persons who are receiving care or treatment in the state. Patients are covered by the legislation for up to 90 days following discharge from a treatment facility -- which is defined to include hospitals, nursing homes, community facilities and boarding and care homes. A fundamental prerequisite of any state advocacy system is that it be independent of agencies which provide treatment or services other than advocacy. The legislation provides access to facilities that provide care and treatment and to the records of individuals for whom a complaint is being investigated. Each system must have provision for an advisory board consisting of attorneys, mental health professionals, knowledgeable members of the public, mental health service providers, consumers of services and members of their families. At least half of the board members must be mental health consumers and family members.

Congress also responded to the needs of the elderly for advocacy services. In the 1973 amendments to the *Older Americans Act*, sub-state plannning and co-ordinating bodies called Area Agencies on Aging were created to determine the needs of the aged for social services and to develop comprehensive and co-ordinated service delivery systems in each area. In addition, advisory councils were formed at the regional level comprised of a majority of elderly people with a mandate to provide the aged an opportunity to act as their own advocates. In 1975, the Administration on Aging developed a nursing home Ombudsman and a legal services program which were combined in 1978. The Ombudsman program focused exclusively on the institutionalized, while the legal program focused predominately on the needs of community-based elderly. In 1978, they were combined into a comprehensive advocacy assistance program for the elderly.

This combined program was enhanced by the passage of the *Comprehensive Older Americans Act Amendments of 1978* which mandated that each state designate an Ombudsman at the state level to investigate and resolve complaints made by long-term care residents; monitor laws, regulations and policies affecting long-term care; provide training for volunteers and promote the participation of citizens groups in the Ombudsman program. It is from this legislation that one of the most successful state Ombudsman programs serving the elderly was established in Massachusetts.

(b) Massachusetts Ombudsman Program

In 1973, Massachusetts established a model project pursuant to the *Older Americans Act* to provide advocacy services to residents of long-term care facilities. The Massachusetts program is currently operating under State legislation and regulations promulgated under the Act by the Massachusetts Office of Elder Affairs. There are 27 regionally-based Ombudsmen covering the entire State and approximately 280 volunteer Ombudsmen working under the local Ombudsmen. The program is administered by the State Long-Term Care Ombudsman who reports to the Secretary of the Department of Elder Affairs. The Secretary is a member of State Cabinet reporting to the Governor.

That State (Central) Office is comprised of seven employees. It is responsible for recruiting and hiring the 27 local program directors responsible for each regional office and also provides training to the 280 volunteer local Ombudsmen. Before a local Ombudsman is permittted to act as an advocate, he or she must be certified by the State Office. The State Office also monitors the services provided by the regional offices and maintains central records of complaints and problems received by the local offices, actions taken, findings and recommendations made in response to the complaints and problems including facilities' responses to complaints. The State Office also develops policies and procedures for the local offices and provides technical assistance to the local offices in implementing them. A further important function of the State Central Office is the establishment of a State-wide uniform reporting system for the collection and analysis of data regarding complaints, problems and conditions in long-term care facilities for the purpose of making submissions for systemic change to the provider agencies and government.

Each of the 27 local Ombudsman offices is staffed by one salaried program director who provides advocacy services to the residents of long-term care facilities in his or her region by recruiting and training volunteer local Ombudsmen assigned to designated long-term care facilities within the area. There are now 280 volunteer Ombudsmen certified in the State who are required to visit their designated nursing home one day per week and to visit every resident of the facility at least once per month. The volunteer Ombudsmen are pure volunteers; volunteers from an Elder Service Corps who receive a stipend of $130 per month for approximately 18 hours' service per week; and Senior Aides who are participating in a federally funded elder employment program for low income elders. The Aides receive the State minimum wage for their service.

As mentioned above, training and certification of local program directors and local Ombudsmen are the responsibility of the Central Office. The training program consists of five sessions of five and a half hours each. Trainees are required to pass a written test prior to certification. In addition, the Central Office conducts monthly in-service training programs for all project directors and a separate program for all local Ombudsmen.

It has been the experience of the volunteer Ombudsmen that approximately two months of visitations are required for the residents to develop the necessary trust to confide problems or complaints to the advocate. Upon receipt of a complaint or problem, the Ombudsman advises the resident of their options, takes instructions, inquires as to whether the resident wishes the Ombudsman to release their name and then meets with the nursing home administrator or designee. The Ombudsman acts only on instructions of the resident.

If the nursing home administrator does not resolve the matter to the satisfaction of the resident, nor respond within a reasonable time frame to the problem, the Ombudsman takes the issue to the local program director for resolution. If the local program director is unable to achieve a satisfactory result the matter is then referred to the Central Office.

The program emphasizes the importance of public education and the constant recruitment of volunteers as the program has experienced a loss of volunteers at the rate of approximately 30% per year. It is felt that the only effective means to deliver advocacy services to the elderly in care facilities is by a visible presence of the Ombudsman in the nursing home and, as noted earlier, it is mandatory that the Ombudsman spend one day a week in a nursing home.

The most common problems or concerns which the Ombudsmen are called upon to deal with relate to patient care and do not ordinarily raise legal or systemic change issues. Emphasis is placed on negotiation and the development of a positive working relationship with the care providers. However, where problems are not resolved at the local level, the Central Office has the capacity to secure necessary legal advice from the State Attorney General's office or, in appropriate cases, from local legal firms.

Advocates do not perform any case management/service co-ordination functions as the program is vigilant in retaining its independence from care providers.

The Ombudsman has the right of access to the patient's medical records with the patient's consent. He or she also has the right to enter long-term care facilities at any time considered necessary and reasonable for the purpose of:

1. investigating/resolving complaints and problems through administrative action;

2. interviewing residents, with their consent and in private;

3. offering his or her services to any resident, in private;

4. interviewing employees or agents of the facility;

5. consulting regularly with the facility administration; and

6. providing services authorized by law or regulation.

There is minimal community control of the operation of the Ombudsman office, in a formal sense at least. While an advisory committee of consumers does exist, it would appear that its impact to date has been minimal. However, the Ombudsman program does utilize community groups who have a demonstrated capacity to provide advocacy services. The Central Office is empowered under the legislation to certify local non-profit organizations who have been established by local initiative to provide advocacy services in their region to residents of long-term care facilities. Once certified, such groups are required to adhere to the standards set by the Central Office and must report to that body and to the local program director in their area. Members of such groups who pass the Central Office training programs receive certification and have the same rights of access to records and facilities as the volunteer field Ombudsman and perform the same functions in the long-term residential facilities.

The Massachusetts legislation also provides a procedure for the termination of the local Ombudsman program. In the event the local program fails to comply with the standards and procedures set by the Central Office, the Department of Elder Affairs may terminate the program after specifying any breach or non-compliance in writing and after allowing a reasonable time, but not less than 15 days for correction. The legislation provides for oral notice and immediate termination of a program where the breach or omission endangers life, health or safety of the residents or staff. There is a statutory right of appeal of the termination decision to the departmental administrative hearing officer.

There is a major commitment to systemic change in the Ombudsman program. The principal responsibility for systemic advocacy is in the Central Office which has staff who are continually drafting legislative amendments and pressing the legislature and care providers for needed changes in the care for the elderly. In the past year, the Central Office has drafted three bills, two of which have been enacted by the State legislature addressing recurring problems encountered by the local Ombudsmen -- Medicaid discrimination, nurses' aides training and the low wages paid to nurses' aides. The local Ombudsmen are required to assist in systemic changes and are regarded as effective lobbyists who organize letter-writing campaigns and stimulate the community to press for needed changes.

The current annual budget of the Ombudsman program in Massachusetts is U.S. $1 million. The office is funded by federal grants. The director and staff of the program have described a need for additional salaried staff to supervise volunteers and to assist with the record keeping.

The Massachusetts Ombudsman program for long-term care residents is an excellent example of an effective centrally structured system which could be adapted to the Ontario context. However, persons who require advocacy in Ontario are not limited to residents of nursing homes. An Advocacy Ombudsman program in Ontario must have a broader reach, also providing advocacy services to developmentally handicapped persons in institutions and in the community; frail elderly persons in the community; and psychiatrically disabled persons in psychiatric facilities and in the community. It would be desirable for the Advocacy Ombudsman to report to an independent body such as a committee of the legislature -- the currently constituted Standing Committee on the Ombudsman may be capable of accepting this added responsibility. In addition to providing independence to the program, the Standing Committee would be an appropriate forum to deal with unresolved complaints or problems requiring systemic change. Such problems could be identified to the Committee in the annual report of the Advocacy Ombudsman and the Committee would be empowered to conduct public hearings to consider the merits of the matter and make recommendations to the Legislature. The public hearings would be a final resort in the event that negotiations with care providers failed to solve systemic problems or even egregious individual complaints.

2.   THE CITIZEN ADVOCACY MODEL

(a) Introduction

As discussed in chapter 3, 20 years ago Wolf Wolfensburger developed the concept and principles of citizen advocacy to address the needs of people with instrumental or expressive disabilities and to facilitate the deinstitutionalization of disabled people and their integration into the community. It is founded upon the establishment of a permanent one-to-one relationship between a volunteer citizen advocate (friend) and a disabled partner (protégé). This innovative program is described in detail in *Citizen Advocacy and Protective Services for the Impaired and Handicapped*, 1973, Wolfensburger and Zauha (*"Citizen Advocacy "*) distributed by the National Institute on Mental Retardation of Canada.

Citizen advocacy recognizes that the continued provision of human services to the disabled can never be sufficient and, to remain effective, there must always be a process of change. It also recognizes that providers are inherently limited in their potential to act as agents of such change, as the role of provider and administrator are only compatible to a limited degree with the role of critic and agent for change. The volunteer citizen advocate, independent of government and service providers, gives expressive and instrumental support to those disabled persons who have no or inadequate personal or family support. Citizen Advocates integrate their partners into their social life, introduce them to the community and represent their partners' interests as if these interests were their own. The essence of citizen advocacy is captured in the following passage from O'Brien, *Learning from Citizen Advocacy Programs*, 1987, Georgia Advocacy Office:

> Ultimately opportunities for people with handicaps to be included in community life can only be provided by ordinary citizens.
>
> People with handicaps are so often isolated and segregated from the rest of their community that, on their own, chances do not exist for them to get to know their neighbors. Segregated schools, and training centers add to this isolation.
>
> Citizens who are already well-connected and involved in the larger community can provide the opportunities for people with disabilities to participate in every day experiences of the community in which they live.
>
> By their very nature services provided by paid professionals are limited in their ability to provide a church family, opportunities for people with handicaps to join the local bowling league, to arrange an evening with neighbors to play cards or get together for dinner, etc. Their job is to provide paid services not to build community.
>
> When professional services are needed we want the best ones available. If a person has trouble seeing well, he/she goes to an eye doctor, if a person needs speech therapy, he/she gets speech therapy. We want the benefit of their training, their expertise.
>
> However, what is occurring in our society is that we are being lulled into believing that only professionals have the answers. If a baby is born handicapped, parents are often urged to put their child in an institution where the child will receive "professional" care. Thus, the parents are robbed of the opportunity to participate in the raising of their child, the community is robbed of knowing their child, and the child is robbed of the experience of being with family and friends. If a teenager is rebelling we can now "fix the problems" by sending our young people to a hospital for as long as the insurance will pay. The parents are robbed of the experience of struggling, suffering and rejoicing. They are made to feel inadequate. The child feels abandoned and gets the impression that he/she is "sick", too "sick" to remain with family and friends.

We need to reclaim our abilities as ordinary citizens and call back
home those that are sent away... everytime we do send someone
away we lose some of our power.

In *Citizen Advocacy*, the authors propose the establishment of advocacy offices on
a provincial or state level comprised of a central office (which is part of -- but
substantially independent from -- an existing government department or Ministry) and
local advocacy offices staffed by the central office with advocacy co-ordinators. This
model was adopted 10 years ago by the state of Georgia and was commended to us in a
number of the written submissions and meetings.

(b) The Georgia Advocacy Office

The Georgia program originated from the federal *Developmentally Disabled
Assistance and Bill of Rights Act, 1975*, which required that states receiving federal
funds for their developmentally disabled citizens establish a program to provide
advocacy services to the disabled independent of the state human service system. The
Georgia Advocacy Office is funded principally by federal grants, though in recent years
there has been an increasing proportion of state funding. The program is currently being
expanded to provide advocacy services to the mentally ill as well as the developmentally
disabled.

The program is operated by a private, non-profit corporation which enables it to
receive charitable donations as well as government funds. There is a seven member
Board of Directors comprised of eminent citizens. Board members do not have to
possess any extensive knowledge of the field and must not be associated with any
service provider. The Board reports to and is accountable to the Governor. It files an
annual report and funding request with the Governor as well as with the federal
Department of Health Education and Welfare. The present annual budget is
approximately U.S. $770,000. To date, the program has operated free of government
interference and, apart from the annual reports, there appears to be limited contact with

government. A prime focus of the Advocacy Office is the matching of disabled persons with citizen advocates and assisting local groups and individuals in deinstitutionalizing disabled persons. The office has not emphasized systemic change as a priority and has only been involved in one test case in its 10 years of operation.

The central office is composed of an Executive Director responsible for the overall administration of the program, an Assistant Executive Director responsible for the six local advocacy offices situated in various regions of the State, a Co-ordinator of Legal Advocacy, a Co-ordinator of Advocacy Development and an Administrative Assistant.

There are citizen advocacy offices in only six communities and consequently central office staff is responsible for the provision of protection and advocacy services throughout the rest of the state. Central office staff investigates complaints of neglect or abuse and assists families and friends of the disabled in efforts to deinstitutionalize the disabled and integrate them into the daily life of the community. As well, an important function of the central office is to provide information and education concerning the concept and principles of citizen advocacy to communities throughout the state.

Of the six local offices providing citizen advocacy services, three do so on a contract basis with the central office through a community Board of Directors which is responsible for the local program. Before funds are advanced to a local board, it must enter into a contract to provide advocacy services to the community in a manner consistent with the principles of citizen advocacy and in compliance with the policies and practices developed by the central office. The staff of the local offices are supervised and accountable directly to the central office.

The six local offices established to date (a seventh is scheduled to open in 1988) are staffed by salaried advocacy co-ordinators. There is usually one co-ordinator and one administrative assistant in each office. The co-ordinator is responsible for the recruitment, screening and training of potential citizen advocates. The principal means of recruitment is meeting with and providing information on citizen advocacy to community groups and seeking commitments from those present to become citizen advocates.

The disabled persons the program seeks to match with a citizen advocate are usually identified by visits to local nursing homes and institutions for the mentally disabled or by referrals from service providers. Though the demands for citizen advocates are large, the local offices prefer to maintain a small working list of approximately 10 vulnerable citizens they are actively engaged in attempting to match with an appropriate citizen advocate.

The advocacy co-ordinator develops a file of names of persons in need of advocacy with their particular needs and interests. He or she brings an appropriate citizen advocate candidate together with the disabled person in a social setting to determine whether the match is appropriate. There is no formal contract between the citizen advocate, the partner or the citizen advocacy office. The co-ordinators seek a clear affirmation from the citizen advocate of his or her commitment to become a citizen advocate willing to accept and integrate the vulnerable person into his or her social life and community. If an affirmative answer is given and the vulnerable adult accepts the relationship, the match is confirmed in writing by the advocacy co-ordinator with the citizen advocate. Thereafter, the co-ordinator is available to the parties to provide support and assistance should it be required.

The program also provides for a corps of crisis advocates. These are usually volunteers having particular skills, such as lawyers, doctors and social workers, who volunteer their services on the basis that they will be available to act as a citizen advocate for a disabled person for a short period of time until a crisis in their lives is resolved.

There is some review of the relationship between the citizen advocate and his or her partner to ensure that it is successful; however, there is concern that the review not be legalistic or excessive. It is pointed out that most advocates are fulfilling roles usually assumed by parents, family and friends, and those relationships are not considered to require ongoing supervision except where there is evidence of abuse.

The local office files monthly reports on its activities and accomplishments with the central office. In addition, educational meetings with the staff of other local offices are held on a quarterly basis and a retreat of all staff involved in the program is held twice per year. To date, the Georgia program has matched a total of 1,000 citizen advocates of which approximately 400 are now active.

The Citizen Advocate model, based as it is on a strong one-to-one personal relationship between a volunteer advocate and his or her disabled partner, offers a strong and direct means of safeguarding and promoting the rights and interests of vulnerable adults. The Georgia model could be enlarged to serve the needs of all of the disability groups in Ontario, although the level of funding required to meet those needs would be many times the level of the Georgia program. Because the Citizen Advocacy model is founded upon the recruitment and matching of citizen advocates with disabled partners in the same community, it is essential that the citizen advocacy co-ordinators be physically located and highly visible in each community having significant numbers of vulnerable adults.

The program could be provided through a central board of directors who would receive funding from government and be accountable to the funding source by means of annual reports and budgeting. Because the program does not emphasize systemic change, there is not a compelling need for the program to be accountable to a Committee of the Legislature as is the case in the Advocacy Ontario and Shared Advocacy models discussed below. However, because of the importance placed on independence of the model from service providers, the Minister of Government to whom the board would report should not be responsible for the service delivery system. Either the Premier or the Attorney General would be appropriate. The central office would fulfill the same functions as the Georgia program for developing uniform policies and procedures for the program, staffing and monitoring the local offices, and providing support and assistance when required. Because a large number of local offices would be required to satisfy the need of all vulnerable adults in the province, it would be more reasonable to operate the program by means of contracts with local community boards who would be responsible for the operation of the local office, subject to annual or quarterly reporting to the central office to ensure compliance with the contract.

3.   THE ADVOCACY ONTARIO MODEL

As previously discussed, in July 1986, Concerned Friends of Ontario Citizens in Care Facilities, a consumer organization representing residents of nursing homes and other long-term care facilities, took the initiative of proposing the implementation of a provincial advocacy system for vulnerable citizens, entitled "Advocacy Ontario". This developmental model was designed to bring those persons and programs currently providing advocacy services together into a comprehensive and professional advocacy system--independent of service providers--with a clear legislated mandate to provide advocacy services to the vulnerable, and with the necessary incidental rights of access to clients, to facilities and to clients' records with their consent. This proposal has received considerable support within the consumer movement.

The Advocacy Ontario model provides a Central Office and five Regional offices situated throughout the province incorporating all of the existing advocacy programs. The program would be operated by a 23-member Board of Directors with at least 60% of Board members being representatives of primary or secondary consumer organizations (service users and their families). To avoid conflicts of interest, no representative of a service provider organization could be a member of the Board of Directors. The program would be funded by the provincial government through an annual grant to the Board of Directors. The Board would be accountable to government through a reporting relationship with both the Attorney General and a Standing Committee of the Legislature.

The Central Office would be managed by an Executive Director and would contain four Departments:

Regional Consultation/Development and Systems Advocacy;
Public Education and Training;
Legal;
Research and Evaluation.

With the exception of the Legal branch, each department would be headed by a Director reporting to the Executive Director. The Regional Consultation/Development department would have two policy analysts, two consultants and two systems advocates. The Public Education and Training Department would be comprised of two staff members devoted to public information, one person responsible for training and one community organizer. The Research and Evaluation Department would be comprised of two researchers and one evaluator. In addition, the office would employ five secretarial staff, one bookkeeper and a comptroller.

The Central Office of Advocacy Ontario would be responsible for:

- disbursement of funds to the five regional offices;

- provision of expert information and consultation services to the regional offices;

- policy development and analysis to support a "systems" advocacy approach which will address trends and issues identified at the regional level which have a provincial impact;

- regular professional evaluation of regional advocacy services;

- development and delivery of programs and services designed to promote public awareness of the rights, needs and contributions of people with disabilities;

- design and implement programs to train and continually upgrade the skills of both professional and lay advocates;

- assist with the development of professional and lay advocacy services on a province-wide basis.

In the Advocacy Ontario model, direct advocacy services would be provided by the five Regional Offices headed by a Regional Director reporting to the Executive Director of the Provincial Advocacy Office. Each office would incorporate two divisions, one responsible for the provision of advocacy services to the vulnerable living in the community and the other responsible for residents of care facilities. The institutional division would have not fewer than 15 staff advocates in addition to the 12 existing psychiatric patient advocates who would be transferred from the Ministry of Health to Advocacy Ontario. The institutional divisions would also include the 27 service co-ordinators in nursing homes and residential homes for special care who are currently attached to the Tri-Ministry program operated by the Ministry of Community and Social Services.

The community advocacy division in each regional office would include all of the 132 Adult Protective Service Workers, who would be transferred from the agencies now funded by the Ministry of Community and Social Services to Advocacy Ontario. In addition, the regional offices would be staffed by 15 new advocates who would be assigned to provide advocacy services to the elderly.

The functions of the five regional advocacy offices would include:

- effective use of funds to provide maximum benefit to clients through the provision of quality "case advocacy" services;

- direct assistance and advice to clients to promote self-advocacy;

- activities to promote community awareness of the rights of elderly individuals and those with disabilities;

- identification of issues and trends at the local level which may have a provincial impact;

- expansion of advocacy services at the local level according to identified needs;

- regular liaison with the Provincial Office to promote uniformly high standards in the provision of advocacy services;

- promoting the development of lay advocacy initiatives at the local level through the effective use of volunteers and the provision of comprehensive training and consultation to community organizations.

The Advocacy Ontario Model has been designed to address the shortcomings of the current mixed advocacy system -- fragmentation, conflicts of interest and lack of support for front-line advocates.

4. THE MIXED ADVOCACY MODEL

(a) Introduction

The Ministry of Community and Social Services has proposed a mixed, or multi-faceted, advocacy model to the Review. This model is essentially based upon the maintenance of the existing diverse methods for delivery of advocacy services, as outlined in chapter 3, with some developmental improvement. It proposes the development of written guidelines or legislation to deal with a number of current issues relating to training and certification of advocates, ethics and standards of practice, powers of entry to facilities and access to records, internal accountability, supervision and external accountability.

In the Mixed Model, advocates are employed by and accountable to separate sources as required by professional training, relationship with the client and the advocacy setting (community, agency, institution, legal clinic...). Three types of advocacy would exist simultaneously in the Mixed Model:

- informal advocacy
- internal advocacy
- independent advocacy

(b) Informal Advocacy

As discussed earlier, informal advocacy is often provided by disabled adults, their family and friends. It is proposed in this Model that this type of advocacy should be enhanced by means of supporting consumer groups, self-help groups and client organizations that promote the self-reliance and independence of the disabled. This would be achieved by providing such groups with professional, administrative and financial support.

(c) Internal Advocacy

Internal advocates, as seen previously, are employed by the service providers (they may be doctors, nurses, service co-ordinators, social workers, nurses' aides, therapists, ...). As such, they are accountable to the provider agency. These internal advocates develop a relationship with the client when they provide professional services and this leads them to attempt to resolve complaints or find a solution to an unmet need within the service system for their clients. These internal advocates usually act on the basis of their perception of the best interests of their patients, rather than on the basis of their patients' instructions.

(d) Independent Advocacy

As noted in chapter 3, at present, two community legal clinics, the Advocacy Resource Centre for the Handicapped (ARCH) and the Advocacy Centre for the Elderly (ACE) have been mandated to represent the interests of the disabled and the elderly. They are funded by and accountable to the Clinic Funding Committee of the Ontario Legal Aid Plan and provide direct legal advocacy services to the physically, mentally and emotionally disabled who are unable to have their legal needs met through the traditional legal system due to communications barriers or lack of specific legal expertise. These clinics also provide a certain amount of non-legal advocacy and are a resource centre providing information, education, advice and assistance to self-advocates, their families, friends and related groups. They act on the instructions of the client.

Independent advocacy is also being provided by a number of volunteer groups as outlined in chapter 3. For example, for the past six years Concerned Friends has been providing volunteer advocacy services to residents of long-term care institutions (nursing homes, homes for the aged...) who have been abandoned or suffered abuse or neglect. Citizen advocacy groups have been established over the past 15 years in a number of centres throughout the province. These groups are dedicated to establishing one-to-one personal relationships between disabled persons and caring volunteer advocates. They encourage a co-operative, non-adversarial relationship with service provider agencies and ministries. Self-help groups of consumers and former consumers of the human service system also provide volunteer advocacy on behalf of vulnerable adults -- carrying forward individual and systemic complaints and problems for resolution and providing community education designed to help normalize the lives of their constituents within the community.

The Mixed Advocacy Model provides a choice of advocacy services to the consumer and integrates advocacy with the service delivery system.

5.   THE SHARED ADVOCACY MODEL

(a) Introduction

It is apparent from our Review that the needs of the vulnerable vary substantially due to factors such as the nature of the disability, the residence of the disabled (at home or in a care facility), the size and location of the community and the resources, both volunteer and professional, available in that locale. As discussed in chapter 3, there is at present a diverse mix of advocacy services being provided to the vulnerable -- internally through service providers (APSWs, PPAO, Service Co-ordinators...), externally through volunteer groups (Concerned Friends, On Our Own, People First, Patients'

Rights...) and through independent community controlled legal clinics (ARCH, ACE). In addition, the vulnerable frequently act as their own advocates with the assistance of family and friends. The needs and resources available are not uniform throughout all of the communities in Ontario. An effective advocacy model must be responsive to local needs and resources. It must also be capable of co-ordinating and strengthening advocacy initiatives of volunteers.

Drawing on the experience of the Ontario Clinic Funding Program, we have developed the Shared Advocacy Model. It is designed to provide a central focus for the co-ordination and provision of advocacy services to vulnerable adults requiring assistance throughout the Province. The structural outline of the Ontario Shared Advocacy Model is set forth in the diagram which accompanies this chapter.

The Shared Advocacy Model is an evolutionary/slow growth model which contemplates the growth of the program over a period of two to three years. The first phase would involve the enactment of legislation establishing a provincial Advocacy Commission, and central office, which would develop standards and procedures for the implementation of the program.

In the second phase, seven regional offices would be established, which would be directed by a community-based Board of Directors and staffed by advocacy co-ordinators. During this phase, the advocacy co-ordinators would be responsible for assuming the advocacy responsibilities contemplated by the Fram Committee as discussed in chapter 3 and for recruiting and training volunteer advocates to provide individual advocacy for the vulnerable adults in the region.

Thereafter, with the assistance of the regional advocacy co-ordinators, local community groups would develop local programs tailored to the needs of the vulnerable adults in their community and seek funding for their implementation from the regional Board and the Commission. Ultimately, it would be these local programs that would bear the primary responsibility for the provision of advocacy services to the vulnerable in the province. This last evolutionary phase of the model would be an ongoing process as local programs are designed and funded.

The Shared Advocacy Model would be funded by and accountable to the government through an independent reporting relationship to either a Standing Committee of the Legislature or to the Attorney General.

Before turning to consider each component of the Shared Advocacy Model in greater detail, it is important to comment on why this model has been so named. First, Shared Advocacy derives its name from the belief that advocacy is everyone's business. Everyone of us must share in the responsibility for advocacy -- whether on behalf of ourselves; for another; or in the interests of social reform.

Second, the Shared Advocacy Model provides co-operation, not confrontation, between and among all participants in the delivery of social services -- from the individual receiving assistance, to the care-giver, to the organization or Ministry providing such services. If the goal of such programs and care providers is an enhanced quality of life for fellow Ontarians, all who share that goal for a vulnerable adult should also have a commitment to recognizing and respecting that individual's rights, wishes and choices.

Third, Shared Advocacy calls for a "team approach" to ensure adequate advocacy on behalf of Ontario's vulnerable. It involves full-time advocates, working with volunteers who may choose to advocate individually and/or in collaboration with others to form an association that addresses the particular situation of certain people -- such as frail elderly residents of nursing homes or former psychiatric patients reintegrating into the community.

Moreover, since the model calls for funding of programs appropriate to different communities, it is the shared responsibility of all residents in each community to identify and address their advocacy needs.

(b) The Advocacy Commission

The Advocacy Commission would be comprised of seven members, including a Chairman and a Vice-Chairman. To ensure independence of the program, Commissioners would be appointed by the Lieutenant-Governor in Council for a fixed term not to exceed five years and could only be removed from office for cause. Commission members should be citizens with a demonstrated commitment to the interests of the disabled. The members should not be employed by a service provider ministry or agency. The Commission would meet at least once per month and Commissioners would receive a modest honorarium in keeping with the amounts paid to members of other provincial boards and commissions.

The Commission would have overall responsibility for the advocacy system in Ontario and its functions would include:

- hiring and supervising a full-time Executive Director to act as chief executive officer responsible for supervision of central office staff;

- funding and terminating funding of regional offices and local programs;

- providing expertise and support to the regional offices and local programs;

- developing policies and standard practices and procedures for the regional offices and the local programs;

- establishing training programs to be given to all advocacy co-ordinators, volunteers and advocates in local programs through the regional offices;

- monitoring the regional offices and local programs;

- establishing a province-wide uniform reporting system to collect and analyze data concerning complaints, problems and responses for the purpose of identifying and promoting the resolution of systemic issues;

- providing information to service providers and government regarding the problems of vulnerable adults and the need for legislative or internal changes to the service delivery system;

- promoting the interests of the vulnerable through publicity, education, lobbying and test case litigation.

It must be emphasized that the selection of appropriate Commissioners to the Advocacy Commission is vital to the effective implementation of the Shared Advocacy Model. The nature of the Commission's important responsibilities calls for persons with unusual experience and a rare combination of qualities. Our work over these past months has included contact with a number of individuals who would serve wisely and well and it has been edifying to meet and learn from such exceptional, eminent Ontarians. Such people do exist and should be given the public trust to implement advocacy.

(c) Commission Staff

The foregoing responsibilities of the Commission will be implemented by a small central office staff. The day-to-day management of the Commission office would be assigned to an Executive Director who would supervise Commission staff, would be responsible for the over-all operations of the Commission's Central Office and would report to the Commissioners.

Of fundamental importance to the system are: (a) the education of consumers, providers and general public as to the role and function of the program; and (b) thorough and proper training of advocacy co-ordinators, volunteer advocates and advocates in the local programs. The Co-ordinator of Training and Public Education, with the assistance of the Commission staff, would be required to develop uniform training programs to be implemented by each regional office. In this regard, Humber College now offers a Case Management/Advocacy course which would provide an excellent resource in the development of appropriate programs. This staff member would also be responsible for publicizing the program and for organizing education and awareness conferences for vulnerable adults, their families, volunteers and providers.

There should also be one member on staff with experience and knowledge of the needs, services and issues pertaining to each of the four principal groups of vulnerable adults (frail elderly; psychiatrically disabled; developmentally disabled and physically handicapped), so that experienced and knowledgeable support may be provided to the regional advocacy co-ordinators, volunteer advocates, and advocates in local programs, as required.

The Commission Office should also include a staff lawyer capable of providing information and advice on legal issues to the advocates in the regional offices and local programs regarding legislation, regulations and administrative rules and policies applicable to the various groups of vulnerable adults. The staff lawyer would also be responsible for all systemic reform activities of the Commission and should be skilled in drafting reports, submissions and proposals for human service, legislative and regulatory reform.

To facilitate the co-operative resolution of systemic problems and issues, the Executive Director and appropriate staff should have regularly scheduled meetings at least four times per year with the Ministries providing services. These meetings should be with a designate of the Minister at the level equivalent to an Assistant Deputy Minister. It is also expected and hoped that, in the pursuit of the best possible care for vulnerable citizens, each provider Ministry would designate a senior official to provide ongoing liaison between the Commission and his Ministry. Test case litigation would not normally be performed by the staff lawyer but would be referred to legal clinics and law offices with appropriate experience.

In addition to the professional staff, the Commission will require support staff to review budgets and funding proposals and to collect and record data from the regional offices. The data referred to would include complaints and problems received, actions taken by advocates and their responses and recommendations.

(d) Regional Offices and Community-Based Boards of Directors

Because the provision of advocacy to vulnerable adults is, in essence, a personal service, it is essential that the advocate be visible and immediately accessible to the vulnerable adults in their community. When vulnerable adults require advocacy services, they often require such assistance within a 24 hour period. All of the successful advocacy programs that we have reviewed provide advocacy through a regional or local office network located in the communities.

The Province of Ontario covers a wide geographic area. In our view, an advocacy system operated from a central office located in Toronto would not be as responsive to local needs, nor be as visible or readily accessible as a program also supported by regional offices. Therefore, in the Shared Advocacy Model, advocacy services are delivered through 7 regional offices, covering the following counties and districts:

1. North

Kenora
Rainy River

Thunder Bay
Algoma
Cochrane
Manitoulin
Sudbury
Timiskaming
Nipissing
Parry Sound

2. East

Prescott/Russell
Stormont/Dundas/
  Glengarry

Ottawa-Carleton
Leeds/Grenville
Lanark
Renfrew
Frontenac
Lennox/Addington
Hastings
Prince Edward

3. Central East

Northumberland
Peterborough

Haliburton
Victoria
Durham
Muskoka
Simcoe
York Region

4. Toronto

Metro Toronto

5. Central West

Peel
Halton
Dufferin
Grey
Wellington
Bruce

6. Central South

Niagara
Haldimand-Norfolk
Hamilton-Wentworth
Brant
Waterloo

7. Southwest

Essex
Kent
Lambton
Elgin
Middlesex
Huron
Oxford
Perth

These 7 regions reflect the research and the recommendation of the *Report of the Ontario Courts Inquiry, 1987*, prepared by The Hon. T. G. Zuber, with respect to the appropriate divisions of the province. The regions have geographic cohesion, are of virtually equal size in terms of population and take account of population trends.

To ensure responsiveness of the program to the particular needs of the region and to safeguard the independence of the system, each regional office should be operated and managed by a community-based Board of Directors. The Board would be responsible for the provision of advocacy services in the region in a manner consistent with the standards and procedures established by the Commission. It would be accountable to the Commission, reporting on a quarterly basis on the activities of the regional office staff and on the activities of the local programs, and would submit an annual budget to the Commission for the provision of advocacy services in the region for the forthcoming year. To receive funds annually, each regional Board would be required to enter into a contract with the Commission stipulating the programs and services to be provided in the region during the year and undertaking to conform with the policies and procedures established by the central office.

The membership of the Regional Board should be large in order to ensure that the interests of all communities in the region are represented, but it should not exceed 25 in number. The majority of the Board should be comprised of primary or secondary consumers of advocacy services (vulnerable adults and their families or friends). Because the advocacy program is new, time will be required for communities to develop a process for electing Regional Boards of Directors. Therefore the initial Board members should be appointed by the Commission for a term of not more than 2 years. These appointments should be an open process and to that end the Commission should invite through the media any interested resident of the region to submit an application and a resumé for consideration by the Commission. These Boards should be broadly representative of the community because all Ontarians have a stake in good advocacy. All of us, acknowledging the need for advocacy, should also be able and ready to participate in its development and delivery. Advocacy must belong to, and be representative of, all Ontarians. During the term of the appointed Board, it would be required to develop a mechanism satisfactory to the Commission for the election of new Board members in a manner which ensures that the majority of the members were primary or secondary consumers and that the Board was reasonably representative of all parts of the region.

The community-based Regional Boards would be responsible for the following:

1. implementing and maintaining advocacy services for the vulnerable adults residing in institutions and communities within the Region;

2. ensuring compliance with the policies and procedures developed by the Advocacy Commission;

3. receiving and considering applications submitted by community groups for funding of advocacy programs in the area and, if appropriate, applying for the funding of such programs to the Commission;

4. hiring and supervising an advocacy co-ordinator to act as the Regional Director responsible for the hiring and supervising of advocacy co-ordinators, and the day-to-day operation of the Regional Office and local programs;

5. overseeing the operation of the Regional Office and the local programs;

6. filing periodic reports with the Commission regarding the activities of the Regional Office and local programs;

7. providing data to the Commission regarding complaints and problems received by the Regional Office, actions taken, findings and recommendations made in response.

(e) Regional Advocacy Co-ordinators

The number of regional office advocates ("advocacy co-ordinators") must be sufficient to fulfill the duty of providing advocacy services to vulnerable adults involved in guardianship, conservatorship and other substitute decision proceedings in accordance with the proposals of the Fram Committee on Substitute Decision Making (see chapter 3, section 2(d)) in addition to ensuring the advocacy needs of all other vulnerable adults in the region are met. It would be a disservice to place one advocate in each regional office with the expectation that he/she will be able to meet the needs of the vulnerable throughout the region in a meaningful way.

At present, there are no available estimates of the number of persons who will require services under the proposed *Substitute Decisions Authority Act*. We do know that approximately 350 guardianship applications under the current legislation are heard by the courts each year. If the legislation is simplified to expedite the appointment of guardians in appropriate cases, this number will undoubtedly increase. Having regard to the serious responsibilities entailed in advocating for those who are the subject of a guardianship or conservatorship application, advocacy co-ordinators will be called upon to spend a considerable amount of time in safeguarding the vulnerable adults against unnecessary guardianship or conservatorship. Thus, it is imperative, if the legislation is enacted, that adequate numbers of advocacy co-ordinators be available in the seven regions of the province to fulfill these statutory responsibilities. It is, therefore, recommended that there be three advocacy co-ordinators in each office, one of whom will act as Regional director responsible for the day to day operation of the office and reporting to the Board of Directors. One advocacy co-ordinator should specialize in and be responsible for the provision of advocacy services to vulnerable adults in the community and one co-ordinator should specialize in and be responsible for the provision of advocacy services to the vulnerable adults living in institutions.

In addition to assisting vulnerable adults involved in guardianship, conservatorship and other substitute decision proceedings, the advocacy co-ordinators would be required to:

1. assist local groups to identify the needs that their community may have for advocacy services and to develop programs for the provision of advocacy services in the community;

2. assist local groups to apply to the regional Board of Directors and the Advocacy Commission for funding local programs to meet the advocacy needs of the community;

3. encourage and monitor the efficacy of local programs in the regions;

4. recruit and train volunteers in sufficient numbers to serve as advocates to the vulnerable adults residing in care facilities within the region and in private residences (Note: the number of regional

office volunteer advocates needed may be higher in the initial stages of implementation of the model, prior to the development of local programs);

5. provide vulnerable adults with non-legal advocacy services within 24 hours of a request for assistance;

6. assign advocates to visit care facilities on a regular basis and to meet with every resident at least once per month (Note: this responsibility of the regional office volunteer advocates may be supplanted in certain regions by the implementation of local programs that are designed to fulfill this function);

7. provide back-up to volunteer advocates when required in resolving problems or complaints;

8. publicize the existence of the advocacy office; educate community members about advocacy and the services the regional office provides;

9. maintain records of complaints and problems received, actions taken, findings, responses and recommendations;

10. assure that all volunteers and advocates in local programs comply with all applicable procedures and policies of the Advocacy Commission;

11. stimulate local groups to establish citizen advocacy programs in their communities based upon principles and practices of Citizen Advocacy as established in consultation with the Advocacy Commission.

(f) Volunteers

The challenge of providing advocacy services to the vulnerable cannot be met by salaried staff advocates alone. It has been evident throughout our review that the spirit of volunteerism is very strong in working to improve the quality of life of the disadvantaged in Ontario. A survey of 22 voluntary associations across the province which are dedicated to helping the disabled indicated that almost all were actively involved in one way or another in providing individual and systemic advocacy on behalf of their constituencies. Volunteers may be found in existing volunteer organizations or self-help groups; in groups of families and friends of vulnerable adults; and also in groups of concerned citizens who choose to contribute their time and efforts to improving the lives of the vulnerable.

These groups and individuals are an experienced and committed resource which ought to be enlisted by the advocacy system to help provide advocacy services to vulnerable adults in the community or in care facilities. By calling on volunteers to become an integral part of the advocacy system, we assure that the system will maintain close ties to the consumer movement; that those who receive advocacy will be readily identified; and that the system is safeguarded from being perceived as another government service system staffed by professionals to help the disabled.

It is recognized that not all existing volunteer groups will wish to become part of the provincial advocacy system. For these groups the regional offices will be a source of expertise. At the same time, it will be essential that the regional advocacy co-ordinators recruit new volunteers from the community to assist in providing advocacy services. To ensure that competent advocacy services are provided by these volunteers, the regional office must provide thorough training programs. All volunteer advocates should receive certification from the Regional Director before they are given the authority to provide advocacy services with the incidental right of entry to care facilities and access to patient records with their permission.

The responsibilities of certified volunteer advocates will include:

1. visiting vulnerable adults in care facilities and in the community on a regular basis;

2. receiving and investigating problems or complaints of vulnerable adults and working to resolve them through consultation and negotiation;

3. reporting problems, complaints and actions taken in response to the regional office;

4. assisting the efforts of the Advocacy Commission for systemic reform and organizing public events such as awareness weeks.

In addition to the volunteer advocacy services that would be provided by the regional office volunteer advocates, it is also recommended that each local program should include, if appropriate, a volunteer component in order to qualify for funding.

(g) Local Programs

While much attention has been given to the Advocacy Commission and the regional offices, it must be stressed that the success of the Shared Advocacy Model is dependent upon the design and implementation of local advocacy programs.

As noted, Ontario is a vast and diverse jurisdiction with a large population and a variety of advocacy needs. Indeed, the needs of our vulnerable adults vary substantially and are affected by such factors as the nature of the disability, their residence (whether at home or in the community), the size and location of their community and the resources, both volunteer and professional, available in that locale. Rather than advocacy being imposed or designed by a central body, it is much more logical for local communities to identify their advocacy needs, to devise local programs to meet those needs, and to implement those programs once funding has been approved.

In the first instance, it will be the responsibility of the regional co-ordinators to stimulate local communities to identify their advocacy needs and to assist them in designing appropriate local programs. Once a local community has devised a particular program, it would submit an application describing the nature of the program to the Regional Board of Directors for approval. As the Board is responsible for the over-all co-ordination of advocacy services in its region, it is appropriate that the Board should first review the application and determine whether, for example, it meets the standards and requirements set by the Advocacy Commission, is needed and not duplicative, and should be submitted to the Advocacy Commission for funding approval.

Examples of local programs might include the following: an advocacy program for residents of long-term care facilities in a particular region where this need is high; a citizen advocacy program; or a small generic program that would be staffed by one or two advocates who would respond to all advocacy needs in the community.

Since certain groups have the need and numbers for specialized advocacy services, local programs could also be spearheaded by associations whose membership is reflective of their needs -- for example, the Ontario Friends of Schizophrenics, and the Canadian Association for Community Living. These associations should be encouraged to develop local programs which identify true advocacy needs and then meet those needs by using association volunteers and perhaps full-time staff who would also receive advocacy training and accreditation.

It is important that such local programs be effective and needed -- and it is for these reasons that their assessment will initially be conducted by the Regional Board of Directors which is to be representative of a cross section of the community. In considering applications for funding, it is vital that both the Regional Board of Directors and the Advocacy Commission allow for a maximum of diversity, flexibility and creativity in local programs. Since advocacy is evolved from the realization of "gaps in the system", no needy vulnerable person should be turned away or disqualified simply because his/her needs are unusual or extraordinary. Indeed, the litmus test of the Shared Advocacy Model will be its efficacy in addressing the legitimate needs of those whose circumstances defy classification and will never conform to general guidelines. The lonely, forgotten and the unusual -- all these must never be regarded as hurdles to be overcome by the new advocacy service. Rather, they are its golden opportunity to prove its true value and need.

Moreover, in our zeal to help the disadvantaged, we must guard against becoming paternalistic.

That is, while every vulnerable citizen should eventually have access to advocacy, no one should have advocacy thrust upon him/her. It is a matter of choice. We must allow for risk-taking. We must also allow people to exercise another option: the right to be left alone.

Thus, local programs must be ambitious in their goals and realistic in their delivery. Communities must take an honest hard look at those in their midst who are vulnerable and need advocates. Then they must ensure that there are sufficient and suitable persons -- be they individual volunteers, association members or full-time paid advocates -- to be accredited and to deliver. Then, with the approbation of the Regional Board, they should apply to the Advocacy Commission for funding and embark with determination and enthusiasm in a work that will be exciting, exhilarating and fulfilling. In generously giving of themselves, they can help the vulnerable improve and even change their lives -- a treasured privilege in anyone's human journey.

"Mary, a retired practical nurse, lived alone with Blackie, her dog, in a one room apartment overrun with cockroaches and smelling badly from her own and the dog's excrement on the floor. Mary could only walk a few inches because of the open ulcers on her feet and legs. Only one person visited her, a friend who occasionally did shopping and cooking. Mary trusted no one to manage her old age pension income or to pay her bills. She would let no one walk the dog outside. She did not take her pills. She gave food purchased for her to the dog. She was often without food herself. Her bills often remained unpaid for weeks and months. She often refused to go in the ambulance for her medical checkups. She was frightened she would be put in a hospital and separated from Blackie."

From a brief submitted by the Home Care Program for Metropolitan Toronto.

ONTARIO
SHARED ADVOCACY MODEL

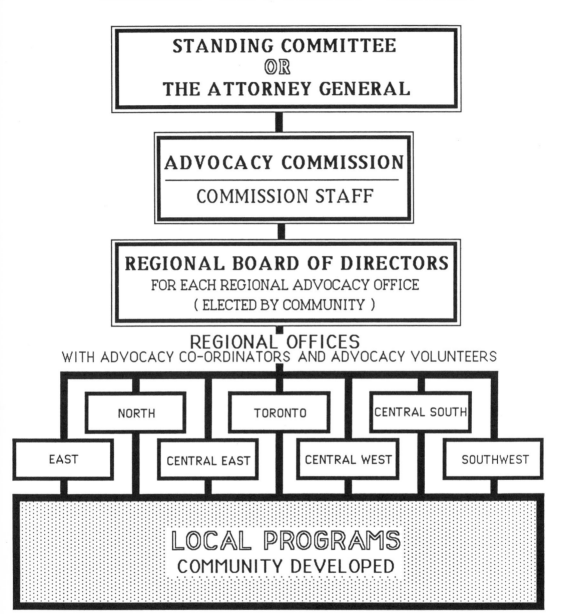

**STANDING COMMITTEE
OR
THE ATTORNEY GENERAL**

ADVOCACY COMMISSION
COMMISSION STAFF

REGIONAL BOARD OF DIRECTORS
FOR EACH REGIONAL ADVOCACY OFFICE
(ELECTED BY COMMUNITY)

REGIONAL OFFICES
WITH ADVOCACY CO-ORDINATORS AND ADVOCACY VOLUNTEERS

NORTH TORONTO CENTRAL SOUTH

EAST CENTRAL EAST CENTRAL WEST SOUTHWEST

LOCAL PROGRAMS
COMMUNITY DEVELOPED

CHAPTER 5

Recommendations

1. Introduction

In evaluating the models described in the foregoing chapter, we have been guided by the following four basic principles of advocacy, identified in Chapter 2, which we feel should be the foundation of an effective advocacy program:

(1) advocacy services must be client directed or "instruction-based": the actions of an advocate must be guided by the instructions of a client and the advocate must serve the client on a voluntary and consensual basis;

(2) advocates must be independent and free of any actual or perceived conflict of interest;

(3) advocacy must be accessible: vulnerable adults, whether residing in institutions or in the community, have the right to advocacy services as required to assure protection of their rights, freedoms and dignity; and advocates should have the right to meet with vulnerable adults on a private basis and, with the client's consent, should have access to the client's clinical records;

(4) advocacy should be seen as a way to achieve co-operation -- where all parties work together, instead of in opposition, to advance the rights of all vulnerable adults and to improve health care and service delivery.

As well, an effective advocacy system should recognize that advocacy services should not only provide one-to-one support, advice and representation to the vulnerable adult, but should also promote needed systemic reforms to meet the changing needs of the vulnerable.

In addition, our evaluation of the models has taken into account the following basic goals of an advocacy system which were developed with the assistance of our three Advisory Committees at a joint meeting held on April 22, 1987:

1. Safeguards against unnecessary guardianship;

2. Independent (from Ministries affected, funding sources, providers);

3. Encourages self-advocacy where possible (self-sufficiency, self-determination);

4. Enhances role of families and volunteers;

5. Educates (families, volunteers, community) - delabels; destigmatizes, identifies gaps in services, promotes awareness that advocacy is everybody's business, ...

6. Flexible (special needs, geographic requirements, multilingual);

7. Responsive (personal concern, carries forward complaints, endeavours to resolve them);

8. Promotes co-operation with Providers and Ministries;

9. Accessible;

10. Seeks improvements in programs (reformative);

11. Has clout;

12. Accountable.

2. Advantages and Shortcomings of the Ombudsman Model

(a) Advantages

- strong reliance on volunteers;

- large number of regional offices results in high visibility of the Ombudsman program;

- independent of service provider system;

- non-bureaucratic (small central office and a one tier delivery system at the regional level);

- strong systemic advocacy capacity based upon the collection and analysis of data provided by the regional offices and the centralization of systemic advocacy efforts through the staff lawyer at the central office;

- provision for training and certification of advocacy co-ordinators and volunteer advocates thereby ensuring the quality of service and promoting confidence in the program in consumers and providers;

- clear legislative mandate to provide advocacy services with legislated rights of access to clients and their records.

(b) Shortcomings

- suitable model for a limited advocacy program; impractical to think one advocacy co-ordinator would have time and range of expertise to co-ordinate advocacy services for all vulnerable groups identified by this Review in each region;

- staffing of regional offices with one advocacy co-ordinator could lead to isolation and lack of backup when co-ordinator absent from office;

- has no capacity for handling guardianship cases;

- lacks community/consumer direction and control;

- in the Ontario setting, a model bearing this title would be confused with the existing Ombudsman program; since public awareness and education are essential to the success of the program this would be considerable obstacle to success in the crucial early years of the program;

- suffers from attrition problems common to volunteer-based programs.

3.   **Advantages and Shortcomings of the Citizen Advocacy Model**

(a) **Advantages**

- independent of service providers;

- strong reliance on volunteers in communities for the provision of individual advocacy;

- clearly articulated ideological principles;

- highly personalized through the establishment of a partnership relationship between the advocate and the partner;

- very effective in integrating vulnerable adults in the community;

- provides expressive support by meeting the partner's needs for friendship and fellowship as well as solving practical day-to-day problems through the representation of the interests of the partner;

- provides volunteers with the backup expertise of advocacy co-ordinators and the central office;

- there is an existing well·developed program available for evaluating the citizen advocacy program;

- relatively low cost.

(b) **Shortcomings**

- will probably never be able to meet all of the demand due to the limited numbers of volunteers available to accept a long-term one-to-one relationship;

- limited efforts at systemic reform;

- has no capacity for handling guardianship cases;

- suffers from attrition problems common to volunteer-based programs;

- minimal review of the relationship between the advocate and the partner;

- there has been noted a tendency to over-emphasize informal, reciprocal and expressive relationships with the result that the more interesting, verbal and lovable vulnerable persons have advocates assigned, while those who are non-communicative, profoundly impaired, institutionalized or otherwise "low profile" are less likely to have an advocate assigned to them. i.e. those most in need of advocates may be the last to receive volunteer advocacy.

4. **Advantages and Shortcomings of the Advocacy Ontario Model**

(a) **Advantages**

- a unified system with a clear legislated mandate to provide advocacy services;

- high visibility;

- capacity to perform advocacy services as outlined in the proposed *Substitute Decisions Authority Act*;

- strong capacity for systemic reform;

- legislated access to clients, facilities and client records;

- standardized quality in service delivery throughout the province;

- strong backup capacity for frontline advocates;

- consumer directed;

(b) **Shortcomings**

- bureaucratic structure with a large number of departments and supervisors;

- lacks flexibility -- single service delivery system for all vulnerable adults in all communities throughout Ontario could result in the program not being responsive to the particular needs and resources of the communities;

- large central Board could be inefficient at the provincial level;

- case managers/service co-ordinators are included in the program as advocates which would either result in the need for the service providers to hire replacements or, if they continue to do service co-ordination, would result in an inferior quality of service co-ordination by reason of the service co-ordinator being external to and, from time to time, in opposition to or a critic of the service providers.

5. Advantages and Shortcomings of the Mixed Advocacy Model

(a) Advantages

- provides some consumer choice between informal, internal and independent advocates;

- integration with existing service delivery system promotes co-operative relationship.

(b) Shortcomings

- lacks independence as a result of the heavy reliance on advocacy services being provided by internal advocates who are employees of the service providers: this results in the perception and, in some cases, the occurrence of conflict of interest;

- number of external advocates is inadequate to meet the demand;

- fragmented system with no clear central focus;

- lacks legislative mandate and legislative rights of access;

- low visibility;

- limited backup support available to self-advocates and internal advocates who have been unsuccessful in their attempts to reach an acceptable resolution of the problem with service providers;

- the internal advocate by reason of his or her position as an employee of the service provider is limited in his or her ability to press for systemic change;

- lacks uniformity in standards of service and training;

- lacks co-ordination: the present system is *ad hoc* with no recognized individual or organization accountable for the delivery of the services or accessible to those who need them;

- internal advocates lack a clear mandate to advocate on behalf of their clients;

- few experienced, full-time advocates who are available to provide the support and assistance and backup required by self-advocates, family advocates and volunteer advocates.

6. Advantages and Shortcomings of the Shared Advocacy Model

(a) Advantages

- independent of service providers;

- clear legislative mandate and right of access to facilities and clients;

- promotes self-advocacy by the disabled, their families and friends by providing advice, assistance and support through regional advocacy co-ordinators and, when necessary, through central office;

- accountable to government through annual funding applications and reports;

- capacity to respond to differing advocacy needs of local communities as determined by those communities;

- provides communities with choice of advocacy programs and permits them to develop innovative programs;

- generic advocacy services available at the regional office level thereby avoiding labelling or stigmatizing based on vulnerability;

- expertise available at central office to support advocacy co-ordinators, volunteer advocates and advocates in local programs;

- enhances existing volunteer programs by providing training and backup resources;

- visibility and accessibility of services obtained through the establishment of regional offices, and through the creation of local programs;

- capacity to provide advocacy services to the disabled involved in guardianship and conservatorship orders and other substitute decision proceedings as contemplated by the proposed *Substitute Decisions Authority Act;*

- capacity for systemic reforms through centralized data collection and analysis system with staff in the central office responsible for systemic reform work;

- capable of being evaluated on a continuing basis through the centralized data retrieval system;

- consumer directed by Regional Board of Directors responsible for the provision of advocacy services to communities in the region.

(b) Shortcomings

- requires salaried full-time professional staff in central office and, when fully operational, salaried advocacy co-ordinators to staff the regional offices;

- utilizes volunteers with the attendant risk of attrition;

- risk that certain communities will be slow to or fail to determine their advocacy needs and propose local advocacy programs.

7.   Recommendations

(a) The Recommended Model -- "Shared Advocacy"

In Chapter 3, the clear need for a cohesive and effective advocacy system in Ontario was demonstrated. As discussed, there exists, at present, a mixture of fragmented advocacy services accessible to a limited number of vulnerable adults. These services are provided to a great extent by internal advocates employed by service provider agencies, and by families and volunteer groups. In the case of internal advocates, there is the perception that the advocacy service is subject to and limited by conflicts of interest, which can seriously undermine the confidence of the clients in the service. Further, the present system lacks a clear mandate to provide advocacy services and those who advocate do not have a clear right of access to care facilities, clients and clients' records. Without a central focus and a clear mandate, the present system lacks uniform standards of service or training of advocates. It is patently clear that the present system is incapable of meeting the needs of the vulnerable adults of the province.

The present system is also discriminatory. Some vulnerable adults by reason of the location of their residence in certain facilities or in particular communities receive advocacy services from dedicated volunteers. Others may receive quality advocacy services if they are fortunate to be assigned care providers who are committed to advocating on behalf of their clients/patients. However, many, if not the majority, of our vulnerable adults, particularly those residing in smaller communities, do not have access to any advocacy programs. For the countless vulnerable adults abandoned by family and friends and now residing in long-term care facilities, the lack of access to the services of an advocate is a profound injustice.

As noted previously, there are over 5,000 developmentally handicapped persons in provincial institutions in Ontario. Most of these residents have lived in such institutions for their entire life and yet do not have access to an advocacy program. In contrast, psychiatric patients who may reside in provincial psychiatric institutions for an average of two months have access to an advocate in the institution. Similarly, residents of nursing homes, homes for the aged and other care facilities, whose needs for advocacy services are equally compelling, have no access to effective advocacy services other than those that may be provided on an *ad hoc* basis by volunteer organizations. Further, physically handicapped persons do not have access to formal advocacy services.

To meet these needs and remedy these injustices, we recommend the Shared Advocacy Model. This model is independent and accessible to all categories of vulnerable adults wherever they may reside in the province. It provides a central focus in the Advocacy Commission which is responsible for training of advocates throughout the province and assuring standards of service. Through the regional offices, the model provides a visible presence in all regions of the province. It is designed to stimulate and encourage communities to identify their particular advocacy needs and to develop advocacy programs that will be best able to meet the needs of their vulnerable adults. It recognizes the need for continual evaluation and analysis of the human service system by mandating the lawyer and other central office staff to press for reforms to meet the changing needs of the vulnerable. It enlists volunteers as front-line advocates to develop a personal relationship with the neglected and abandoned and provides the volunteers with the necessary professional support, information and advice they may require to effectively present the problems, complaints and concerns of their partners for resolution.

(b) Accountability of the Shared Advocacy Model

Because the Shared Advocacy Model will be publicly funded, there must be a credible system for the program to account to government for the use and application of public funds. The Shared Advocacy Model has an internal accountability mechanism together with external accountability to government.

Internally, local programs will be reviewed and evaluated by the regional Board of Directors by means of quarterly reporting, monitoring of the programs by the regional advocacy co-ordinators and the annual applications for funding submitted by the local programs to the Regional Board. Each of these internal mechanisms will ensure compliance by the local programs with the terms and conditions of the contracts they enter with the Regional Board when they receive funding. Similarly, compliance by the regional Board of Directors with the terms and conditions of their funding contracts with the Commission will be ensured through quarterly reports, reviews by Commission staff, and their annual reports and applications for funding to the Advocacy Commission. The Commission itself will account to government for its administration of the provincial program through its annual report on operations and annual application for funding.

On the question of which agency of government should be responsible for the operation of the Advocacy Commission and its funding, several alternatives have been considered. There is a clear consensus that the advocacy program must be independent of service providers and therefore must not be funded or administered by any ministry

providing services to vulnerable adults. There is, however, a diversion of opinion as to
the appropriate government department to which an independent advocacy program
should be accountable. We have concluded that the independence and effectiveness of
the Shared Advocacy Model could be best maintained by vesting responsibility for the
administration and funding of the program in either the Ministry of the Attorney General
or a Standing Committee of the Legislature.

(i) Attorney General

The Ministry of the Attorney General has a demonstrated independence from other
ministries. The Attorney General frequently is called upon to provide legal advice and
opinions as to the propriety and legality of actions and policies of other ministries. The
Ministry's ability to do so in an uncompromising manner is well recognized. Further,
the Ministry has been the agency of government responsible for the Legal Aid Plan and
the Community Legal Clinics throughout the terms of a number of governments and
Attorneys General, without compromising the vital independence of these programs. On
many occasions, Attorneys General have effectively championed the interests of the
Legal Aid Plan and the Clinic Funding program both publicly and within government
and secured levels of funding which have made the Legal Aid Plan and the Clinic
Funding Program among the most progressive and highly regarded services of their kind
in the common law world.

By assigning responsibility for the administration and funding of the program to
the Attorney General, the Shared Advocacy Model will have a strong voice in Cabinet
not only in regard to funding issues but also in regard to systemic reform measures.
Further, as the Minister responsible for the provision of legal advocacy services to
government and to the citizens of Ontario through the Legal Aid Plan, and as Minister
responsible for the Offices of the Public Trustee, Official Guardian and for the
administration of the anticipated substitute decision making legislation, the Attorney
General and his/her staff would be most knowledgeable of and sensitive to the mandate,
objectives and requirements of the non-legal advocacy program.

While enlisting the assistance and support of the Attorney General in dealing with systemic issues or egregious individual cases of neglect or mistreatment is a distinct advantage of this reporting relationship, it must be recognized that these issues will not always be capable of resolution even by the Attorney General. Therefore, we would recommend that the legislation include a requirement that the Attorney General table the annual report of the Advocacy Commission in the Legislature. In this way, unresolved issues would be reported to the House and Members could refer the report to a Committee of the Legislature for a public hearing to address the unresolved problems.

(ii) Standing Committee of the Ombudsman

Vesting responsibility for the Advocacy Commission in the Standing Committee of the Ombudsman also has a number of advantages. First, the Standing Committee has a well-recognized tradition of independence and non-partisanship. It has the capacity to hold hearings to investigate and report to the Legislature regarding instances of government neglect or administrative failure. Such hearings offer a powerful means to bring to public attention those needs for systemic change when service providers have failed to respond to the demonstrated needs of vulnerable adults and could also draw attention to individual cases of abuse or neglect.

A reporting relationship to government through a redefined Standing Committee of the Ombudsman and Advocacy would result, however, in an inherent threat of referring a matter to the Standing Committee for public hearings which would prevail on any occasion where an advocate was attempting to resolve a particular problem or complaint. This may characterize the role of the advocate in the eyes of service providers as investigators or adversaries, and could be counterproductive to the efforts of the advocate to resolve issues by negotiation with care providers. Understandably, care providers could respond to advocates in a self-protective manner. While this problem might be ameliorated by a reporting relationship through the Attorney General, the recommendation that the annual report of the Advocacy Commission be tabled in the Legislature will still result in the possibility that the role of the advocate will be perceived as unduly adversarial. Notwithstanding this concern, we are convinced that the advocacy system ought to have ultimate recourse to the Legislature in those cases where needed systemic reforms cannot be obtained through the co-operative approach. In order to avoid the perception of the advocate as an adversary and to foster a co-operative relationship, it would be imperative that training programs for advocates recognize this inherent problem and educate the advocates in fostering a co-operative, non-threatening relationship with care providers.

Finally, it should be noted that the Standing Committee has only a small staff available to assist them with their work, while the Ministry of the Attorney General has greater resources. On the other hand, the Attorney General does have a multitude of programs and responsibilities to engage his/her staff, whereas the Standing Committee is not so burdened. We have concluded that the advantages and shortcomings of a reporting relationship with either the Standing Committee or the Attorney General are relatively equal and would recommend either as an appropriate body to be assigned responsibility for the Shared Advocacy Model.

(c) Funding the Shared Advocacy Program

Each year, the Regional Board of Directors would be required to submit a budget covering the provision of advocacy services in the region for the forthcoming year. This budget would include not only the funds required for the operation of the regional office but would also include a request for new funding or continued funding of those advocacy programs developed at the community level by volunteer groups or individuals which are considered by the Board to merit funding. The Advocacy Commission would be responsible for reviewing the budget requests of each of the seven Regional Boards and determining the level of funding that it will recommend to the Attorney General or Legislature through its designated Standing Committee.

Funds would be disbursed by the Commission to the Regional Boards pursuant to a contract which each Board would be required to enter with the Commission undertaking to provide advocacy services in conformity with their application for accordance with the standards and procedures established by the Commission. Similarly, local Boards will disburse funds pursuant to contracts with the local community groups or individuals containing terms and conditions of funding which require delivery of advocacy in compliance with their application for funding and the standards and procedures set by the Commission. This annual process will provide an opportunity for the Regional Boards to review and evaluate the effectiveness of the local programs on a regular basis. Those programs that are no longer effective or required will not receive further funding. A decision of the Board to deny applications for funding by local individuals and groups should be subject to review by the Advocacy Commission.

(d) Federal-Provincial Cost Sharing

It is recommended that the legislation establishing the provincial advocacy system be structured, if possible, to qualify for funding under the federal *Canada Assistance Plan Act* (CAP). This legislation provides for federal government funding of one-half of the cost of provincial welfare services. The Act is administered by the Minister of National Health and Welfare. Programs or services within a program can qualify for cost-sharing under the following conditions:

1. They satisfy the definition of a "welfare service". These are services having as their object the lessening, removal or prevention of the causes and effects of poverty, child neglect or dependence on public assistance, and, without limiting the generality of the foregoing, includes:

    (a) rehabilitation services,

    (b) case work, counselling, assessment and referral services

    ....

    (e) community development services,

    (f) consulting, research and evaluation services with respect to welfare programs...

2. They are provided by "provincially approved agencies" -- that is agencies that are non-profit, and mandated by provincial law or by the "provincial authority" (i.e. in Ontario, the Minister of Community and Social Services) to deliver these services. The term "provincial law" refers to

Acts of the legislature that provide for financial assistance or welfare services and are administered by the Minister of Community and Social Services.

3. They serve "persons in need" (i.e. people receiving Family Benefits or General Welfare Assistance) or persons who are likely to be in need. The likelihood of need is decided on the basis of the income of the family or the individual. This is generally determined by some kind of proxy indicator such as random sampling or reference to available statistics rather than by income testing each individual using the service.

Cost-sharing for welfare services is limited to the following sharable costs: salaries and wages, benefits (pensions, UIC, CPP, health insurance ...) staff travel and training (including volunteer staff) professional fees, computer costs. Office administration costs, such as rent, telephone, and stationery, are not considered sharable costs.

While advocacy services would appear to qualify as "welfare services" under the CAP definition, there may be difficulty with respect to the requirement that the program be administered or mandated by the Minister of Community and Social Services. While the fundamental principle that the advocacy program be independent of service providers must not be compromised, it is clear that the advocacy model is consonant with the purposes and principles of the federal Act . We recommend, therefore, that there be consultation with the federal Minister of Health and Welfare with a view to qualifying the program for federal assistance in a manner that would preserve the independence of the program.

(e) Implementation of the Shared Advocacy Program--
The Need for Legislation

We recommend that the first priority of implementing the Shared Advocacy Program should be the enactment of legislation to establish the Advocacy Commission. The legislation should include a list of the duties and responsibilities of the Commission, Commission staff, Regional Boards of Directors, and Advocacy Co-ordinators. Further, it should provide for the right of access to institutions in which vulnerable adults reside to all advocacy co-ordinators, volunteer advocates, and advocates in local programs who have received certification as an advocate upon successful completion of an appropriate training program.

In addition, in the case of vulnerable adults residing in the community, the legislation should provide that all co-ordinators and advocates have the right to meet privately with the vulnerable adult at his or her residence. While recognizing the right of privacy of the owners and occupants of residences where vulnerable adults live, we are of the view that the right of the vulnerable adult to have access to an advocate should be accorded priority--in the event that reasonable alternative arrangements cannot be made for the advocate to access the vulnerable adult outside of his or her home. The right of access to vulnerable adults ought to be available to certified advocates at any time considered necessary and reasonable by them for the purpose of: investigating complaints and problems; interviewing vulnerable adults in private with their consent; interviewing employees or agents of care facilities; or offering any other services of an advocate to any vulnerable adult.

The legislation should also provide for the advocate to have access to the client's records as maintained by the care facility, with his or her consent. This information should be treated as confidential and must not be released without the consent of the client. In addition, it is imperative that the proposed legislation ensure the confidentiality of advocate/client communications. As discussed earlier, it is extremely difficult for clients to feel free to seek assistance from an advocate unless confidentiality is assured. It is recommended, however, that the legislation should incorporate the following two limited exceptions to this right of confidentiality as identified by the Fram Committee in its "Statement of Principles Regarding the Provision of Advocacy Services to Mentally Disadvantaged Persons":

(i) where access is required to ascertain whether the advocate has acted negligently; and

(ii) where a client dies in circumstances in which it would be in the public interest for the advocate to testify at an inquest.

(f) Need for Clear Standards and Procedures to be Set by Advocacy Commission

Following enactment of legislation and the appointment of seven Commissioners, the Commission will establish a central commission office and recruit an executive director and staff with the qualifications and expertise outlined above. Among the first priorities of the Commission and its staff should be the development of clear and uniform policies, practices and standards of service applicable throughout the entire advocacy system. In devising such standards and procedures, it is suggested that the Commission look to the experience of such agencies as the Clinic Funding Committee and the Ombudsman's Office for guidance.

With respect to the provision of advocacy services in general, it is recommended that the Commission should ensure that the basic principles of advocacy are adhered to--for example, that advocacy should be primarily non-adversarial and instruction-based. In addition, as discussed earlier, it would be important for the Commission to establish training, testing and certification programs for all advocates and to ensure that advocates' skills are upgraded on an ongoing basis.

With respect to the funding of local programs, it is proposed that the Commission should devise detailed criteria that each local program would be required to meet before approval would be given for their implementation. For example, we recommend that every local program should be required to demonstrate that it includes a public education component and will utilize, if appropriate, volunteer advocates. In addition, we are of the view that local programs should be required to devote a portion of their time and resources to identifying appropriate systemic advocacy issues and advising the central office of them on a regular basis. It will be recalled that it was recommended earlier that systemic advocacy should be one of the important functions of the central office, which is in the best position to co-ordinate this type of advocacy activity.

As well, we recommend that every local program that is proposed for funding must demonstrate that it will be accessible to the types of vulnerable adults that it has been designed to serve. For example, if the program is to serve physically handicapped persons, the facilities should be wheel-chair accessible. Further, it would be important to demonstrate that vulnerable adults with communication problems would be able to communicate with the advocates--that the program had access to persons who can sign and/or had proposed the purchase of Bliss boards, TTY services or other appropriate communication devices.

In addition, we recommend that all applications for the funding of local programs should not only contain a description of the group (groups) of vulnerable adults that the program will serve and the reasons why there is a need to serve this group, but should also identify the needy vulnerable groups that will not be served by the proposed program or other local initiatives, and to justify their omission. If the applicants are unable to do so, then the Regional Board should not carry forward the application to the Advocacy Commission. In this way, the Regional Board would be reminded that there are groups who are not being served by the local programs and will ensure that these groups are not forgotten in subsequent applications for the funding of other local programs. Throughout the Review, the concern was expressed that the interest of one group of vulnerable adults could be neglected in favour of "high profile" disabled or those who receive greater public sympathy. This concern is a valid one and it is hoped that this proposed funding guideline will assist to ameliorate it.

(g) Problems Associated with Instruction-Based Advocacy

Throughout the Report, it has been noted that one of the basic principles of advocacy is that it be client-directed or "instruction-based"--that the actions of an advocate must be guided by the instructions of a client and that the advocate serve the client on a voluntary and consensual basis. While we have clearly endorsed the concept of instruction-based advocacy, it is important to acknowledge that certain problems can arise in attempting to fulfill this obligation and to suggest appropriate ways to deal with them.

Ironically, those who may need an advocate most are frequently those least able to give direction. They may be unable to speak; they may be confused; or for some other reason be unable to communicate with ease or clarity. In such cases, a trained advocate must first make every effort to come to know and understand his or her clients, so as to have some insight into their wishes.

In addition, we are of the view that, in certain circumstances, advocates must be given the right to presume direction on behalf of their clients--based upon reasonable discretion. For example, if an advocate should encounter a non-communicative vulnerable adult who has been left in wet clothes due to incontinence, or whose bandages remain unchanged, he or she can reasonably presume direction to alter those unacceptable circumstances. This is the simple application of good common sense and should be allowed.

However, advocacy on a non-directed basis of less clear needs (for example, change of residence or treatment) should be made only after consultation with others involved in the person's care--and after asking another non-involved advocate for peer evaluation of the circumstances, and suggested plan of action. We recommend that it would be appropriate and useful for the Advocacy Commission to devise guidelines for the rare use of non-directed advocacy. Advocates, such as PPAs, APSWs and Tri-Ministry service co-ordinators, could provide invaluable assistance in this regard.

Another problem with respect to instruction-based advocacy concerns those situations where a client is able to give instruction, but the advocate finds that those instructions constitute a danger to the health or well-being of the client or others. For example, a psychiatric patient, confused as a result of over-medication and their psychiatric condition, may insist upon receiving drugs which should no longer be administered. In this case, the advocates must be free to advise their client of their objections to the direction and offer support in seeking alternatives.

Ultimately, if an impasse persists the advocate must be prepared to withdraw from the relationship. The advocate should not, however, simply abandon the vulnerable partner without having first outlined the reasons for rejecting his or her wishes and presenting the option of an alternate advocate. Again, peer evaluation in such circumstances should be employed--and caring common sense be the guiding standard.

(h) Who will be Advocates?

An understandable concern at this point is: who will serve as advocates? From the perspective of the needs identified in this Review, it is to be hoped that the advocates will be reflective of our population and the vulnerable. Whether they be part-time volunteers or full-time employees of the Commission, advocates will have to possess a range of qualities that are appropriate to the important tasks they will undertake.

Foremost, they should be people of genuine caring and compassion; good listeners; with a particular regard for the rights and aspirations of others. Their altruism will be translated into action as desired by their advocacy partner -- and consistent with that increasingly rare commodity, common sense.

While they will require training and accreditation, advocates should come from a variety of backgrounds and be generalists in the sense that they remain open to the exigencies of the human condition. During the course of this Review, it has been clear that there are already individuals well suited to the responsibilities of advocacy -- gifted with those dimensions of trust and persistence that will be the hallmark of successful advocates. For the initial phase of Ontario's new advocacy program, it is to be hoped that advocacy co-ordinators will be drawn from the ranks of the current APSWs, service co-ordinators, chaplains, social workers, nurses and other individuals with a demonstrated commitment to the well-being of others.

For reasons detailed elsewhere, it is important that the expertise of the psychiatric patient advocates be an integral part of the advocacy services, while maintaining the best features of their special advocacy.

Typically, volunteer advocates could be recruited from among the ranks of those who have "been there". For example, an individual whose parent was subjected to inferior nursing home care who now wishes to ensure that others made vulnerable by age, infirmity and absence of caring family will not be ignored or overlooked. Or the former psychiatric patient, now enjoying a return to good health, who understands the difficulties faced by a newly-discharged patient reintegrating into community life -- with bleak prospects for employment or suitable housing.

Similarly, retirement at age 65 can also offer a freedom and opportunity for some of our most experienced Ontarians to put their time, good health and savvy at the disposal of those who are vulnerable and need such effective advocates. The possibilities for rewarding and effective advocacy are as great as Ontario's human resources -- and certainly a match for the tremendous needs of those desiring of an advocacy partner.

(i) Data Collection and Analysis

In its first year, the Advocacy Commission and its staff should establish a comprehensive system for collecting, recording and analyzing data to be reported by the regional offices to the central office on a quarterly basis. This data would include complaints and problems received, actions taken by advocates, responses and recommendations. This data would be available to monitor and evaluate the effectiveness of the program and would also be a valuable resource for the Advocacy Commission and staff in carrying out their mandate to promote and lobby for systemic reforms.

(j) Legal Component

While the basic approach of the advocacy program is non-adversarial with front-line advocates resolving the problems and complaints of partners through consultation and negotiation, it is essential that the program have a strong legal component to provide credibility and clout. The legislation, regulations and administrative practices and policies applicable to vulnerable adults are complex. All of the ministries and many agencies which provide services employ full-time legal experts to assist their staff. There are, however, very few lawyers in the community with expertise in these areas. Therefore, it is recommended that the central office employ a full-time staff lawyer to give legal advice and assistance to advocates when required. The lawyer should also participate in the training of advocates so that they will be able to recognize those matters that require legal, as opposed to non-legal, advocacy. While the staff lawyer should provide summary advice and assistance to advocates, it is recommended that if the matter cannot be resolved through consultation and negotiation, and litigation is required, the matter should be referred to an appropriate community legal clinic or lawyer in private practice. It is our view that the other pressing responsibilities of the staff lawyer will not afford sufficient time to properly prosecute such cases through the courts.

(k) Research Component

It is recommended that the central office should include a research component to aid the staff in their work towards systemic reform. In addition to their other responsibilities outlined earlier, the central staff advocates should also assist the staff lawyer in gathering research, writing papers and making recommendations for reform. To help prevent "burnout", a rotational arrangement, similar to a rotating fellowship, could be devised whereby experienced advocacy co-ordinators could exchange positions for a year with the central office advocate. This would give the co-ordinator a creative outlet to reflect on and develop solutions to problems encountered in the field and would give the central office advocate the opportunity to be involved directly in front-line advocacy work.

(l) Public Education and Outreach

The concept of non-legal advocacy services for vulnerable adults will be new to many citizens. Consumers and providers of services who have been exposed to the present fragmented advocacy system will be unaware of the mandate, rights and accountability of the advocacy co-ordinators, volunteer advocates and the advocates in the local programs. We recommend that the Advocacy Commission should aggressively publicize the program through a variety of media and conduct education and awareness conferences for vulnerable adults, their families, volunteers and providers. While this effort should be led by the central office Co-ordinator of Training and Public Education, all Commission staff should be enlisted in this work in order to publicize the program and promote as much understanding and goodwill as possible. Public education and outreach should also be an early priority once the regional offices are established and the regional advocacy co-ordinators should devote a major portion of their time in the early stages to this activity. Through education and outreach activities, vulnerable adults will be informed of the mandate and availability of the program, providers will understand the role and rights of advocates, potential volunteer advocates will be encouraged to offer their services, and local communities will be encouraged to identify their needs and design effective local advocacy programs.

(m) Trusteeship

In the event the Commission determines that a Regional Board of Directors is failing in a material way to fulfill the obligations set forth in its contract, it should have the power, after giving the local Board at least fifteen days within which to comply, to appoint a trustee of the regional office program until such time as the Commission determines that the trusteeship is no longer required. Similarly, in the event the Regional Board of Directors determines that those responsible for the operation of a local program are failing in a material way to comply with the contractual obligations accompanying funding of the program, it should have the power, after giving at least fifteen days' notice to rectify the matter, to appoint a trustee of the local program. The ability to appoint trustees to assume responsibility for advocacy services at the regional or local level will enable the provision of advocacy services to continue on an uninterrupted basis notwithstanding the occurrence of a material breach of the terms and conditions of the funding contract.

We also recommend that there be a right of appeal of the appointment of a regional board trustee to the Standing Committee or Attorney General and a right of appeal of a local program trustee to the Advocacy Commission. Pending the determination of an appeal, the trustee should continue to operate the program and be accorded full co-operation and assistance of all persons responsible for the provision of advocacy services.

(n) Regional Boards of Directors

As discussed earlier, the Advocacy Commission should be responsible for appointing the founding members of the Board of Directors for each region to hold office for a term of not longer than two years. It is recommended that the Commission publicly invite applications from any interested citizen in the region for appointment to the Board. The Commission will then appoint not more than 25 of the applicants to the Board. Within two years, the Regional Board of Directors would be required to develop a procedure for the election of their successors which procedure must be approved by the Commisison.

The Regional Board of Directors should be representative of interests of consumers and communities throughout the region and *comprised of a majority* of primary and secondary users (consumers and their families). With respect to the balance of the membership of the Board, we do not share the view that persons be excluded from eligibility for membership on the Board by reason of their affiliation with an organization, agency or Ministry which is a service provider. Based upon the meetings and briefs we have received, we are confident that such persons can and will bring an open and unbiased mind to their duties and will provide a wealth of knowledge, experience and support to the advocacy program. When issues arise on the Board's agenda in which conflicts of interest occur, the member can disqualify him or herself (or, if necessary, be disqualified by a majority vote) from participating in the discussion or vote on the issue.

(o) Psychiatric Patient Advocate Office

When the Review on Advocacy commenced in January, an evaluation of the Psychiatric Patient Advocate program, which is discussed in Chapter 3, was being conducted by a Committee appointed by the Minister of Health under the chairmanship of Professor Manson. This external evaluation of the program is extensive, incorporating both qualitative and empirical research. While we have had the opportunity of meeting with the Chairman on several occasions throughout our Review, unexpected delays encountered by the Committee in completing the collection and analysis of data precluded formal consideration of its research or recommendations. The Psychiatric Patient Advocate Office evaluation remains pending and in these circumstances, we are unable to provide any commentary on the findings, conclusions or recommendations of the evaluation.

However, the following compelling reasons were presented to us during the course of the Review for the integration of the Psychiatric Patient Advocate Office into a provincial advocacy system:

(1) integration would ensure that co-ordinated and consistent services would be available to psychiatric patients in both institutions and in the community. This is a particularly compelling reason for integration when one considers that the average length of stay of psychiatric patients in institutions is two months;

(2) integration will help to avoid confusion as to the mandates and responsibilities of the two programs, prevent duplication of service or gaps in services, particularly in the case of dual-diagnosis clients (e.g. developmentally disabled and psychiatriclly disabled) and would be more cost effective;

(3) the knowledge and experience gained in the past four years by those active in the P.P.A. program would be of considerable assistance to the Commission in its initial organizational phase;

(4) integration would facilitate the exchange of data, information, and experience which would strengthen both the systemic and individual advocacy work of both psychiatric patient advocates and the advocates working with other vulnerable groups;

(5) a program whose principal mandate is the provision of advocacy services should be independent of service providers and must be accountable to the funding body. If the PPA program is transferred from the Ministry of Health, it would be logical and consistent that it be funded under the provincial Shared Advocacy Program;

(6) integration would promote delabelling and destigmatizing clients based on disability and would prevent the Psychiatric Patient Advocate program, its staff and clients from becoming isolated and ghettoized on the basis of disability;

(7) there would be accumulated benefits to the Psychiatric Patient Advocates as they are given greater career flexibility and mobility. They would become part of an association of fellow advocates that will provide support and offer an opportunity to exchange experiences and ideas.

It has been submitted that integration of the Psychiatric Patient Advocate Office into a provincial advocacy system will ultimately result in the weakening of the program as the interests of psychiatrically disabled persons will be subordinated to the needs of more appealing groups of vulnerable adults. To ensure that the PPA program is not so compromised, we recommend that the Psychiatric Patient Advocate Co-ordinator be appointed to the central office staff, assigned responsibility for the provision of advocacy services to the psychiatrically disabled in institutions and in the community and that the psychiatric patient advocates continue to report to and be supervised by the Co-ordinator. We also recommend that the PPA Co-ordinator be given responsibility for liaison with the Ministry of Health on issues affecting the psychiatrically disabled.

(p) Case Managers/Service Co-ordinators and Advocacy

An important issue raised early in the Review was whether case managers/service co-ordinators should be included in an independent advocacy system. Service co-ordinators have primary responsibility for co-ordinating the provision of appropriate services and monitoring the delivery of services to their clients. It was submitted by a major service provider ministry that the service co-ordination function was a cornerstone of the service delivery system in orchestrating co-operation among services, programs, agencies and service professionals to facilitate clients' access to information and appropriate services. The more closely the service co-ordinator is integrated into the service system, the more knowledgeable and effective he or she can be. If the advocate performs service co-ordination in an independent and sometimes adversarial program to the service provider, the result will be a diminution in the specialized expertise and contacts necessary to provide effective co-ordination and implementation of the client's service plan -- to the ultimate detriment of the client.

It must be noted that service co-ordinators also have a responsibility to advocate for their clients as part of their job functions. In the case of APSWs, the duty to provide advocacy services is specifically set out in their operating guidelines. Many service co-ordinators have submitted that their advocacy role is seriously compromised by their employment as part of the service delivery system. Frequently, they are called to advocate on behalf of their clients against their employer in pressing for new programs or reforms to existing programs. The ability of service co-ordinators to advocate freely and vigorously is limited by fear of reprisal or fear of loss of employment or promotion opportunities. Further,vulnerable clients lack confidence in their advocacy because of the perceived conflict of interest.

There are also conflicting client mandates which guide advocates and service co-ordinators. Advocates must act on the instructions of their client. On the other hand, service co-ordinators cannot always act on instructions when they conflict with their perception of the client's best interests. For example, if a service co-ordinator concludes that an individual client is at risk by reason of physical or economic exploitation, he or she has a duty to report that to the appropriate agencies--whether or not the client gives instructions to do so.

The inclusion of service co-ordination responsibilities in an independent advocacy system presents another serious conflict. In a report entitled, *Further Explorations of Advocacy Models for the Mentally Disabled*, 1982, Valerie J. Bradley, an investigator with the Human Services Research Institute in Boston, pointed out that where service co-ordination becomes part of the advocacy system, there is a substantial likelihood that the advocacy function will become secondary to the pressing demands for service co-ordination.

Further, if the service co-ordination function were merged in an advocacy system, there would no longer be the capacity to independently monitor the effectiveness of the service co-ordinator. Because of the importance of the service co-ordination function to the client, it would be necessary to create another independent person to carry out that function.

We therefore conclude that it is not desirable to include service co-ordinators in an independent advocacy system. In making this recommendation, we have also taken into account the fact that none of the existing advocacy systems in the United States which we have studied include a service co-ordination component. Indeed, those responsible for the operation of these programs have advised against the inclusion of service co-ordination responsibilities in a program. The submission of the Ontario Psychiatric Patient Advocate Office also advised that it would not be desirable to include both advocacy and service co-ordination services in the mandate of an advocacy model.

However, we would recommend that advocacy should continue to be an important component of the internal service co-ordinator's functions. Where the service co-ordinator's advocacy efforts reach the point where they are compromised by his or her position, the service co-ordinator should refer the matter to a local advocacy co-ordinator or the Commission staff. We also recommend that, in special circumstances, an advocate should be permitted to perform some service co-ordination services where no service co-ordinators are available to assume this responsibility. However, this would be an exceptional case and the advocate should only perform such services in "acute" situations.

In summary, we are of the view that, in most cases, advocacy is an essential component of case management/service co-ordination. Service co-ordination, however, is not an essential aspect of advocacy.

(q) Legislative Protection of Vulnerable Adults

It was startling to discover in the course of the Review, that apart from the amendments to the nursing home legislation enacted this year requiring the reporting of instances of abuse or neglect of residents, there is no similar protective legislation in Ontario for the elderly living in other institutions or in the community, or for other vulnerable adults. The lack of any legislative protective provisions was raised by many advocates and care providers who have seen the effects of abuse and neglect of the vulnerable on a first hand basis in the course of their work.

There is in the statutes, legislation which protects children from abuse and neglect. The *Child and Family Services Act* requires that any instance of child abuse or neglect which comes to the attention of a care provider be reported to the police and the Children's Aid Society for investigation. Persons who fail to report are subject to prosecution. Significantly, there is also legislative protection in Ontario for animals that have been abused or neglected. *The Ontario Society for the Prevention of Cruelty to Animals Act* empowers Humane Society workers to access property and seize animals when they believe their lives are endangered. In the absence of an effective and comprehensive advocacy service delivery system, the omission of legislative protection for vulnerable adults leaves at serious risk countless disabled citizens of Ontario who have been abandoned by their families and friends.

The problem is particularly acute in the case of frail elderly people. As noted in Chapter 3, approximately 11% of the population in this province is over 65 years of age and by 2030 seniors will represent 23% of the population. Statistics confirm the perception that advances in medicine and greater attention to personal health have resulted in more people living into their 70s, 80s and 90s than ever before. We have heard of the abuse and neglect which the frail elderly suffer not only in private and public care facilities but also in their homes. Those who exploit and abuse them include close family members, as well as friends, tradesmen and strangers. As mentioned earlier, the Federal Government's National Clearing House on Family Violence estimates that between 2-4% of senior citizens in our country are victims of elder abuse. Further, in a 1980 study on elder abuse conducted by sociologist Donna J. Shell for the Government of Manitoba Council on Aging, it was estimated that 2.2% of the 18,000 elderly Manitobans receiving care from relatives or home-service agencies were suffering abuse. This amounted to .3% of the provincial population over 65 years of age. Financial abuse was encountered most frequently followed by emotional and physical abuse.

It is obvious that the enactment of protective legislation for vulnerable adults is not free from complexity: there must be reasonable alternative residences available to which the abused can be removed; the removal of vulnerable adults from their homes is contrary to the current social policy of promoting deinstitutionalization and reducing the warehousing of the vulnerable; and some abused adults would prefer to endure their home circumstances rather than accept the alternative of removal to an institution, however safe. Fortunately, there are a number of precedents of adult protection legislation in jurisdictions in the United States and in other provinces which have dealt with these issues. For example, Nova Scotia and Minnesota have developed effective enactments to address these concerns.

Under the Nova Scotia Act, (Appendix 9) every person who has information indicating that an adult is in need of protection is required to report the information, whether or not it is confidential or privileged, to the Minister of Social Services. Under the aegis of the Co-ordinator of Adult Protection Services, a system has been established to investigate the reports and develop solutions for individual cases. In the first year of operation, investigators reviewed 180 reported instances of neglect among Nova Scotia's elderly and 73 cases of abuse. Attempts are made to avoid the institutionalization of those suffering abuse by providing supportive and counselling services to the family and arranging for staff investigators to make periodic visits to the residence of the abused adult.

The Minnesota legislation (Appendix 10) defines a vulnerable adult as any person 18 years of age or older who is resident of a long-term care facility, or who, regardless of residence, is unable or unlikely to report abuse or neglect without assistance because of impairment of mental or physical functions or emotional status. Abuse is the intentional and nontherapeutic infliction of physical pain or injury, or any persistent course of conduct intended to produce mental or emotional distress. Neglect is defined as the failure by a care provider to supply a vulnerable adult with necessary food, clothing, shelter, health care or supervision. The Minnesota legislation stipulates that it is the public policy of the State to protect vulnerable adults, to provide safe institutional residential services or living environments for adults who have been abused or neglected and to assist persons charged with the care of vulnerable adults to provide safe environments. The operative section of the legislation with regard to the duty to report is as follows:

> (3)   A professional or his delegate who is engaged in the care of
> vulnerable adults, education, law enforcement, or any of the regulated
> occupations referenced in subdivision 2, clause (g)(3) and (4), or an
> employee of or person providing services in a facility who has
> knowledge of the abuse or neglect of a vulnerable adult, has
> reasonable cause to believe that a vulnerable adult is being or has been
> abused or neglected, or who has knowledge that a vulnerable adult
> has sustained a physical injury which is not reasonably explained by
> the history of injuries provided by the caretaker or caretakers of the
> vulnerable adult shall immediately report the information to the local
> police department, county sheriff, local welfare agency, or
> appropriate licensing or certifying agency. The police department or
> the county sheriff, upon receiving a report, shall immediately notify
> the local welfare agency. The local welfare agency, upon receiving a
> report, shall immediately notify the local police department or the
> county sheriff and the appropriate licensing agency or agencies.
>
> A person not required to report under the provisions of this
> subdivision may voluntarily report as described above. Medical

examiners or coroners shall notify the police department or county sheriff and the local welfare department in instances in which they believe that a vulnerable adult has died as a result of abuse or neglect.

Persons required to report under section (3) are required to make an oral report "immediately by telephone or otherwise" and a written report "as soon as possible" to the "appropriate police department, county sheriff, local welfare agency or appropriate licensing agency." The written report is required to be of sufficient content to identify the vulnerable adult, the nature and extent of the suspected abuse or neglect, any evidence of previous abuse or neglect, name and address of the reporter and any other information the reporter believes might be helpful in investigating the suspected abuse or neglect.

A failure to report as required by the Act is a misdemeanour offence. In addition, persons who are required to report and fail to do so are statutorily liable for a civil suit for damages caused by the failure to report.

The Minnesota legislation also provides that any person who reports in good faith suspected abuse or neglect, and any vulnerable adult with respect to whom a report is made, will be protected from acts of retaliation. Any person or facility which retaliates is subject to a fine of $1,000 and liable to the person retaliated against for actual damages.

This protection against retaliation is given particular force by virtue of section 17(c) of the Act:

> (c)   There shall be a rebuttable presumption that any adverse action, as defined below, within 90 days of a report is retaliatory. For purposes of this clause, the term "adverse action" refers to action taken by a facility or person involved in a report against the person making the report or the person with respect to whom the report was made because of the report, and includes, but is not limited to:
>
> (1) Discharge or transfer from the facility;
> (2) Discharge from or termination of employment;
> (3) Demotion or reduction in remuneration for services;
> (4) Restriction or prohibition of access to the facility or its residents; or

(5) Any restriction of rights set forth in section 144.651.

Finally, any person who has care of a vulnerable adult and any operator, employee or volunteer worker at care facilities who intentionally abuses or neglects a vulnerable adult or who "permits conditions to exist which result in the abuse or neglect of a vulnerable adult" is guilty of a gross misdemeanour under the Act.

The Act also mandates the Commissioner of Public Welfare to establish "an aggressive program to educate those required to report, as well as the general public, about the requirements of the legislation by using a variety of media".

The Nova Scotia and Minnesota legislation could be readily adapted to the Ontario context and the services of the Advocacy Commission could be enlisted as part of an Ontario protective scheme. Where there is reasonable proof that there has been abuse or neglect and the vulnerable adult has by reason of choice or otherwise remained in the residence where the neglect or abuse occurred, an advocate could be assigned by the regional office to develop a relationship with the vulnerable adult which would provide an independent monitoring of the situation and facilitate reporting of subsequent abuse by the vulnerable adult. We recommend that the enactment and implementation of protective legislation for vulnerable adults be given the highest possible priority.

(r) Cost of the Shared Advocacy Program

The projected cost of the recommended Shared Advocacy Model has not been quantified in this Report for two reasons.

First, because of the evolutionary nature of the model, it is difficult to ascertain a specific cost at this stage. As discussed, the Model contemplates an evolutionary growth of the program over a period of several years. The first phase will largely involve the establishment of the Commission and central office staff and the development of standards and procedures for the program. In the second year, Regional Boards will be established, advocacy co-ordinators hired and assigned to recruit volunteers to assist in the provision of advocacy services throughout the region. Thereafter, with the assistance of the advocacy co-ordinators, local community groups will develop local programs tailored to the needs of the vulnerable adults in their community. This last evolutionary phase of the model will be an ongoing process as the local programs are developed, funded and, when the need is no longer present, discontinued. Therefore, the calculation of the immediate costs and the projected costs over the life of the program is best left to the budgetary analysts in government who have the required expertise.

The second and more important reason is our belief that the determination of whether or not to establish a provincial system to provide advocacy services can only be fairly and properly made when the cost of providing the service is compared with the cost of not doing so. It is not possible to measure the cost to our society of failing to make available effective advocacy services to all of our vulnerable citizens who have been abandoned, neglected or abused. The loss of their human dignity and self-respect, the denial and infringement of their legal rights and the diminution the community experiences when one of its members is neglected and unable to participate and contribute to the life of the community to the fullest possible extent cannot be measured.

While responsible government officials must consider the cost of providing effective advocacy services, we believe that when proper account is taken of the human cost of failing to provide these services, the interests of vulnerable adults will prevail.

155

"John was labelled retarded, and because he had that label he had to live a life of poverty, no freedom of choice or privacy; he was a man crying out for help, and he died because the community didn't hear his cry... John needed friends in the community, but he was never given that chance. He never had the chance to say I want a real job and I want to live in the community in a decent home and make friends like every other average person. Like many People First members, John was well-serviced, but the service system didn't care about his needs; the service system didn't support John."

Reference to John Dimun, a developmentally handicapped man who died in a rooming house in Toronto in December, 1986. From a brief submitted by People First of Ontario, a self-help association for developmentally handicapped people.

In Closing...

Having been the beneficiary of countless hours of volunteer help with the Review and this Report, we know that the spirit of volunteerism is alive and healthy within our province.

It needs to be enhanced and encouraged. Volunteer advocates provide the possibility for more wide-spread and locally-sensitive advocacy services.

The training of such volunteer advocates is consistent with our belief that advocacy is not just a function of government: it is part of our responsibility to care for one another as family members, friends and concerned citizens.

Volunteer advocacy will make a positive contribution to the lives of both the vulnerable adult and the advocate who will experience the satisfaction of learning that we still need one another, and that we can still make a difference in the well-being of others and our society.

Moreover, we wish to endorse the insights offered us by an individual whose remarkable life's journey includes long-term institutionalization, labelling as mentally retarded, a decision to strike out on his own, and who today offers advocacy and hope to many others.

This man spoke compellingly of a basic difference, from the partner's point of view, between a paid advocate and a volunteer advocate.

As he put it, the paid advocate would be regarded as a professional who has a job to do. But the volunteer advocate, exactly because he/she is there voluntarily," is also my friend."

We have found no better description of the advocate *par excellence.*

While recognizing the need for a corps of equally dedicated, professionally trained, and suitably paid advocates, this Review has concluded that the heart and soul of advocacy services will depend upon caring volunteers.

Sometimes there is frustratingly little that can be done to change or improve the sad circumstances of some of our vulnerable fellow citizens.

But volunteer advocacy can advance the possibility of assistance, and at the very least, provide vulnerable citizens with the hope and satisfaction that they no longer face their circumstances with the additional handicap of loneliness or abandonment.

Shared Advocacy in Ontario, once implemented, will say to those in need that, at least, you've got a friend.

Sometimes that is the biggest and best difference in all our lives.

It is a difference that we should be willing to make as we learn with renewed resolve to stop acting as strangers when confronted by those to whom life has been less than kind.

If Ontario is to continue to be a caring, compassionate and progressive society, we must replace fear with friendship, and inaction with advocacy.

Regardless of physical or mental illness and/or impairment, vulnerable persons must have the power to make decisions and exercise their right of choice. People are people, whether or not they have identifiable handicaps. The advocacy system is designed to foster a vulnerable individual's sense of dignity as a valuable contributing citizen of Ontario.

There is nothing in this Report that cannot be achieved if there is the political will to recognize the genuine needs of Ontario's vulnerable citizens.

This Review has been, in the Attorney General's words, "the first step on the road to a more effective and sensitive delivery of services to vulnerable adults in Ontario."

May we now move forward -- and never turn back.

ENDNOTES

CHAPTER 2

1.	See Crosson, *Advocacy and the Developmentally Disabled: An Overview* (1977), at 1.

2.	Wolfensberger, *A Balanced Multi-Component Advocacy/Protection Schema* (1977), at 18-19.

3.	Submission received from Ministry of Community and Social Services (April 15, 1987).

4.	See Wolfensberger, *A Multi-component Advocacy/Protection Schema* (1977), at 25.

5.	Advisory Committee on Substitute Decision Making for Mentally Incapable Persons, *"Statement of Principles Regarding theProvision of Advocacy Services to Mentally Disadvantaged Persons"*, at 4-5 (see Appendix 8).

6.	Intagliata,*"Improving the Quality of Community Care for the Chronically Mentally Disabled: The Role of Case Management"* (1982), 8 Schizophrenia Bulletin 655, at 657.

7.	*Ibid.*, at 658.

8.	See *Ibid.*

9.	*Ibid.*, at 659.

CHAPTER 3

1.	Statistic provided by Office for Senior Citizens' Affairs (Ontario).

2.	Statistic provided by Office Responsible for Disabled Persons (Ontario).

3.	Hurst, *"Health Care Crisis Looms as Elderly Live Longer"*, Toronto Star (May 31, 1987).

4.	Statistic provided by Office for Senior Citizens' Affairs (Ontario).

5. Statistic provided by Ministry of Health.

6. Statistic provided by Ministry of Health (as of June 30, 1987).

7. Statistic provided by Ministry of Community and Social Services (as of June 30, 1987).

8. Ministry of Health, *Hospital Statistics (1985-86)*.

9. Statistic provided by Ministry of Health (as of April 15, 1987).

10. See *First Report of the Psychiatric Patient Advocate Office* (1985), at 1.

11. *Ibid.*

12. *Living Room II: A City Housing Policy Review*, Housing Policy Review Committee, City of Toronto, 1986.

13. Statistic provided by Ministry of Community and Social Services.

14. *Ibid.*

15. Statistic provided by Ministry of Citizenship and Culture.

16. *Ibid.*

17. Silversides, *"Long-term care deadens the spirit VON speakers tell gerontologists"*, Globe and Mail (October 19, 1985).

18. Submission received from the Advocacy Centre for the Elderly .

19. Ministry of Community and Social Services, *Program Guildelines for the Adult Protective Service Worker* (November 1983), at 1.

20. Statistic provided by the Ministry of Community and Social Services.

21. Wolfensberger, *A Balanced Multi-Component Advocacy Protection Schema* (1977), at 30.

22. Statistic provided by Ministry of Community and Social Services.

23. O'Brien, *Learning from Citizen Advocacy* (1987), Georgia Advocacy Office Inc.

APPENDICES

1. Terms of Reference

2. Statement by the Honourable Ian Scott, Attorney General

3. Advertisement placed in Newspapers

4. Submissions

5. Meetings and Consultations

6. Advisory Committee Members

7. Statement of Principles Regarding the Provision of Advocacy Services to Mentally Disadvantaged Persons

8. Government Programs and Initiatives for Vulnerable Adults

9. Nova Scotia Legislation

10. Minnesota Legislation

APPENDIX NO. 1

January 1987

REVIEW OF ADVOCACY FOR VULNERABLE ADULTS

A review of advocacy would be primarily concerned with advocacy that ensures the rights of disadvantaged individuals and groups.

TERMS OF REFERENCE:

1.   To consider the need for advocacy for adults in institutitonal care settings as well as those adults that may require such services and are living in the community.

2.   To analyze thoroughly the concept of advocacy in relation to disadvantaged adult populations in Ontario, e.g. frail elderly, physically handicapped, psychiatrically disabled, developmentally handicapped.

3.   To develop options concerning the establishment of advocacy services, including organizational structure and accountability for each option.

4.   The consideration of need will include a detailed review relating to the co-ordination of advocacy with:

a)   existing case management and other delivery systems; and

b)   existing legal and volunteer advocacy services.

APPENDIX NO. 2

Statement by The Honourable Ian Scott, Attorney General, to The Legislature

Re: Review of Advocacy for Vulnerable Adults

Tuesday, December 16, 1986

I am pleased to announce the appointment of Father Sean O'Sullivan to conduct a Review of Advocacy for vulnerable adults in Ontario.

The impetus for this review comes, in part, from a Submission made last summer from an organization called Concerned Friends of Ontario Residents in Care Facilities and entitled "Advocacy Ontario". It was a submission that I encouraged the organization to prepare because of my own conviction that there is an unmet need for non-legal advocacy for vulnerable adults living in institutional care settings and in the community. Vulnerable adult populations include the frail elderly, the developmentally handicapped and the psychiatrically disabled.

In part, also, the impetus for this review comes from the many other organizations which agree on the need for more and better non-legal advocacy but want careful consideration to be given to ascertaining the best method, or methods, for delivering advocacy services. These organizations, which also represent vulnerable adults, have put forward a variety of other models for the establishment of independent advocacy services in Ontario.

My colleagues, the Minister of Health, the Minister of Community and Social Services, the Minister responsible for Senior Citizens' Affairs, the Minister responsible for Disabled Persons and I share the conviction that vulnerable adults must be heard and that health and social services must respond to their needs. While we agree on this basic principle, there are still many unanswered questions. It is important to ensure that whatever system of advocacy we put in place will respond to the real needs of vulnerable adults. Advocacy must be structured so as to be effective and meaningful. It would be a disservice to everyone to act hastily and to cobble together a solution that failed to address the real problems facing our vulnerable citizens.

Accordingly, I have asked Father Sean O'Sullivan to conduct a review of independent advocacy for vulnerable adults living in institutional care settings and in the community. Father O'Sullivan will provide an independent and thorough review of the concept of advocacy and develop various options for the establishment of advocacy services. He will also consider ways in which advocacy might be co-ordinated with existing case management and other service delivery systems and with existing legal and volunteer advocates in the community. Father O'Sullivan will be supported by three advisory groups representing consumers, providers of services and affected Ministries.

I have asked Father O'Sullivan to report within six months so that the government can give timely consideration to his recommendations. This review should be seen as the first step on the road to a more effective and sensitive delivery of services to vulnerable adults in Ontario.

APPENDIX NO. 3

Advertisement Placed in Newspapers

REVIEW OF ADVOCACY FOR
VULNERABLE ADULTS
IN ONTARIO

The Review of Advocacy has been initiated to consider the issue of non-legal advocacy services for vulnerable adults, such as the frail elderly, the mentally disadvantaged, the psychiatrically disabled and adults with physical disabilities, who are living in institutional care settings and in the community. The nature of advocacy services, in general, involves assisting disadvantaged individuals to obtain services to which they are entitled, offering them advice in order to help them make their own decisions, and make representations on their behalf to improve and supplement the services that currently are available to them.

The Review of Advocacy will involve a thorough study of the need for non-legal advocacy in this province, as well as an analysis of the concept of advocacy and the consideration of options for the effective delivery of non-legal advocacy services in Ontario. An important aspect of the Review will be to consider ways in which the advocacy programme could be coordinated with existing government social service programmes, as well as with existing legal and volunteer advocacy agencies, groups and individuals in the community.

Written briefs are welcomed and should be submitted before April 1, 1987 to:

Review of Advocacy for Vulnerable Adults
180 Dundas Street West
22nd Floor   ATTN: Paul J. Podesta
Toronto, Ontario   Executive Assistant
(416) 965-6335

Publication

Barrie Examiner
Belleville Intelligencer
Brampton Guardian
Brandford Expositor
Brockville Recorder Times
Cambridge Daily Reporter
Chatham Daily News
Cobourg Daly Star
Cornwall Standard-Freeholder
Fort Francis Daily Bulletin
Guelph Mercury
Hamilton Spectator
Kenora Daily Miner & News
Kingston Whig Standard
Kirkland Lake Northern Daily News
Kitchener-Waterloo Record
Lindsay Post
London Free Press
Niagara Falls Review
North Bay Nugget
Oshawa Times
Ottawa Citizen (E)
Ottawa L'Droit (F)
Owen Sound Times
Pembroke Observer
Peterborough Examiner
Port Hope Guide
St. Catharines Standard
St. Thomas Times-Journal
Sarnia Observer
Sault Ste. Marie Star
Simcoe Reformer
Sioux Lookout N'West Explorer
Stratford Beacon-Herald
Globe & Mail (Ont. Edition)
Toronto Star
Toronto Sun
Welland-Port Colbourne Tribune
Windsor Star
Woodstock-Ingersol Sentinel Review

APPENDIX NO. 4

Submissions

Adult Protection Service Association
 of Ontario
90 Albert Street
London, Ontario, N6A 1L8

Adult Protection Service Association
 of Ontario
Eastern Chapter APSAO
Winchester District Memorial Hospital
Winchester, Ontario, K0C 2K0

Advocacy Centre for the Elderly
120 Eglinton Avenue East
Suite 902
Toronto, Ontario, M4P 1E2

Advocacy Resource Centre for the
 Handicapped
40 Orchard View Boulevard
Suite 255
Toronto, Ontario, M4R 1B9

Alzheimer Association of Ontario
131 Bloor Street West
Suite 423
Toronto, Ontario, M5S 1R1

Amity Goodwill Industries
225 King William Street
Hamilton, Ontario, L8R 1B1

Ms. Flo Armstrong
Toronto, Ontario

Association of General Hospital
  Psychiatric Service
Woodstock General Hospital
270 Riddell Street
Woodstock, Ontario, N4S 6N6

Association of Local Official
 Health Agencies
277 Lakeshore Road East
Suite 218
Oakville, Ontario, L6J 6J3

Association of Nursing Directors and
 Supervisors of Ontario Official
 Health Agencies
30 Lorraine Drive
Willowdale, Ontario, M2N 2E3

Avenue II Community Program Services
 (Thunder Bay) Incorporated
122 S. Cumberland Street
Thunder Bay, Ontario, P7B 2V3

The Barrie & District Association
 for the Mentally Retarded
P.O. Box 1017
Barrie, Ontario, L4M 5E1

Mr. A. Boles
Stouffville, Ontario

Brockville Psychiatric Hospital
P.O. Box 1050
Brockville, Ontario, K6V 5W7

Canadian Diabetes Association
Ontario Division
P.O. Box 2603
London, Ontario, N6A 4G9

The Canadian Hearing Society
Head Office
271 Spadina Road
Toronto, Ontario, M5R 2V3

Canadian Hearing Society
Hamilton Regional Office
402 Concession Street
Hamilton, Ontario, L9A 7B7

Canadian Mental Health Association
Kingston Branch
388 King Street East
Kingston, Ontario, K7K 2Y2

Canadian Mental Health Association
Mental Health/Waterloo Region
607 King Street West
Kitchener, Ontario, N2G 1C7

Canadian Mental Health Association
North Bay Branch
129 Main Street West
North Bay, Ontario, P1B 2T6

Canadian Mental Health Association
Sudbury Branch
73 Elm Street West
Suite 202
Sudbury, Ontario, P3C 1T3

Canadian Mental Health Association
56 Wellesley Street West
Suite 410
Toronto, Ontario, M5S 2S3

Canadian Mental Health Association
Windsor-Essex County Branch
880 Ouellette Avenue
Suite 201
Windsor, Ontario, N9A 1C7

Canadian Neurological Coalition
100 College Street, Suite 126
Toronto, Ontario, M5G 1L5

Canadian Pensioners Concerned
Ontario Division
51 Bond Street
Toronto, Ontario, M5B 1X1

Canadian Rehabilitation Council for
 the Disabled
Information Resources & Communication
1 Yonge Street, Suite 2110
Toronto, Ontario, M5E 1E5

Canadian Schizophrenia Foundation
816-150 Park Street West
Windsor, Ontario, N9A 7A2

Chatham-Kent Community & Family Services
P.O. Box 880
59 Adelaide Street South
Chatham, Ontario, N7M 5L3

Christian Horizons
354 Charles Street East
Kitchener, Ontario, N2G 4L5

Citizen Advocacy – Ottawa Carleton
107- 219 Argyle Avenue
Ottawa, Ontario, K2P 1B8

The Citizen Advocacy Windsor/Essex
1522 Ouellette Avenue
Windsor, Ontario, N8X 1K8

City of Sudbury
Sudbury Citizen Advocacy
P.O. Box 1000
200 Brady Street
Sudbury, Ontario, P3E 4S5

City of Toronto
Department of Public Health
City Hall
Toronto, Ontario, M5H 2N2

Civil Liberties Association
National Capital Region
323 Chapel Street
Suite B1
Ottawa, Ontario, K1N 7Z2

Mr. Robert Clarke
Victoria Clarke
Ms. M.V. Clarke-Beechley
Mr. Roy M. Beechley
Kingston, Ontario

Committee on Adequate & Affordable
 Housing in York Region
52 Clarendon Avenue
Toronto, Ontario, M4V 1J1

Community Legal Services of
 Niagara South
27 Division Street
P.O. Box 128
Welland, Ontario, L3B 3Z5

Community Living Mississauga
2444 Hurontario Street, 4th Floor
Mississauga, Ontario, L5B 2V1

Community Occupational Therapy
 Associates
3101 Bathurst Street
Suite 200
Toronto, Ontario, M6A 2A6

Community Resources Consultants
 of Toronto
120 Eglinton Avenue East
Suite 200
Toronto, Ontario, M4P 2E2

Concerned Friends of Ontario
 Citizens in Care Facilities
Station "Q", P.O. Box 1054
Toronto, Ontario, M4T 2P2

Mary Connell
Whitby, Ontario

Mrs. Doris Constable
Peterborough, Ontario

Mr. Eric Constable
Peterborough, Ontario

Mr. Gianni Corini
Adult Protective Service Worker
York Community Services
1651 Keele Street
Toronto, Ontario, M6M 3W2

Corporation of the City of Waterloo
S.H.I.N.E. Home Support Services
20 Erb Street West
Marsland Centre
P.O. Box 337
Waterloo, Ontario, N2J 4A8

Corporation of the City of Windsor
755 Louis Avenue
Windsor, Ontario, N9A 1X3

Corporation of the County of Essex
Department of Social and
 Family Services
360 Fairview Avenue West
Essex, Ontario, N8M 1Y6

Mr. Sam L. Cureatz, Q.C., M.P.P.
Room 105, North Wing
Legislative Building
Toronto, Ontario, M7A 1A2

The District Health Council
 of Eastern Ontario
P.O. Box 1478
Cornwall, Ontario, K6H 5V5

District Municipality of Muskoka
Pine Street
P.O. Box 1720
Bracebridge, Ontario, POB 1C0

Dufferin Association for the
 Mentally Retarded
53 Zina Street
Orangeville, Ontario, L9W 1E5

Dundurn Community Legal Services
Suite 119
10 West Avenue South
Hamilton, Ontario, L8N 3Y8

Durham Region District Health Council
40 King Street West
Suite 300
Oshawa, Ontario, L1H 1A4

East Toronto Community Legal
 Services Inc.
930 Queen Street East
Toronto, Ontario, M4M 1J5

Mr. Noel Elson, M.A.
Toronto, Ontario

Hon, Murray J. Elston, M.P.P.
Minister of Health
Hepburn Block, 10th Floor
80 Grosvenor Street
Toronto, Ontario, M7A 2C4

Emergency Food & Clothing Centre
507 Bank Street
Ottawa, Ontario, K2P 1Z5

Etobicoke Social Development Council
35 Saskatoon Drive
Etobicoke, Ontario, M9P 2E8

Extendicare/Oakville
Residents' Council
599 Lyons Lane
Oakville, Ontario, L6J 2Y2

Family Service Association of
 Metropolitan Toronto
22 Wellesley Street East
Toronto, Ontario, M4Y 1G3

Family Services Centre of Sault Ste.
 Marie and District
421 Bay Street
Suite 603
Station Tower
Sault Ste. Marie, Ontario, P6A 1X3

Food & Shelter Assistance Advisory
 Committee
Region of Municipality of
 Hamilton—Wentworth
P.O. Box 910
Hamilton, Ontario, L9N 3V9

Friends and Advocates
10 Jamestown Crescent
2nd Floor
Rexdale, Ontario, M9V 3M5

The Geneva Centre
204 St. George Street
Toronto, Ontario, M5R 2N5

Gerontological Nursing Association
P.O. Box 368, Station "K"
Toronto, Ontario, M4P 2G7

Gerontology Research Council
 of Ontario
88 Maplewood Avenue
Hamilton, Ontario, L8M 1W9

Greater Niagara Association for the
 Mentally Retarded
4625 Ontario Avenue
Niagara Falls, Ontario, L2E 3P8

Haliburton, Kawartha & Pine Ridge
 District Health Council
P.O. Box 544
Peterborough, Ontario, K9J 6Z6

Hamilton-Wentworth District
 Health Council
Sanatorium Road
P.O. Box 2085, M.P.O.
Hamilton, Ontario, L8N 3R5

Hastings & Prince Edward Counties
 Health Unit
Adult Protective Service
179 North Park Street
Belleville, Ontario, K8P 4P1

Hastings & Prince Edward Legal
Services
158 George Street
Belleville, Ontario, K8N 3H3

Home Care Program for
 Metropolitan Toronto
45 Sheppard Avenue East, 7th floor
Willowdale, Ontario, M2N 5W9

The Homewood Sanitarium of Guelph
 Ontario Limited
150 Delhi Street
Guelph, Ontario, N1E 6K9

House of Friendship of Kitchener
P.O. Box 1837, Station "C"
63 Charles Street East
Kitchener, Ontario, N2G 4R3

Huntington Society of Canada
13 Water Street North
Suite 3
Cambridge, Ontario, N1R 5T8

Injured Workers Organization
Welland District
P.O. Box 781
Welland, Ontario, L3B 5T5

Independent Living Brokerage
New Model of Service Development
Coordination and Delivery
141 Erskine Avenue
Toronto, Ontario, M4P 1Y9

Mr. Cam Jackson, M.P.P.
Burlington South
Legislative Building
Queen's Park
Toronto, Ontario, M7A 1A2

Kent County District Health Council
75 Thames Street
Chatham, Ontario, N7L 1S4

The Kidney Foundation of Canada
 (Ontario Branch)
1300 Yonge Street
Suite 508
Toronto, Ontario, M4T 1X3

Kingston, Frontenac & Lennox &
 Addington District Health Council
544 Princess Street
P.O. Box 1690
Kingston, Ontario, K7L 5J6

K-W Counselling Services
235 King Street East, 1st Floor
Kitchener, Ontario, N2G 4N5

Legal Assistance of Windsor
85 Pitt Street East
Windsor, Ontario, N9A 2V3

Mennonite Central Committee (Ontario)
50 Kent Avenue
Kitchener, Ontario, N2G 3R1

Metropolitan Toronto Association for
   the Mentally Retarded
8 Spadina Road
Toronto, Ontario, M5R 2S7

Ms. Norma McCormack
Bancroft, Ontario

Ministry of Community and
 Social Services (Smiths Falls)
Rideau Regional Center
P.O. Box 2000
Smiths Falls, Ontario, K7A 4T7

Ministry of Community and
 Social Services (Chaplaincy Services)
700 Bay Street, Room 216
Toronto, Ontario, M7A 1E9

Ministry of Correctional Services
2001 Eglinton Avenue East
Scarborough, Ontario, M1L 4P1

I. Mitchell
Kenora, Ontario

Municipality of Metropolitan Toronto
Metropolitan Clerk's Department
City Hall
Toronto, Ontario, M5H 2N1

Municipality of Metropolitan Toronto
Metropolitan Community Services Dept.
Policy and Planning Division
City Hall, 5th Floor, East Tower
Toronto, Ontario, M5H 2N1

Hon. Lily Munro, M.P.P.
Minister of Citizenship & Culture
77 Bloor Street West, 6th Floor
Toronto, Ontario, M7A 2R9

New Democrats
Suite 218 North
Queen's Park
Toronto, Ontario, M7A 1A2

Niagara District Health Council
1440 Pelham Street
P.O. Box 1059
Fonthill, Ontario, L0S 1E0

Niagara North Community Legal
 Assistance
P.O. Box 1266
8 Church Street
St. Catharines, Ontario, L2R 7A7

Nipissing Community Legal Clinic
466 First Avenue West
North Bay, Ontario, P1B 3C4

North Bay & District Association
 for the Mentally Retarded
161 Main Street East, Ste. #4
North Bay, Ontario, P1B 1A9

North Frontenac Community Services
  Corporation
P.O. Box 250
Sharbot Lake, Ontario, K0H 2P0

Oakville Association for the
 Mentally Retarded
1108 Speers Road
Oakville, Ontario, L6L 2X4

Oakville Senior Citizens
 Recreation Centre
263 Kerr Street
Oakville, Ontario, L6K 3B4

Office of the Official Guardian
Ministry of the Attorney General
180 Dundas Street W., 6th Floor
Toronto, Ontario, M5G 1E4

Office of the Public Trustee
145 Queen Street West
Toronto, Ontario, M5H 2N8

Office Responsible for Disabled
  Persons
700 Bay Street, 3rd Floor
Toronto, Ontario, M5G 1Z6

On Our Own
1860-A Queen Street East
Toronto, Ontario, M4L 1H1

Ontario Association for Children and
   Adults with Learning Disabilities
1901 Yonge Street, 3rd Floor
Toronto, Ontario, M4S 1Y6

Ontario Association of Family
   Service Agencies
1243 Islington Avenue, Ste. 802
Toronto, Ontario, M8X 1Y9

Ontario Association of Homes for
   the Aged
8 Director Court, Ste. 201
Woodbridge, Ontario, L4L 3Z5

Ontario Association for the Mentally
 Retarded
1376 Bayview Avenue
Toronto, Ontario, M4G 3A3

Ontario Association of Professional
 Social Workers
410 Jarvis Street
Toronto, Ontario, M4Y 2G6

Ontario Association of Residents
   Councils
Castleview-Wychwood Towers
351 Christie Street
Toronto, Ontario, M6G 3C3

Ontario Coalition of Senior Citizens'
    Organizations
3995 Bathurst Street
Suite 208
North York, Ontario, M3H 5V3

Ontario Friends of Schizophrenics
Administration Office
P.O. Box 217, Station "O"
Toronto, Ontario, M4A 2W3

Ontario Gerontology Association
2201 St. David's Road
P.O. Box 1042
Thorold, Ontario, L2V 4T7

Ontario Hospital Association
150 Ferrand Drive
Don Mills, Ontario, M3C 1H6

Ontario March of Dimes
Timmins Regional Office
P.O. Box 1121
841 Pine Street South
Timmins, Ontario, P4N 7H9

Ontario Nurses' Association
85 Grenville Street
Suite 600
Toronto, Ontario, M5S 3A2

Ontario Public Service Employees
    Union (OPSEU)
1901 Yonge Street
Toronto, Ontario, M4S 2Z5

Ontario Social Development Council
OSOC Task Force on
 De-Institutionalization
60 Bloor Street West, Ste. #208
Toronto, Ontario, M4W 3B8

Ontario Society for Autistic Citizens
8108 Yonge Street
Suite 203
Thornhill, Ontario, L4J 1W4

Oshawa Senior Citizens Centre
43 John Street West
Oshawa, Ontario, L1H 1W8

Ottawa Carleton Citizen Advocacy
107-219 Argyle Avenue
Ottawa, Ontario, K2P 1B8

Ottawa Carleton Regional District
 Health Council
955 Green Valley Crescent
Suite 350
Ottawa, Ontario, K2C 3V4

Ottawa Carleton Friends of
 Schizophrenics
11 Lizner Crescent
Kanata, Ontario, K2K 1A3

Ottawa Council for Low Income
  Support Services
95 Beech Street
Ottawa, Ontrio, K1S 3J7

Owen Sound & District Association
 for the Mentally Retarded
259 - 8th Street East
Owen Sound, Ontario, N4K 1L2

Parkdale Community Legal Services Inc.
1239 Queen Street West
Toronto, Ontario, M6K 1L5

Mr. Ray Peters
Peterborough, Ontario

Penetanguishene Mental Health Centre
P.O. Box 698
Penetanguishene, Ontario, L0K 1P0

People First of Ontario
1376 Bayview Avenue
Toronto, Ontario, M4G 3A3

Peterborough Hearing Handicapped
  Group Home Society
Civitan Home
P.O. Box 2078
Peterborough, Ontario, K9J 7Y4

Persons United for Self Help
 in Ontario
Suite 204
597 Parliament Street
Toronto, Ontario, M4X 1W3

Physically Handicapped Citizens
 Association (Halton North)
28 Chapel Street
Georgetown, Ontario, L7G 2L9

Port Hope-Cobourg & District
 Association for the Mentally
 Retarded
West Northumberland Advocacy Office
P.O. Box 835
Cobourg, Ontario, K9A 4S3

Mr. Gilles Pouliot, M.P.P.
Lake Nipigon
Room 330
Parliament Buildings
Toronto, Ontario, M7A 1A2

Prince Edward Heights Advocacy
 Organization
R. R. #1
Carrying Place, Ontario, K0K 1L0

Psychiatric Nursing Interest Group
Registered Nurses' Association of Ont.
Satelite 1
RANO
2040 Balfour Boulevard
Windsor, Ontario, N8T 2S7

Psychiatric Patient Advocate Office
880 Bay Street, 2nd floor
Toronto, Ontario, M5S 1Z8

The Queen Elizabeth Hospital Toronto
550 University Avenue
Toronto, Ontario, M5G 2A2

Queen Street Mental Health Centre
1001 Queen Street West
Toronto, Ontario, M6J 1H4

Ms. Sharon Rayment
Peterborough, Ontario

Reena Foundation
99 Cartwright Avenue
Toronto, Ontario
M6A 1V4

Regional Municipality of
    Hamilton/Wentworth
Community Mental Health Promotion
    Programme
P.O. Box 897
Hamilton, Ontario, L8N 3P6

Regional Municipality of Halton
Social Services Department
P.O. Box 7000
1151 Bronte Road
Oakville, Ontario, L6J 6E1

Regional Municipality of York
Health and Social Services Home
  Care Program
615 Davis Drive, Ste. 202
Newmarket, Ontario, L3Y 2R2

Registered Nurses' Association of
    Ontario
33 Price Street
Toronto, Ontario, M4W 1Z2

Renfrew County & District Health Unit
75 Wallace Street
P.O. Box 58
Eganville, Ontario, K0J 1T0

Rideau Valley District Health Council
P.O. Box 487
1 Abel Street
Smith Falls, Ontario, K7A 4T4

St. Clair Tri-County Region
Adult Protective Services Workers
c/o Chatham-Kent Community & Family
  Services
P.O. Box 800
59 Adelaide Street South
Chatham, Ontario, N7M 5L3

Service Co-ordination Program
Carewell Muskoka
Box 970
Gravenhurst, Ontario, P0C 1G0

Service Employees International Union
1 Credit Union Drive
Toronto, Ontario, M4A 2S6

Shepherds of Good Hope
Les Bergers De L'Espoir
P.O. Box 340
Station 'A'
Ottawa, Ontario, K1N 8V3

Simcoe Legal Services Clinic
43 West Street North
Box 275
Orillia, Ontario, L3V 6J6

South Essex Community Council
Selkirk Community Centre
18 Selkirk Avenue
Leamington, Ontario, N8H 1G3

South Riverdale Commuity Health Centre
126 Pape Avenue
Toronto, Ontario, M4M 2V8

Spruce Lodge
Senior Citizens Residence
643 West Gore Street
Stratford, Ontario, N5A 1L4

St. Elizabeth Visiting Nurses'
   Association of Ontario
600 Eglinton Avenue East, Ste. #300
Toronto, Ontario, M4P 1P3

St. Joseph's Health Centre
30 The Queensway
Toronto, Ontario, M6R 1B5

St. Joseph's Hospital
50 Charlton Avenue East
Hamilton, Ontario, L8N 4A6

St. Joseph's Hospital
Volunteer Department
50 Charlton Avenue East
Hamilton, Ontario, L8N 4A6

Sunnybrook Medical Centre
2075 Bayview Avenue
North York, Ontario, M4N 3M5

Hon. John Sweeney, M.P.P.
Minister of Community & Social Services
Hepburn Block, 6th Floor
Queen's Park
Toronto, Ontario, M7A 1E9

The Association for Severely
   Handicapped - Ontario
P.O. Box 283
Commerce Court Postal Station
Toronto, Ontario, M5L 1E9

Teck Pioneer Resident Home for the Aged
Churchhill Drive
Kirkland, Ontario
P2N 1V1

Tender Loving Care Nursing Inc.
9 Melrose Avenue
Ottawa, Ontario, K1Y 1T8

Thunder Bay District Health Council
516 Victoria Avenue, Ste. 8
Thunder Bay, Ontario, P7C 1A7

Toronto Citizen Advocacy
455 Spadina Avenue, Ste. #306
Toronto, Ontario, M5S 2G8

Toronto Mayor's Committee on Aging
Department of the City Clerk
City Hall
Toronto, Ontario, M5H 2N2

Mr. R. G. Tredgett
Willowdale, Ontario

The United Senior Citizens of
 Ontario Inc.
3033 Lakeshore Boulevard West
Toronto, Ontario, M8V 1K5

Maureen Upper, R.N.
Toronto, Ontario

Hon. Ron Van Horne, M.P.P.
Office for Senior Citizens' Affairs
76 College Street, 6th Floor
Queen's Park
Toronto, Ontario, M7A 1N3

Victoria House
361 Queen Street South
Kitchener, Ontairo
N2G 1W6

Waterloo Region District Health Council
75 King Street South, Ste. 218
Waterloo, Ontario, N2J 1P2

Waterloo Regional Homes for the Mental
   Health Inc.
P.O. Box 42
Kitchener, Ontario, N2G 3W9

Welland & District Citizen Advocacy
135 East Main Street
Welland, Ontario, L3B 3W5

West End Legal Services of Ottawa
104-1305 Richmond Road
Ottawa, Ontario, K2B 8Y4

West Park Hospital
82 Buttonwood Avenue
Toronto, Ontario, M6M 2J5

Whitby Psychiatric Hospital
Patient Government
Patient Advocate Office
P.O. Box 613, c/o Cottage 12
Whitby, Ontario, L1N 5S9

Windsor Association for the
    Mentally Retarded,
2090 Wyandotte Street East
Windsor, Ontario

Mr. Kirk Wood
Georgetown, Ontario

York Central Association for
  the Mentally Retarded
475 Edward Avenue
Richmond Hill, Ontario, L4C 5E5

York Support Services Network
289 Yonge Street South
Newmarket, Ontario, L3Y 4V7

York Community Services
1651 Keele Street
Toronto, Ontario, M6M 3W2

APPENDIX NO. 5

Meetings and Consultations

Judge Rosalie Abella — Ontario Labour Board
Advocacy Resource Centre for the Handicapped — Board of Directors
Mr. Phil Andrewes, M.P.P. — Lincoln
Ms. Louise Allen — Canadian Mental Health Association
                        Windsor-Essex

Ms. Arlene Babad — Ontario Nurses' Association
Mr. David Baker — Advocacy Resource Centre for the Handicapped
Mr. Ted Ball — PoliCorp
Mr. Harry Beatty — Advocacy Resources Centre for the Handicapped
Ms. June Beeby — Ontario Friends of Schizophrenics
Ms. Laurie Bell — Toronto Citizen Advocacy*
Ms. Sue Biersteker — Advocacy Resource Centre for the Handicapped
Mr. John Boys — Ontario Association for the Living
Ms. Carolyn Braithwaite — On Our Own
Mr. Nick But — Ministry of Housing

Ms. Sheril Carden — Ontario Association of the Mentally Retarded
Concerned Friends in Care Facilities and Other Consumers and
    Providers Organizations — Representatives
Mr. David Cooke, M.P.P. — Windsor-Riverside
Mr. Gianni Corini — York Community Services
Mr. Justin Clarke — Partage House Group Home
Ms. Jo Cork — Daybreak
Ms. Marianne Cunliffe — Extendicare
Ms. Marilyn Currie — Action Awareness

Mr. Roland D'Abadie — Ministry of the Attorney General
Mr. Jack D'Ambrosio, Jr. — Office of the Ombudsman for the
                        Institutionalized Elderly
Mr. Brian Davidson — Canadian Mental Health Association
Mr. Glen Davies — York Manor Home for the Aged
Mr. William Dillane — Lincoln Place Nursing Home
Mr. Peter Dill — Metropolitan Toronto Association for the
                        Mentally Retarded
Mr. Greg Douglas — Community Occupational Therapists Association

Mr. John Eaker — Social Assistance Review
Mr. Garry W. Eason — Prince Edward Heights
Mr. Rawle Elliott — York Community Services
Honourable Murray Elston, M.P.P. — Minister of Health
Mr. Douglas Ewart — Ministry of the Attorney General

* Denotes more than one meeting.

Dr. Reid Finlayson -- Woodstock General Hospital
Mr. Stephen V. Fram -- Ministry of the Attorney General
Ms. Joan Fussell -- Concerned Friends of Ontario Citizens
                    in Care Facilities

Ms. Jennie Gilbert -- Ontario Coalition of Senior
                      Citizens Organizations
Mr. David Giuffrida -- Queen Street Mental Health Centre
Mr. George Glover -- Villa Colombo
Ms. Mary Ellen Glover -- Ontario Association of Residents' Councils
Dr. Barry Goldlist -- Ontario Medical Association
Mr. Peter Gooch -- Ministry of Housing
Mr. John Gross -- Baycrest Home for the Aged

Ms. Marnie Hacker -- Penetanguishene Mental Health Centre
Ms. Robin Harris -- Concerned Friends of Ontario Citizens in
                    Care Facilities
Mr. Glen Heagle -- Office for Senior Citizens' Affairs
Ms. Ivy Hill -- Riverdale Hospital
Mr. David Hodgson -- Ministry of Housing
Mr. Ian Hofford -- Prince Edward Heights
Mr. Les Horne -- Office of Child and Family Service Advocacy
Mr. Carl Hunt -- Extendicare
Ms. Jill Hutcheon -- Ministry of Solicitor General

Mr. Ross Irwin -- Legal Aid Clinic Funding

Rev. David Janzen -- Ministry of Community and Social Services
Dr. Fred Jervis -- The Center for Constructive Change
Ms. Deana Johnson -- Canadian Mental Health Association
                     Windsor-Essex
Mr. Patrick Johnston -- Social Assistance Review
Mr. Richard Johnston, M.P.P. -- Scarborough West

Mr. Darwin Kealey -- Principal Secretary to Larry Grossman, M.P.P.
Honourable Ken Keyes, M.P.P. -- Minister of Correctional Services
Rev. W.G. Kidnew -- Prince Edward Heights
Ms. Joyce King -- United Senior Citizens of Ontario
Dr. James Kirkland -- Queen Elizabeth Hospital
Ms. Susan Kitchener -- Ontario March of Dimes
Dr. Shio Loon Kong -- Ontario Advisory Council on Multiculturalism
Mr. John Krauser -- Ontario Medical Association
Mr. George Kytayko -- Penetanguishene Mental Health Centre

Ms. Paula Lackstone -- Lincoln Place Nursing Home
Mr. Frederick Ladly -- Extendicare
Ms. Marie Lauzier -- York Support Services Network

Legal Aid Clinic Funding Committee
Dr. Harold Livergant -- Extendicare
Ms. Cecile Lynes -- Toronto Citizen Advocacy*
Ms. Gloria Lynn -- Ontario Nurses' Association

Mrs. M. MacDonald -- Home for Special Care
Ms. Joyce Maine -- Blind Organization of Ontario with
                   Self-Help Tactics
Professor Allan Manson -- Psychiatric Patient Advocate Office
                   Evaluation Committee*
Ms. Norma McDonald -- Rideau Regional Centre
Mr. Robert McDonald -- Ministry of Correctional Services
Ms. Susan McDonough -- Office of Elder Affairs
Mr. Henry McErlean -- Ontario Advisory Council on Multiculturalism
Mr. David McFadden, M.P.P. -- Eglinton
Mrs. Dianne MacFarlane -- Whitby Psychiatric Hospital
Mr. Peter McKenna -- Adult Protective Service Worker,
                   County of Lanark
Mr. Alan McLaughlin -- Senior Citizen Affairs
Ms. Cathy McPherson -- People United for Self-Help Ontario
Ms. Marjory McPherson -- Ontario Association of the Mentally
                   Retarded
Dr. Judith Meeks -- St. Peter's Centre
Ms. Lisa Mendelson -- Ministry of Housing
Ms. Sarah Mitchell -- Office of the Public Advocate
Mr. Patrick Monahan -- Ministry of the Attorney General
Mr. Barry Monahagan -- West Park Hospital
Angela Morris -- Alzheimer Association of Ontario
Mr. Denis Morrice -- Canadian Hearing Society
Ms. Julie Morris -- Public Advocacy Committee Alzheimer
                   Association of Ontario
Mr. Michael Mullan -- Queen Street Mental Health Centre

Mr. Barry Napier -- Social Assistance Review
Mr. Jeff Nault -- County of Lanark, Community and Social Services
Mr. Peter D. Ness -- Canadian Mental Health Association
Mr. Alan Nickell -- York Support Services Network*
Ms. Eva Nichols -- Ontario Association for Children and
                   Adults with Learning Disabilities
Mr. Harvey Nightingale -- Ontario Nursing Homes Association

Mr. Terry O'Connor, M.P.P. -- Oakville
Ontario Municipal Social Service Association -- Representatives
Mr. Scott Orfold -- Prince Edward Heights

Ms. Louise Paul -- York Support Services*
Rev. Don. Peake -- Ministry of Community & Social Services
Mr. Don Pease -- Multiple Sclerosis Society of Canada

Dr. Bryan Pell -- Woodstock General Hospital
Mr. Norman Pellerin -- Partage House Group Home
Ms. Lou Anne Peroff-Williams -- Community Occupational
                              Therapists Association
Ms. Beryl Potter -- Action Awareness
Ms. Trish Powell -- Georgia Advocacy Office
Psychiatric Patient Advocate Office Conference

Mr. Bob Rae, M.P.P. -- Leader of the New Democratic Party
Ms. Judy Rebick -- Canadian Hearing Society
Ms. Diane Roberts -- Toronto Citizen Advocacy*
Ms. Sue Ronald -- Rideau Regional Center
Ms. Linda Rosenweig -- Office of the Public Advocate
Mr. Ron Ross -- Handicapped Action Group
Mr. Kirby Rowe -- Canadian Paraplegic Association
Honourable Tony Ruprecht, M.P.P. -- Minister Responsible
                              for Disabled Persons

Mr. Gary Sandor -- York Support Services Network
Mr. Ron Sapsford -- Nursing Homes Branch
Dr. Jack Saunders -- Ontario Medical Association
Mr. Clem Sauve -- Office Responsible for Disabled Persons
Dr. K.R. Schell -- Home For Special Care
Mr. Steven Schwartz -- Northhampton State Hospital
Mr. Graham Scott -- MacMillan Binch
The Honourable Ian G. Scott, M.P.P. -- Attorney General
Ms. Barbara Selkirk -- Queen Street Mental Health Centre
Ms. Jan Sharette -- Harrisburg State Hospital
Ms. Glenna Cole Slattery -- Ontario Nurses' Association
Ms. Sharlotte Snedden -- Service Employees International Union
Mr. John Southern -- Blind Organization of Ontario With
                    Self-Help Tactics (BOOST)
Mr. Dominic Spadafora -- Social Assistance Review
Ms. Patricia Spindel -- Concerned Friends of Ontario Citizens
                    in Care Facilities
Mr. Tim Stainton -- Ontario Association of the
                    Mentally Retarded
Ms. Verna Steffler -- Ontario Coalition for Nursing Home Reform
Dr. Donald Stevens -- Ontario Medical Association
Honourable John Sweeney, M.P.P. -- Minister of Community
                    and Social Services

Ms. Jane Taylor -- Queen Street Mental Health Centre
Mr. George Thomson -- Social Assistance Review
Ms. Alma Thompson -- Leisure World
Ms. Linda Till -- Concerned Friends of Ontario Citizens
                    in Care Facilities
Mr. Bernard Travis -- Rideau Regional Center

Tri Ministry Service Co-ordinators Conference
Mr. William Trott - Queen Street Mental Health Centre*
Ms. Elaine Turcotte -- Shepherds of Good Hope
Dr. Tyrone Turner -- Willenby House

Ms. Mary Beth Valentine -- Queen Street Mental Health Centre*
Mr. John Van Beek -- Service Employees International Union

Ms. Judith Wahl -- Advocacy Centre for the Elderly
Ms. Jacqueline Walker -- State Ombudsman
Ms. Karen Walker -- Whitby Psychiatric Hospital
Mr. Rod Walsh -- Ontario Association for the Mentally Retarded
Ms. Winifred W. White -- Canadian Mental Health Association
Mrs. Janis P. Williams -- The Center for Constructive Change
Mr. Rick Williams -- Prince Edward Heights
Ms. Lisa Wilson -- Office for Senior Citizens' Affairs
Ms. Sherri Wiseberg -- York Support Services Network
Ms. Jean Woodsworth -- Canadian Pensioners Concerned
Mr. Patrick Worth -- People First of Ontario*

Mr. Harry Zwerver -- Ontario Association of the Mentally Retarded

APPENDIX NO. 6
Consumers Advisory Committee Members

Mrs. Anne Coy
President
Patients' Rights Association
Toronto

Dr. Dorothea Crittenden
Past Chairperson
Nursing Home Residents
Complaints Committee
Toronto

Ms. Carla McKague
Senior Litigation Counsel
Advocacy Resource Cenre for the
Handicapped in Toronto
Toronto

Mrs. Ivy St. Lawrence, Chairman
Ontario Advisory Council on
Senior Citizens, Toronto

Ms. Patricia Spindel
Consultant to the Board
Concerned Friends of Ontario
Citizens in Care Facilities
Toronto

Ms. Pat Woode
Persons United for Self Help
in Ontario
Georgetown

Mr. Patrick Worth, President
People First of Ontario
Toronto

Ministerial Advisory Committee Members

Ms. Arna Banack
Manager, Policy Services
Secretariat for Disabled Persons

Mr. Stephen V. Fram, Q.C.
Counsel, Policy Development
Division, Ministry of the
Attorney General

Mrs. Debi Mauro
Director, Community Mental
Health, Operations Branch
Ministry of Health

Mr. Alan McLaughlin, Policy
Advisor, Program Development
and Strategic Planning, Office
of Senior Citizen Affairs

Mr. John Wilson
Manager, Planning
Ministry of Community and
Social Services

Mr. Michael Irvine, Manager
Corporate Policy, Ministry
of Correctional Services

Providers Advisory Committee Members

Mr. David Baker
Executive Director, Advocacy
Resource Centre for the
Handicapped, Toronto

Ms. Lea Caragata
Executive Director
Houselink Community Homes
Toronto

Dr. W. B. Dalziel
Associate Professor of
Medicine; Head, Division
of Geriatrics
Ottawa Civic Hospital

Mr. Stephen Lurie
Executive Director
Canadian Mental Health
Association, Toronto

Mr. David R. Mitchell
Case Manager
Pembroke General Hospital
Nursing Home Case Management
Services, Pembroke

Ms. Judith A. Wahl
Executive Director
Advocacy Centre for the
Elderly, Toronto

Ms. Kay Wigle
Chairperson
Adult Protective Service
Association of Ontario
London

APPENDIX NO. 7

Statement of Principles Regarding the Provision of Advocacy Services to Mentally Disadvantaged Persons

The Advisory Committee on Substitute Decision-Making for Mentally Incapable Persons has been given responsibility for developing new legislation to govern conservatorship and personal guardianship for mentally incapable persons. An important facet of this responsibility is to consider the related role of supportive services such as consensual advocacy in meeting the needs of the mentally disadvantaged and in helping to ensure that guardianship and trusteeship are never used inappropriately.

It must be emphasized that the presence of a mental disability does not, in itself, indicate a need for guardianship. Appointment of a substitute decision-maker is necessary and justifiable to the extent that an individual lacks the mental capacity to make the decision and as a result is at risk of harm. Many mentally disadvantaged persons are capable of making decisions for themselves, but require assistance to understand the implications of a decision or lack of decision and alternative courses of action. An individual's mental capacity may be such that he/she is able to make some types of decisions but not others, depending on the level of complexity. In the community and in institutional settings, the autonomy of individuals thought to be mentally disadvantaed may be vunerable. The Advisory Committee has identified a need for advocacy services to provide support and assistance where required by a client in his/her decision-making and to advocate for the client and on behalf of mentally disadvantaged persons collectively.

1.   Population to be Served

Persons to be served by the advocacy services include individuals in institutional care settings as well as those individuals living in the community who may require such services. In particular, the advocacy services should be available to persons whose competence may be the subject of proceedings under the Substitute Decisions Authority Act (or the current legislation it is intended to replace).

2.   Objectives of Advocacy Services

The advocacy services for mentally disadvantaged persons should have the following objectives:

to promote respect for the rights,
freedoms and dignity of the persons they
serve, both individually and collectively;

to ensure that their clients' legal and
human rights are recognized and protected;

to assist their clients to receive the
health care and social services to which
they are entitled and which they wish to
receive;

to enhance the autonomy of their clients by
advocating on their behalf, both
individually and collectively;

to assist their clients to lead lives that
are as independent as possible, and in the
least restrictive environment possible;

to help protect mentally disadvantaged
persons from financial, physical and
psychological abuse;

to fully explain the implications of and
provide advice with respect to guardianship
and conservatorship under the Substitute
Decisions Authority Act (or the current
legislation it is intended to replace).

3.   Design of The Advocacy Services

This statement of principles applies to the advocacy
services that are funded by the government.

(a)   The advocacy services should be designed
        having regard to:

        (i)   the varying needs of persons to
                be served;
        (ii)   the variety of institutions and
                communities in which these persons
                live;
        (iii)   the most effective means of
                delivering advocacy services;
        (iv)   the need for advocacy services to
                function independently of health
                care and residential facilities.

(b)   An advocacy services should have a means by
        which to advise the government or agenices
        providing services to its clients, on systematic
        problems affecting the rights of its clients,
        and recommended solutions.

(c)   If an advocacy service is established to serve
        clients in care facilities, its advocates should
        be free to establish a physical presence in the
        facility.

(d)   An advocacy service should have an outreach
        component to ensure that persons in need of
        the service will be aware of its existence.
        A client should have the right to free and
        unimpeded access to and confidential
        communication with an advocate.

4.   The Nature of the Advocate-Client Relationship

The advocate serves his/her client on a voluntary,
consensual basis. The actions of an advocate are guided by
instructions, usually given by the client, and in some cases
(described below) by a substitute decision-maker. The
advocate is not authorized to make substitute decisions and,
therefore, must not substitute for instructions his or her
own personal or professional view of how to serve the best
interests of the client.

In law, individuals are presumed to be mentally competent.
In determining if a client is competent to instruct, the
advocate begins with this presumption. In respect of a
subject matter about which the client has been found to be
mentally incompetent (e.g., financial management) and a
substitute decision maker is authorized to make decisions
(e.g., conservator or guardian), an advocate's function is
restricted. The advocate can do on behalf of the client no
more than the client has legal authority to do. The
advocate can convey to the substitute decision maker and
others the client's wishes and preferences. Where the
client and the substitute decision maker are not in
conflict, the advocate may take the requested action. If
the advocate has reason to believe that a substitute
decision maker is acting improperly he/she should report
this situation to the Public Guardian and Trustee. The
advocate may also assist an incapable person to exercise his
or her rights under the legislation governing substitute
decision making and other legal rights the incapable person
may have with respect to liberty and security.

5.   Role of the Advocate

In addition to providing one-to-one support and advice, the advocate represents the client's interests and intercedes on his/her behalf. The advocate also has a role in lobbying for systemic change on behalf of mentally disadvantaged persons.

The advocate must be able to respond to therapeutic and other non-legal issues by representing the client directly or by making appropriate referrals. The advocate may provide rights advice and shall ensure there is legal representation if requested.

An important role for the advocate is to provide service to individuals who are the subject of mental incompetency applications. The advocate should be promptly notified of individuals in this situation so that he/she may provide rights advice and ensure there is legal representation if requested.

6.   Access and Confidentiality

In order to fulfill their role and responsibilities, advocates must be assured of the opportunity for access to their clients and the confidentility of advocate-client communications must be protected. The Committee recommends that the following principles with respect to rights of access and confidentiality be embodied in a statute.

(a)   An advocate should not be obstructed in his/
       her attempts to serve a client. The advocate
       should have the opportunity to determine
       whether or not a person wishes to become or
       remain a client of the advocate. Where an
       advocate-client relationship has been
       established, the advocate should be free to
       contact the client without interference from
       others.

(b)   The client should have a right of access to his
       or her records. With the client's consent, the
       advocate should have the same right of access
       to the client's clinical records as the client
       has himself/herself.

(c)   As a general rule, without the client's consent,
       or the gurdian or conservator's consent if the
       client is incapable of expressing an opinion,
       an advocate should not be a compellable witness
       and should not be compelled to produce records
       regarding confidential communications undertaken
       as part of advocacy for the client. In certain

circumstances, there will be exceptions to this right of confidentiality. For example,

(i)   where access is required to ascertain whether or not the advocate has acted negligently

(ii)   where a client dies in circumstances in which it would be in the public interest for the advocate to testify at an inquest.

7.   The Implementation of the Substitute Decisions Authority Act and Advocacy Services

If the Substitute Decisions Authority Act becomes law in Ontario, some of the cumbersome, expensive, and time-consuming processes which are currently available to authorize substitute decision-making will be replaced by more streamlined alternatives. While this legislation has been drafted to respect the rights of the individual, the committee does not wish to increase the risk that people who are competent to make decisions will lose their right to do so.

To make people subject to this legislation without providing them advocacy services should therefore be avoided. The committee recommends that the Substitute Decisions Authority Act not come into force until advocacy services, supported by appropriate legislation, are operational and are available to the persons that would be affected by the Substitute Decisions Authority Act.

APPENDIX NO. 8

Government Programs and Initiatives
For Vulnerable Adults

There are a number of programs and initiatives which demonstrate this province's continuing commitment to meeting the needs of vulnerable citizens. Following is a representative list of such measures which would be enhanced by the introduction of advocacy services -- the next logical and needed step.

o Homemakers and Nurses Services

o Support Service Living Unit Program

o Attendant Care Outreach Program

o Interpreter Service

o Intervenor Service (increase the independence of deaf-blind adults living in the community through the use of an "intervenor")

o Vocational Rehabilitation Services and Workshops for Disabled Persons

o Adult Development and Life Skills Programs

o Adult Protective Service Workers Program

o Special Services at Home Program

o Parent Relief and Respite Care Programs

o Family Support Workers Program

o Communications Programs

o Assessment and Diagnostic Services

o Supported Independent Living

o Assistive Devices Program

o Approved Homes Program (for psychiatric patients and developmentally handicapped)

o Homes for Special Care Program

o Extended Home Care Program

o Chronic Home Care Program

o School Health Service Program

o Community Mental Health Services Program

o Integrated Homemaker Program

o The Extended Care Program

o Geriatric Day Hospitals Programs

o Community Health Centers

o The Integrated Homemakers Program

o Respite Care Program

APPENDIX NO. 9

Nova Scotia Legislation

CHAPTER A-27

AN ACT TO PROVIDE FOR PROTECTION
OF ADULTS FROM ABUSE AND NEGLECT
cited as
S.N.S., 1985, Chapter 2

SHORT TITLE
1   This Act may be cited as the *Adult Protection Act.*
1985, c. 2, s. 1.

PURPOSE OF ACT
2   The purpose of this Act is to provide a means
whereby adults who lack the ability to care and fend
adequately for themselves can be protected from abuse and
neglect by providing them with access to services which will
enhance their ability to care and fend for themselves or
which will protect them from abuse or neglect. 1985, c. 2,
s. 2.

INTERPRETATION
3   In this Act,

(a)   "adult" means a person who is or is
apparently sixteen years of age or older;

(b)   "adult in need of protection" means an adult
who, in the premises where he resides,

(i)   is a victim of physical abuse, sexual
abuse, mental cruelty or a combination thereof,
is incapable of protecting himself therefrom by
reason of physical disability or mental infirmity,
and refuses, delays or is unable to make provision for his protection therefrom, or

(ii) is not receiving adequate care and attention, is incapable of caring adequately for himself by reason of physical disability or mental infirmity, and refuses, delays or is unable to make provision for his adequate care and attention;

(c) "Co-ordinator" means the Co-ordinator of Adult Protection Services appointed pursuant to this Act;

(d) "court" means the Family Court;

(e) "Minister" means the Minister of Social Services;

(f) "prescribed" means prescribed by the regulations;

(g) "regulations" means the regulations made pursuant to this Act. 1985, c. 2, s. 3.

ADMINISTRATION OF ACT
4   (1) The Minister is charged with the general administration of this Act and may from time to time designate in writing the Co-ordinator or any other person to have, perform and exercise any of the powers, privileges, duties and functions of the Minister or the Co-ordinator under this Act, and shall, when so designating, specify the powers, privileges, duties and functions to be had, performed and exercised by the person so designated.

DOCUMENT EXECUTED BY DESIGNATED PERSON
        (2) Where a designation is made pursuant to subsection (1) and the person designated signs or executes a document pursuant to the designation, he shall refer to the name of his office together with the words "Authorized pursuant to Section 4 of the Adult Protection Act" and where a document contains such reference, the document

(a)   shall be received in evidence without further proof of the authority of the person who signs or executes the same; and

(b)   may be relied upon by the person to whom the document is directed or given and by all other persons as an effective exercise of the power or function to which the document relates.

APPOINTMENT OF CO-ORDINATOR
(3)   A Co-ordinator of Adult Protection Services may be appointed in accordance with the Civil Service Act. 1985, c. 2, s. 4.

DUTY TO REPORT INFORMATION
5   (1)   Every person who has information, whether or not it is confidential or privileged, indicating that an adult is in need of protection shall report that information to the Minister.

NO ACTION LIES
(2)   No action lies against a person who gives information under subsection (1) unless the giving of the information is done maliciously or without reasonable and probable cause. 1985, c. 2, s. 5.

INQUIRY AND ASSESSMENT BY MINISTER
6   Where the Minister receives a report that a person is an adult in need of protection, he shall

(a)   make inquiries with respect to the matter; and

(b)   if he finds there are reasonable and probable grounds to believe the adult is in need of protection, cause an assessment to be made, and the Minister may, if he deems it advisable, request a qualified medical practitioner to assess the adult, the care and attention the adult is receiving and whether the adult has been abused. 1985, c. 2, s. 6.

ASSISTANCE BY MINISTER
7   Where, after an assessment, the Minister is satisfied that a person is an adult in need of protection, the Minister shall assist the person, if the person is willing to accept the assistance, in obtaining services which will enhance the ability of the person to care and fend adequately for himself or will protect the person from abuse or neglect. 1985, c. 2, s. 7.

ORDER FOR ENTRY
8   Where the adult who is being assessed refuses to consent to the assessment or a member of the family of the adult or any person having care or control of the adult interferes with or obstructs the assessment in any way, the Minister may apply to the court for an order authorizing the entry into any building or place by a peace officer, the Minister, a qualified medical practitioner or any person named in the order for the purpose of making the assessment, and where

(a)   the Minister has given at least four days notice of the hearing to the adult or the person having care or control of the adult; or

(b)   the Minister has applied ex parte and the court is satisfied there are reasonable and probable grounds to believe that the person who is being assessed is in danger,

the court may grant the order after making due inquiry and being satisfied that there are reasonable and probable grounds to believe that the person who is being assessed is an adult in need of protection. 1985, c. 2, s. 8.

APPLICATION FOR COURT ORDER
    9   (1)   Where on the basis of an assessment made pursuant to this Act the Minister is satisfied that there are reasonable and probable grounds to believe a person is an adult in need of protection, he may apply to a court for an order declaring the person to be an adult in need of protection and, where applicable, a protective intervention order.

NOTICE
          (2)   The Minister shall give at least ten days notice of the application in the prescribed form to the person in respect of whom the application is made or some person having custody or control of that person and, where applicable, the person against whom a protective intervention order may be made.

ORDER OF COURT
          (3)   Where the court finds, upon the hearing of the application, that a person is an adult in need of protection and either

              (a)   is not mentally competent to decide whether or not to accept the assistance of the Minister; or

              (b)   is refusing the assistance by reason of duress,

the court shall so declare and may, where it appears to the court to be in the best interest of that person,

              (c)   make an order authorizing the Minister to provide the adult with services, including placement in a facility approved by the Minister, which will enhance the ability of the adult to care and fend adequately for himself or which will protect the adult from abuse or neglect;

(d)   make a protective intervention order directed to any person who, in the opinion of the court, is a source of danger to the adult in need of protection

(i)   requiring that person to leave the premises where the adult in need of protection resides unless that person is the owner or lessee of the premises,

(ii)   prohibiting or limiting that person from contact or association with the adult in need of protection,

(iii) requiring that person to pay maintenance for the adult in need of protection in the same manner and to the same extent as that person could be required to pay pursuant to the Family Maintenance Act.

NOTICE TO PUBLIC TRUSTEE

(4)   Where a court makes an order pursuant to clause (c) or (d) of subsection (3), it may advise the Public Trustee that there appears to be no guardian to act on behalf of the adult in need of protection or that it appears that there is a guardian or a person acting pursuant to a power of attorney who is neglecting or dealing with the estate contrary to the best interests of the adult in need of protection.

EXPIRY OF ORDER

(5)   An order made pursuant to subsection (3) expires six months after it is made.

VARIATION OR RENEWAL OF ORDER

(6)   An application to vary, renew or terminate an order made pursuant to subsection (3) may be made by the Minister, the adult in need of protection or an interested person on his behalf, or a person named in a protective intervention order upon notice of at least ten days to the

parties affected which notice may not be given in respect of a protective intervention order earlier than three months after the date of the order.

FACTOR CONSIDERED BY COURT

(7)   An order made pursuant to subsection (3) may be varied, renewed or terminated by the court where the court is satisfied that it is in the best interests of the adult in need of protection.

EXPIRY OF RENEWAL ORDER

(8)   A renewal order expires six months after it is made.

BALANCE OF PROBABILITIES

(9)   The determination of all matters by a court pursuant to this Section shall be made on the balance of probabilities.

APPEAL

(10) An order made pursuant to this Section may be appealed in accordance with the Summary Proceedings Act and on appeal the order may be confirmed, with or without modification, terminated or remitted with direction to the court appealed from, or another order authorized by this Act may be substituted. 1985, c. 2, s. 9.

REMOVAL FOR PROTECTION

10   (1)   Where on the basis of an assessment made pursuant to this Act the Minister is satisfied that there are reasonable and probable grounds to believe that

(a)   the life of a person is in danger;

(b)   the person is an adult in need of protection; and

(c)   the person is not mentally competent to decide whether or not to accept the assistance

of the Minister or is refusing the assistance by
reason of duress,

the Minister may authorize the immediate removal of the
person to such place as the Minister considers fit and proper
for the protection of the person and the preservation of his
life, and a person so authorized may take reasonable
measures to remove the person whose life is in danger.

APPLICATION FOR COURT ORDER
          (2)   Within five days after a person is removed
pursuant to subsection (1), the Minister shall apply to the
court for an order declaring that the person is an adult in
need of protection unless the person is sooner returned.

NOTICE
          (3)   Prior to the hearing of an application
pursuant to subsection (2), the Minister shall give notice of
the application in the prescribed form to the person in
respect of whom the application is made or some person
having custody or control of that person.

HEARING BY COURT
          (4)   The court shall proceed forthwith to hear
the application of the Minister.

POWERS OF COURT
          (5)   Upon the completion of the hearing, the
court may

          (a)   dismiss the application and direct the
          return of the person removed; or

          (b)   make an order in accordance with
          subsection (3) of Section 9.

SUBSECTIONS 9(4) to (10) APPLY
          (6)   Subsections (4) to (10) of Section 9 apply
mutatis mutandis to an order made pursuant to this Section.
1985, c. 2, s. 10.

COSTS
11   Costs may be awarded against the Minister in the discretion of the court dismissing an application by the Minister pursuant to this Act and the amount shall be determined in accordance with the rules of the Family Court. 1985, c. 2, s. 11.

WELFARE OF ADULT IS PARAMOUNT CONSIDERATION
12   In any proceeding taken pursuant to this Act the court or judge shall apply the principle that the welfare of the adult in need of protection is the paramount consideration. 1985, c. 2, s. 12.

PUBLIC TRUSTEE INFORMED OF REMOVAL OF ADULT
13   (1)   Where an adult is removed from the premises where he resides to another place pursuant to this Act and it appears to the Minister that there is an immediate danger of loss of, or damage to, any property of his by reason of his temporary or permanent inability to deal with the property, and that no other suitable arrangements have been made or are being made for the purpose, the Minister shall inform the Public Trustee.

POWERS OF PUBLIC TRUSTEE
(2)   Where the Public Trustee receives information pursuant to subsection (1) and where he is of the opinion that his intervention is appropriate, the Public Trustee may assume immediate management of the estate of that person and may take possession of the property of that person and shall safely keep, preserve and protect the same until

(a)   the Public Trustee determines that it is no longer necessary to manage the estate of the person;

(b)   the Supreme Court or a Judge thereof has appointed the Public Trustee or another person to be guardian of the estate of the adult in need of protection;

(c)   a court finds that the person is not an adult in need of protection; or

(d)   the order that a person is an adult in need of protection expires, terminates or is rescinded. 1985, c. 2, s. 13.

OTHER REMEDY OR RIGHT OF ACTION UNAFFECTED
14   (1)   Nothing in this Act limits a remedy available or affects an action that may be taken pursuant to another enactment.

OBLIGATION OF OTHERS UNAFFECTED
(2)   Nothing in this Act limits or affects the responsibility of a municipal unit pursuant to the provisions of the Social Assistance Act or the obligation of a person to provide maintenance. 1985, c. 2, s. 14.

ASSISTANCE BY PEACE OFFICER
15   A peace officer shall assist with the execution of an order issued pursuant to this Act or with the conveyance of an adult in need of protection to a place directed in accordance with this Act when requested to do so by a person acting for the Minister or pursuant to an order of the court. 1985, c. 2, s. 15.

FAILURE TO REPORT INFORMATION IS OFFENCE
16   (1)   Every person who has information, whether or not it is confidential or privileged, indicating that an adult is in need of protection and who fails to report that information to the Minister is guilty of an offence under this Act.

TIME LIMIT FOR PROSECUTION
(2)   A prosecution for an offence referred to in this Section shall be commenced within one year after the

day on which the offence was committed and not thereafter. 1985, c. 2, s. 16.

CONTRAVENTION OF ACT OR ORDER IS OFFENCE
    17   Every person who violates this Act or a protective intervention order is guilty of an offence punishable on summary conviction and is liable to a fine of not more than one thousand dollars or to imprisonment for not more than one year, or both. 1985, c. 2, s. 17.

JURISDICTION OF FAMILY COURT
    18   The Family Court has exclusive original jurisdiction over offences against this Act. 1985, c. 2, s. 18.

REGULATIONS
    19   (1)   The Governor in Council may make regulations

        (a)   respecting the provision of services for adults in need of protection;

        (b)   respecting the procedure for an assessment pursuant to this Act;

        (c)   respecting forms to be used pursuant to this Act;

        (d)   respecting the contents and service of documents to be used pursuant to this Act;

        (e)   defining any word or expression used in this Act and not defined herein;

        (f)   respecting any matter necessary or advisable to carry out effectively the intent and purposes of this Act.

REGULATIONS ACT
     (2)   The exercise by the Governor in Council of the authority contained in subsection (1) shall be regulations within the meaning of the Regulations Act. 1985, c. 2, s. 19.

PROCLAMATION
     20   This Act comes into force on and not before such day as the Governor in Council orders and declares by proclamation. 1985, c. 2, s. 20.

                    Proclaimed   - December 17, 1985
                    In Force   - January 6, 1986

───────────

APPENDIX NO. 10

Minnesota Legislation

626.557. Reporting of maltreatment of vulnerable adults

Subdivision 1. Public policy. The legislature declares that the public policy of this state is to protect adults who, because of physical or mental disability or dependency on institutional services, are particularly vulnerable to abuse or neglect; to provide safe institutional or residential services or living environments for vulnerable adults who have been abused or neglected; and to assist persons charged with the care of vulnerable adults to provide safe environments.

In addition, it is the policy of this state to require the reporting of suspected abuse or neglect of vulnerable adults, to provide for the voluntary reporting of abuse or neglect of vulnerable adults, to require the investigation of the reports, and to provide protective and counseling services in appropriate cases.

Subd. 2. Definitions. As used in this section, the following terms have the meanings given them unless the specific context indicates otherwise.

(a) "Facility" means a hospital or other entity required to be licensed pursuant to sections 144.50 to 144.58; a nursing home required to be licensed pursuant to section 144A.02; an agency, day care facility, or residential facility required to be licensed pursuant to sections 245.781 to 245.812; a mental health program receiving funds pursuant to section 245.61; or any entity required to be certified for participation in Titles XVIII or XIX of the Social Security Act, 42 U.S.C. 1395 et seq.

(b) "Vulnerable adult" means any person 18 years of age or older:

(1) Who is a resident or patient of a facility;

(2) Who receives services at or from a facility required to be licensed pursuant to sections 245.781 to 245.812; or

(3) Who, regardless of residence, is unable or unlikely to report abuse or neglect without assistance because of impairment of mental or physical function or emotional status.

(c) "Caretaker" means an individual or facility who has responsibility for the care of a vulnerable adult as a result of family relationship, or who has assumed responsibility for all or a portion of the care of a vulnerable adult voluntarily, or by contract, or agreement.

(d) "Abuse" means:

(1) Any act which constitutes a violation of sections 609.322, 609.342, 609.343, 609.344, or 609.345; or

(2) The intentional and nontherapeutic infliction of physical pain or injury, or any persistent course of conduct intended to produce mental or emotional distress.

(e) "Neglect" means failure by a caretaker to supply the vulnerable adult with necessary food, clothing, shelter, health care or supervision.

(f) "Report" means any report received by the local welfare agency, police department, county sheriff, or licensing agency pursuant to this section.

(g) "Licensing agency" means:

(1) The commissioner of health, for facilities as defined in clause (a) which are required to be licensed or certified by the department of health;

(2) The commissioner of public welfare, for facilities required by sections 245.781 to 245.813 to be licensed;

(3) Any licensing board which regulates persons pursuant to section 214.01, subdivision 2; and

(4) Any agency responsible for credentialing human services occupations.

Subd. 3. Persons mandated to report. A professional or his delegate who is engaged in the care of vulnerable adults, education, law enforcement, or any of the regulated occupations referenced in subdivision 2, clause (g)(3) and (4), or an employee of or person providing services in a facility who has knowledge of the abuse or neglect of a vulnerable adult, has reasonable cause to believe that a vulnerable adult is being or has been abused or neglected, or who has knowledge that a vulnerable adult has sustained a physical injury which is not reasonably explained by the history of injuries provided by the caretaker or caretakers of the vulnerable adult shall immediately report the information to the local police department, county sheriff, local welfare agency, or appropriate licensing or certifying agency. The police department or the county sheriff, upon receiving a report, shall immediately notify the local welfare agency. The local welfare agency, upon receiving a report, shall immediately notify the local police department or the county sheriff and the appropriate licensing agency or agencies.

A person not required to report under the provisions of this subdivision may voluntarily report as described above. Medical examiners or coroners shall notify the police department or county sheriff and the local welfare department in instances in which they believe that a vulnerable adult has died as a result of abuse or neglect.

Nothing in this subdivision shall be construed to require the reporting or transmittal of information regarding an incident of abuse or neglect or suspected abuse or neglect if the incident has been reported or transmitted to the appropriate person or entity.

Subd. 4. Report. A person required to report under subdivision 3 shall make an oral report immediately by telephone or otherwise. A person required to report under subdivision 3 shall also make a report as soon as possible in writing to the appropriate police department, the county sheriff, local welfare agency, or appropriate licensing agency. The written report shall be of sufficient content to identify the vulnerable adult, the caretaker, the nature and extent of the suspected abuse or neglect, any evidence of previous abuse or neglect, name and address of the reporter, and any other information that the reporter believes might be helpful in investigating the suspected abuse or neglect. Written reports received by a police department or a county sheriff shall be forwarded immediately to the local welfare agency. The police department or the county sheriff may keep copies of reports received by them. Copies of written reports received by a local welfare department shall be forwarded immediately to the local police department or the county sheriff and the appropriate licensing agency or agencies.

Unless the local welfare agency has notified a licensing agency, records maintained by local welfare agencies, local police departments, or county sheriffs under this section shall be destroyed as follows:

(a) All records relating to reports which, upon investigation, are found to be false shall be destroyed, but only after notice of intent to destroy has been mailed to the alleged abuser. At that party's request the records shall be maintained as confidential. The request must be mailed within 30 days of the mailing date of the original notice or the records will be destroyed;

(b) All records relating to reports which, upon investigation, are found to be substantiated shall be destroyed seven years after the date of the final entry in the case record; and

(c) All records of reports which, upon initial investigation, cannot be substantiated or disproved to the satisfaction of the local welfare agency, local police department or county sheriff shall be kept for a period of two years. If the local welfare agency, local police department or county sheriff is unable to substantiate the report within that period, each agency unable to substantiate the report shall destroy its records relating to the report.

If a licensing agency has been notified, records maintained by local welfare agencies, local police departments, or county sheriffs shall be destroyed upon receiving notice of record destruction from all licensing agencies notified about the report.

Subd. 5. Immunity from liability. A person, including a person voluntarily making reports and a person required to make reports under subdivision 3, participating in good faith in making a report pursuant to this section shall have immunity from any civil liability that otherwise might result from making the report.

Subd. 6. Falsified reports. A person who intentionally makes a false report under the provisions of this section shall be liable in a civil suit for any actual damages suffered by the person or persons so reported and for any punitive damages set by the court or jury.

Subd. 7. Failure to report. (a) A person required to report by this section who intentionally fails to report is guilty of a misdemeanor.

(b) A person required by this section to report who negligently or intentionally fails to report is liable for damages caused by the failure.

Subd. 8. **Evidence not privileged.** No evidence regarding the abuse or neglect of the vulnerable adult shall be excluded in any proceeding arising out of the alleged abuse or neglect on the grounds of lack of competency under section 595.02.

Subd. 9. **Mandatory reporting to a medical examiner or coroner.** When a person required to report under the provisions of subdivision 3 has reasonable cause to believe that a vulnerable adult has died as a direct or indirect result of abuse or neglect, he shall report that information to the appropriate medical examiner or coroner in addition to the local welfare agency, police department, or county sheriff or appropriate licensing agency or agencies. The medical examiner or coroner shall complete an investigation as soon as feasible and report the findings to the police department or county sheriff and the local welfare agency.

Subd. 10. **Duties of local welfare agency upon a receipt of a report.** (a) The local welfare agency shall immediately investigate and offer emergency and continuing protective social services for purposes of preventing further abuse or neglect and for safeguarding and enhancing the welfare of the abused or neglected vulnerable adult. Local welfare agencies shall have the right to enter facilities and inspect and copy records as part of investigations. In cases of suspected sexual abuse, the local welfare agency shall immediately arrange for and make available to the victim appropriate medical examination and treatment. The investigation shall not be limited to the written records of the facility but shall include every other available source of information. When necessary in order to protect the vulnerable adult from further harm, the local welfare agency shall seek authority to remove the vulnerable adult from the caretaker in whose care the neglect or abuse occurred. The local welfare agency shall also investigate to determine whether the conditions which resulted in the reported abuse or neglect place other vulnerable adults in jeopardy of being abused or neglected and offer protective social services that are called for by its determination. In performing any of these duties, the local welfare agency shall maintain appropriate records.

(b) If the report indicates, or if the local welfare agency finds that the suspected abuse or neglect occurred at a facility, or while the vulnerable adult was or should have been under the care of or receiving services from a facility, or that the suspected abuse or neglect involved a person licensed by a licensing agency to provide care or services, the local welfare agency shall immediately notify the appropriate licensing agency or agencies, and provide the licensing agency with a copy of the report and of its investigative findings.

Subd. 11. **Duties of licensing agencies upon receipt of report.** Whenever a licensing agency receives a report, or otherwise has information indicating that a vulnerable adult may have been abused or neglected at a facility it has licensed, or that a person it has licensed or credentialed to provide care or services may be involved in the abuse or neglect of a vulnerable adult, or that such a facility or person has failed to comply with the requirements of this section, it shall immediately investigate. Subject to the provisions of chapter 13, the licensing agency shall have the right to enter facilities and inspect and copy records as part of investigations. The investigation shall not be limited to the written records of the facility, but shall include every other available source of information. The licensing agency shall issue orders and take actions with respect to the license of the facility or person that are designed to prevent further abuse or neglect of vulnerable adults.

Subd. 12. Records. Each licensing agency shall maintain summary records of reports of suspected abuse or neglect and suspected violations of the requirements of this section with respect to facilities or persons licensed or credentialed by that agency. These records shall state the nature of the suspected abuse or neglect or violation of the requirements of this section and the results of the agency's investigation. These records, which shall not contain the name of the person making the report or the vulnerable adult, shall be public. All other records maintained pursuant to this section shall be private data on individuals, except that the records shall be made available to a prosecuting authority and law enforcement officials, local welfare agencies, and other licensing agencies in investigating the alleged abuse or neglect. The records shall be collected and maintained in accordance with the provisions of chapter 13, and an individual subject of a record shall have access to the record in accordance with those sections, except that the name of the reporter shall be disclosed only upon a finding by the court that the report was false and made in bad faith.

Records maintained by licensing agencies under this section shall be destroyed as follows:

(a) All records relating to reports which, upon investigation, the licensing agency finds to be false shall be destroyed in accordance with provisions of subdivision 4, clause (a) ;

(b) All records relating to reports which, upon investigation, the licensing agency finds are substantiated shall be destroyed seven years after the date of the final entry in the case record; and

(c) All records of reports which, upon initial investigation, cannot be substantiated or disproved to the satisfaction of the licensing agency shall be kept for two years. If the licensing agency is unable to substantiate the report within that period, the agency shall destroy the records. The licensing agency shall notify the appropriate local welfare agency, local police department, or county sheriff of the agency's destruction of records relating to reports made pursuant to this section and the reasons for the destruction.

Subd. 12a. Application of data practices act. The classification of reports and records created or maintained for the purposes of this section shall be determined as provided by this section, notwithstanding any other classifications established by chapter 13.

Subd. 13. Coordination. (a) Any police department or county sheriff, upon receiving a report shall notify the local welfare agency pursuant to subdivision 3. A local welfare agency or licensing agency which receives a report pursuant to that subdivision shall immediately notify the appropriate law enforcement, local welfare, and licensing agencies.

(b) Investigating agencies, including the police department, county sheriff, local welfare agency, or appropriate licensing agency shall cooperate in coordinating their investigatory activities. Each licensing agency which regulates facilities shall develop and disseminate procedures to coordinate its activities with (i) investigations by police and county sheriffs, and (ii) provision of protective services by local welfare agencies.

Subd. 14. Abuse prevention plans. (a) Each facility shall establish and enforce an ongoing written abuse prevention plan. The plan shall contain an assessment of the physical plant, its environment, and its population identifying factors which may encourage or permit abuse, and a statement of specific measures to be taken to minimize the risk of abuse. The plan shall comply with any rules governing the plan as are promulgated by the licensing agency.

(b) Each facility shall develop an individual abuse prevention plan for each vulnerable adult residing there. Facilities designated in subdivision 2. clause (b)(2) shall develop plans for any vulnerable adults receiving services from them. The plan shall contain an individualized assessment of the person's susceptibility to abuse, and a statement of the specific measures to be taken to minimize the risk of abuse to that person. For the purposes of this clause, the term "abuse" includes self-abuse.

Subd. 15. Internal reporting of abuse and neglect. Each facility shall establish and enforce an ongoing written procedure in compliance with the licensing agencies' rules for insuring that all cases of suspected abuse or neglect are reported promptly to a person required by this section to report abuse and neglect and are promptly investigated.

Subd. 16. Enforcement. (a) A facility that has not complied with this section within 60 days of the effective date of passage of temporary rules is ineligible for renewal of its license. A person required by subdivison 3 to report and who is licensed or credentialed to practice an occupation by a licensing agency who willfully fails to comply with this section shall be disciplined after a hearing by the appropriate licensing agency.

(b) Licensing agencies shall as soon as possible promulgate rules necessary to implement the requirements of subdivisions 11, 12, 13, 14, 15, and 16, clause (a). Agencies may promulgate temporary rules pursuant to sections 14.29 to 14.36.

(c) The commissioner of public welfare shall promulgate rules as necessary to implement the requirements of subdivision 10.

Subd. 17. Retaliation prohibited. (a) A facility or person shall not retaliate against any person who reports in good faith suspected abuse or neglect pursuant to this section, or against a vulnerable adult with respect to whom a report is made, because of the report.

(b) Any facility or person which retaliates against any person because of a report of suspected abuse or neglect is liable to that person for actual damages and, in addition, a penalty up to $1,000.

(c) There shall be a rebuttable presumption that any adverse action, as defined below, within 90 days of a report, is retaliatory. For purposes of this clause, the term "adverse action" refers to action taken by a facility or person involved in a report against the person making the report or the person with respect to whom the report was made because of the report, and includes, but is not limited to:

(1) Discharge or transfer from the facility;

(2) Discharge from or termination of employment;

(3) Demotion or reduction in remuneration for services;

(4) Restriction or prohibition of access to the facility or its residents; or

(5) Any restriction of rights set forth in section 144.651.

Subd. 18. Outreach. The commissioner of public welfare shall establish an aggressive program to educate those required to report, as well as the general public, about the requirements of this section using a variety of media.

Subd. 19. Penalty. Any caretaker, as defined in subdivision 2, or operator or employee thereof, or volunteer worker thereat, who intentionally abuses or neglects a vulnerable adult, or being a caretaker, knowingly permits conditions to exist which result in the abuse or neglect of a vulnerable adult, is guilty of a gross misdemeanor.

Laws 1980, c. 542, § 1, eff. Jan. 1, 1981. Amended by Laws 1981. c. 311, § 39; Laws 1982, c. 393, §§ 3, 4; Laws 1982, c. 424, § 130; Laws 1982, c. 545, § 24; Laws 1982, c. 636, §§ 5, 6, eff. March 24, 1982.

Historical Note

Laws 1981, c. 311, § 39, directed statutory cross reference changes generally throughout the statutes to correct references to provisions formerly numbered as §§ 15.1611 to 15.1699.

Laws 1982, c. 393, and Laws 1982, c. 636, both in subd. 19 inserted "knowingly".

In addition, Laws 1982, c. 393, in subd. 2(g)(3) inserted ", subdivision 2".

Laws 1982, c. 636, in addition to the insertion noted above, in subd. 19 substituted "is guilty of a gross misdemeanor" for "may be charged with a violation of section 609.23".

Laws 1982, c. 424, § 130, directed references to the administrative procedure act be changed to reflect renumbering. The references appear generally throughout the statute.

Laws 1982, c. 545, § 24, directed statutory cross reference changes generally throughout the statutes to correct references to provisions formerly numbered as §§ 15.1611 to 15.1699, including those contained in Laws 1981, c. 311.

Cross References

Community social services act, adults in need of protection and vulnerable under this section, see § 256E.03.

Nursing homes,

Correction orders, facilities not in compliance with this section, see § 144A.10, subd. 4.

Suspension or revocation of license proceedings, violations of this section, see § 144A.11, subd. 2.

Sexual assault counselors, competency of witnesses, no exemption from compliance with this section, see § 595.02(10).

Library References

Asylums ⟸3.
Mental Health ⟸1, 20, 21, 31.

C.J.S. Asylums and Institutional Care Facilities §§ 5 to 8.
C.J.S. Insane Persons §§ 3, 40, 58, 61, 67.

AMENDMENTS

626.557. Reporting of maltreatment of vulnerable adults

[See main volume for text of subdivision 1]

Subd. 2. Definitions. As used in this section, the following terms have the meanings given them unless the specific context indicates otherwise.

(a) "Facility" means a hospital or other entity required to be licensed pursuant to sections 144.50 to 144.58; a nursing home required to be licensed to serve adults pursuant to section 144A.02; an agency, day care facility, or residential facility required to be licensed to serve adults pursuant to sections 245.781 to 245.812; or a home health agency certified for participation in titles XVIII or XIX of the Social Security Act, United States Code, title 42, sections 1395 et seq.

(b) "Vulnerable adult" means any person 18 years of age or older:

(1) who is a resident or inpatient of a facility;

(2) who receives services at or from a facility required to be licensed to serve adults pursuant to sections 245.781 to 245.812, except a person receiving outpatient services for treatment of chemical dependency or mental illness;

(3) who receives services from a home health agency certified for participation under titles XVIII or XIX of the Social Security Act, United States Code, title 42, sections 1395 et seq. and 1396 et seq.; or

(4) who, regardless of residence or type of service received, is unable or unlikely to report abuse or neglect without assistance because of impairment of mental or physical function or emotional status.

(c) "Caretaker" means an individual or facility who has responsibility for the care of a vulnerable adult as a result of a family relationship, or who has assumed responsibility for all or a portion of the care of a vulnerable adult voluntarily, by contract, or by agreement.

(d) "Abuse" means:

(1) any act which constitutes a violation under sections 609.221 to 609.223, 609.23 to 609.235, 609.322, 609.342, 609.343, 609.344, or 609.345;

(2) nontherapeutic conduct which produces or could reasonably be expected to produce pain or injury and is not accidental, or any repeated conduct which produces or could reasonably be expected to produce mental or emotional distress;

(3) any sexual contact between a facility staff person and a resident or client of that facility; or

(4) the illegal use of a vulnerable adult's person or property for another person's profit or advantage, or the breach of a fiduciary relationship through the use of a person or a person's property for any purpose not in the proper and lawful execution of a trust, including but not limited to situations where a person obtains money, property, or services from a vulnerable adult through the use of undue influence, harassment, duress, deception, or fraud.

(e) "Neglect" means:

(1) failure by a caretaker to supply a vulnerable adult with necessary food, clothing, shelter, health care or supervision;

(2) the absence or likelihood of absence of necessary food, clothing, shelter, health care, or supervision for a vulnerable adult; or

(3) the absence or likelihood of absence of necessary financial management to protect a vulnerable adult against abuse as defined in paragraph (d), clause (4). Nothing in this section shall be construed to require a health care facility to provide financial management or supervise financial management for a vulnerable adult except as otherwise required by law.

(f) "Report" means any report received by a local welfare agency, police department, county sheriff, or licensing agency pursuant to this section.

(g) "Licensing agency" means:

(1) the commissioner of health, for facilities as defined in clause (a) which are required to be licensed or certified by the department of health;

(2) the commissioner of human services, for facilities required by sections 245.781 to 245.813 to be licensed;

(3) any licensing board which regulates persons pursuant to section 214.01, subdivision 2; and

(4) any agency responsible for credentialing human services occupations.

Subd. 3. Persons mandated to report. A professional or the professional's delegate who is engaged in the care of vulnerable adults, education, social services, law enforcement, or any of the regulated occupations referenced in subdivision 2, clause (g)(3) and (4), or an employee of a rehabilitation facility certified by the commissioner of jobs and training for vocational rehabilitation, or an employee of or person providing services in a facility who has knowledge of the abuse or neglect of a vulnerable adult, has reasonable cause to believe that a vulnerable adult is being or has been abused or neglected, or who has knowledge that a vulnerable adult has sustained a physical injury which is not reasonably explained by the history of injuries provided by the caretaker or caretakers of the vulnerable adult shall immediately report the information to the local police department, county sheriff, local welfare agency, or appropriate licensing or certifying agency. The police department or the county sheriff, upon receiving a report, shall immediately notify the local welfare agency. The local welfare agency, upon receiving a report, shall immediately notify the local police department or the county sheriff and the appropriate licensing agency or agencies.

A person not required to report under the provisions of this subdivision may voluntarily report as described above. Medical examiners or coroners shall notify the police department or county sheriff and the local welfare department in instances in which they believe that a vulnerable adult has died as a result of abuse or neglect.

Nothing in this subdivision shall be construed to require the reporting or transmittal of information regarding an incident of abuse or neglect or suspected abuse or neglect if the incident has been reported or transmitted to the appropriate person or entity.

Subd. 3a. Report not required. (a) Where federal law specifically prohibits a person from disclosing patient identifying information in connection with a report of suspected abuse or neglect under Laws 1983, chapter 273, section 3, that person need not make a required report unless the vulnerable adult, or the vulnerable adult's guardian, conservator, or legal representative, has consented to disclosure in a manner which conforms to federal requirements. Facilities whose patients or residents are covered by such a federal law shall seek consent to the disclosure of suspected abuse or neglect from each patient or resident, or a guardian, conservator, or legal representative, upon the patient's or resident's admission to the facility. Persons who are prohibited by federal law from reporting an incident of suspected abuse or neglect shall promptly seek consent to make a report.

(b) Except as defined in subdivision 2, paragraph (d), clause (1), verbal or physical aggression occurring between patients, residents, or clients of a facility, or self-abusive behavior of these persons does not constitute "abuse" for the purposes of subdivision 3 unless it causes serious harm. The operator of the facility or a designee shall record incidents of aggression and self-abusive behavior in a manner that facilitates periodic review by licensing agencies and county and local welfare agencies.

(c) Nothing in this section shall be construed to require a report of abuse, as defined in subdivision 2, paragraph (d), clause (4), solely on the basis of the transfer of money or property by gift or as compensation for services rendered.

Subd. 4. Report. A person required to report under subdivision 3 shall make an oral report immediately by telephone or otherwise. A person required to report under subdivision 3 shall also make a report as soon as possible in writing to the appropriate police department, the county sheriff, local welfare agency, or appropriate licensing agency. The written report shall be of sufficient content to identify the vulnerable adult, the caretaker, the nature and extent of the suspected abuse or neglect, any evidence of previous abuse or neglect, name and address of the reporter, and any other information that the reporter believes might be helpful in investigating the suspected abuse or neglect. Written reports received by a police department or a county sheriff shall be forwarded immediately to the local welfare agency. The police department or the county sheriff may keep copies of reports received by them. Copies of written reports received by a local welfare department shall be forwarded immediately to the local police department or the county sheriff and the appropriate licensing agency or agencies.

Subd. 5. Immunity from liability. (a) A person making a voluntary or mandated report under subdivision 3 or participating in an investigation under this section is immune from any civil or criminal liability that otherwise might result from the person's actions, if the person is acting in good faith.

(b) A person employed by a local welfare agency or a state licensing agency who is conducting or supervising an investigation or enforcing the law in compliance with subdivision 10, 11, or 12 or any related rule or provision of law is immune from any civil or criminal liability that might otherwise result from the person's actions, if the person is acting in good faith and exercising due care.

[See main volume for text of subds. 6 to 8]

Subd. 9. **Mandatory reporting to a medical examiner or coroner.** A person required to report under the provisions of subdivision 3 who has reasonable cause to believe that a vulnerable adult has died as a direct or indirect result of abuse or neglect shall report that information to the appropriate medical examiner or coroner in addition to the local welfare agency, police department, or county sheriff or appropriate licensing agency or agencies. The medical examiner or coroner shall complete an investigation as soon as feasible and **report the findings to the police department or county sheriff**, the local welfare agency, **and, if applicable, each licensing agency.**

Subd. 10. **Duties of local welfare agency upon a receipt of a report.** (a) The local welfare agency shall immediately investigate and offer emergency and continuing protective social services for purposes of preventing further abuse or neglect and for safeguarding and enhancing the welfare of the abused or neglected vulnerable adult. Local welfare agencies may enter facilities and inspect and copy records as part of investigations. In cases of suspected sexual abuse, the local welfare agency shall immediately arrange for and make available to the victim appropriate medical examination and treatment. The investigation shall not be limited to the written records of the facility, but shall include every other available source of information. When necessary in order to protect the vulnerable adult from further harm, the local welfare agency shall seek authority to remove the vulnerable adult from the situation in which the neglect or abuse occurred. The local welfare agency shall also investigate to determine whether the conditions which resulted in the reported abuse or neglect place other vulnerable adults in jeopardy of being abused or neglected and offer protective social services that are called for by its determination. In performing any of these duties, the local welfare agency shall maintain appropriate records.

(b) If the report indicates, or if the local welfare agency finds that the suspected abuse or neglect occurred at a facility, or while the vulnerable adult was or should have been under the care of or receiving services from a facility, or that the suspected abuse or neglect involved a person licensed by a licensing agency to provide care or services, the local welfare agency shall immediately notify each appropriate licensing agency, and provide each licensing agency with a copy of the report and of its investigative findings.

(c) When necessary in order to protect a vulnerable adult from serious harm, the local agency shall immediately intervene on behalf of that adult to help the family, victim, or other interested person by seeking any of the following:

(1) a restraining order or a court order for removal of the perpetrator from the residence of the vulnerable adult pursuant to section 518B.01;

(2) the appointment of a guardian or conservator pursuant to sections 525.539 to 525.6198, or guardianship or conservatorship pursuant to chapter 252A;

(3) replacement of an abusive or neglectful guardian or conservator and appointment of a suitable person as guardian or conservator, pursuant to sections 525.539 to 525.6199, or

(4) a referral to the prosecuting attorney for possible criminal prosecution of the perpetrator under chapter 609.

The expenses of legal intervention must be paid by the county in the case of indigent persons, under section 525.703 and chapter 563.

In proceedings under sections 525.539 to 525.6198, if a suitable relative or other person is not available to petition for guardianship or conservatorship, a county employee shall present the petition with representation by the county attorney. The county shall contract with or arrange for a suitable person or nonprofit organization to provide ongoing guardianship services. If the county presents evidence to the probate court that it has made a diligent effort and no other suitable person can be found, a county employee may serve as guardian or conservator. The county shall not retaliate against the employee for any action taken on behalf of the ward or conservatee even if the action is adverse to the county's interest. Any person retaliated against in violation of this subdivision shall have a cause of action against the county and shall be entitled to reasonable attorney fees and costs of the action if the action is upheld by the court.

Subd. 10a. **Notification of neglect or abuse in a facility.** (a) When a report is received that alleges neglect, physical abuse, or sexual abuse of a vulnerable adult while in the care of a facility required to be licensed under section 144A.02 or sections 245.781 to 245.812, the local welfare agency investigating the report shall notify the guardian or conservator of the person of a vulnerable adult under guardianship or conservatorship of the person who is alleged to have been abused or neglected. The local welfare agency shall notify the person, if any, designated to be notified in case of an emergency by a vulnerable adult not under guardianship or conservatorship of the person who is alleged to have been abused or neglected, unless consent is denied by the vulnerable adult. The notice shall contain the following information: the name of the facility; the fact that a report of alleged abuse or neglect of a vulnerable adult in the facility has been received; the nature of the alleged abuse or neglect; that the agency is conducting an investigation; any protective or corrective measures being taken pending the outcome of the investigation; and that a written memorandum will be provided when the investigation is completed.

(b) In a case of alleged neglect, physical abuse, or sexual abuse of a vulnerable adult while in the care of a facility required to be licensed under sections 245.781 to 245.812, the local welfare agency may also provide the information in paragraph (a) to the guardian or conservator of the person of any other vulnerable adult in the facility who is under guardianship or conservatorship of the person, to any other vulnerable adult in the facility who is not under guardianship or conservatorship of the person, and to the person, if any, designated to be notified in case of an emergency by any other vulnerable adult in the facility who is not under guardianship or conservatorship of the person, unless consent is denied by the vulnerable adult, if the investigative agency knows or has reason to believe the alleged neglect, physical abuse, or sexual abuse has occurred.

(c) When the investigation required under subdivision 10 is completed, the local welfare agency shall provide a written memorandum containing the following information to every guardian or conservator of the person or other person notified by the agency of the investigation under paragraph (a) or (b): the name of the facility investigated; the nature of the alleged neglect, physical abuse, or sexual abuse; the investigator's name; a summary of the investigative findings; a statement of whether the report was found to be substantiated, inconclusive, or false; and the protective or corrective measures that are being or will be taken. The memorandum shall be written in a manner that protects the identity of the reporter and the alleged victim and shall not contain the name or, to the extent possible, reveal the identity of the alleged perpetrator or of those interviewed during the investigation.

(d) In a case of neglect, physical abuse, or sexual abuse of a vulnerable adult while in the care of a facility required to be licensed under sections 245.781 to 245.812, the local welfare agency may also provide the written memorandum to the guardian or conservator of the person of any other vulnerable adult in the facility who is under guardianship or conservatorship of the person, to any other vulnerable adult in the facility who is not under guardianship or conservatorship of the person, and to the person, if any, designated to be notified in case of an emergency by any other vulnerable adult in the facility who is not under guardianship or conservatorship of the person, unless consent is denied by the vulnerable adult, if the report is substantiated or if the investigation is inconclusive and the report is a second or subsequent report of neglect, physical abuse, or sexual abuse of a vulnerable adult while in the care of the facility.

(e) In determining whether to exercise the discretionary authority granted under paragraphs (b) and (d), the local welfare agency shall consider the seriousness and extent of the alleged neglect, physical abuse, or sexual abuse and the impact of notification on the residents of the facility. The facility shall be notified whenever this discretion is exercised.

(f) Where federal law specifically prohibits the disclosure of patient identifying information, the local welfare agency shall not provide any notice under paragraph (a) or (b) or any memorandum under paragraph (c) or (d) unless the vulnerable adult has consented to disclosure in a manner which conforms to federal requirements.

[See main volume for text of subd. 11]

Subd. 11a. Duties of prosecuting authorities. Upon receipt of a report from a social service or licensing agency, the prosecuting authority shall immediately investigate, prosecute when warranted, and transmit its findings and disposition to the referring agency.

Subd. 12. **Records.** (a) Each licensing agency shall maintain summary records of reports of alleged abuse or neglect and alleged violations of the requirements of this section with respect to facilities or persons licensed or credentialed by that agency. As part of these records, the agency shall prepare an investigation memorandum. Notwithstanding section 13.46, subdivision 3, the investigation memorandum shall be accessible to the public pursuant to section 13.03 and a copy shall be provided to any public agency which referred the matter to the licensing agency for investigation. It shall contain a complete review of the agency's investigation, including but not limited to: the name of any facility investigated; a statement of the nature of the alleged abuse or neglect or other violation of the requirements of this section; pertinent information obtained from medical or other records reviewed; the investigator's name; a summary of the investigation's findings; a statement of whether the report was found to be substantiated, inconclusive, or false; and a statement of any action taken by the agency. The investigation memorandum shall be written in a manner which protects the identity of the reporter and of the vulnerable adult and may not contain the name or, to the extent possible, the identity of the alleged perpetrator or of those interviewed during the investigation. During the licensing agency's investigation, all data collected pursuant to this section shall be classified as investigative data pursuant to section 13.39. After the licensing agency's investigation is complete, the data on individuals collected and maintained shall be private data on individuals. All data collected pursuant to this section shall be made available to prosecuting authorities and law enforcement officials, local welfare agencies, and licensing agencies investigating the alleged abuse or neglect. Notwithstanding any law to the contrary, the name of the reporter shall be disclosed only upon a finding by the court that the report was false and made in bad faith.

(b) Notwithstanding the provisions of section 138.163:

(1) all data maintained by licensing agencies, treatment facilities, or other public agencies which relate to reports which, upon investigation, are found to be false may be destroyed two years after the finding was made;

(2) all data maintained by licensing agencies, treatment facilities, or other public agencies which relate to reports which, upon investigation, are found to be inconclusive may be destroyed four years after the finding was made;

(3) all data maintained by licensing agencies, treatment facilities, or other public agencies which relate to reports which, upon investigation, are found to be substantiated may be destroyed seven years after the finding was made.

Subd. 12a. Repealed by Laws 1983, c. 273, § 8.

[See main volume for text of subd. 13]

Subd. 14. **Abuse prevention plans.** (a) Each facility, except home health agencies, shall establish and enforce an ongoing written abuse prevention plan. The plan shall contain an assessment of the physical plant, its environment, and its population identifying factors which may encourage or permit abuse, and a statement of specific measures to be taken to minimize the risk of abuse. The plan shall comply with any rules governing the plan promulgated by the licensing agency.

(b) Each facility shall develop an individual abuse prevention plan for each vulnerable adult residing there. Facilities designated in subdivision 2. clause (b)(2) or clause (b)(3) shall develop plans for any vulnerable adults receiving services from them. The plan shall contain an individualized assessment of the person's susceptibility to abuse, and a statement of the specific measures to be taken to minimize the risk of abuse to that person. For the purposes of this clause, the term "abuse" includes self-abuse.

[See main volume for text of subd. 15]

Subd. 16. **Enforcement.** (a) A facility that has not complied with this section within 60 days of the effective date of passage of emergency rules is ineligible for renewal of its license. A person required by subdivision 3 to report and who is licensed or credentialed to practice an occupation by a licensing agency who willfully fails to comply with this section shall be disciplined after a hearing by the appropriate licensing agency.

(b) Licensing agencies shall as soon as possible promulgate rules necessary to implement the requirements of subdivisions 11, 12, 13, 14, 15, and 16, clause (a). Agencies may promulgate emergency rules pursuant to sections 14.29 to 14.36.

(c) The commissioner of human services shall promulgate rules as necessary to implement the requirements of subdivision 10.

[See main volume for text of subd. 17]

Subd. 18. **Outreach.** The commissioner of human services shall establish an aggressive program to educate those required to report, as well as the general public, about the requirements of this section using a variety of media.

[See main volume for text of subd. 19]

Amended by Laws 1983, c. 273, §§ 1 to 7; Laws 1984, c. 640, § 32, eff. May 3, 1984; Laws 1984, c. 654, art. 5, § 58; Laws 1985, c. 150, §§ 1 to 6; Laws 1985, c. 293, §§ 6, 7; Laws 1985, 1st Sp., c. 14, art. 9, § 75; Laws 1986, c. 444.

1983 Amendment. In subd. 2, inserted "to serve adults", and substituted "a home health agency" for "any entity required to be" and "United States Code, Title 42, sections 1395 et seq." for "42 U.S.C. 1395 et seq." in clause (a); substituted "inpatient" for "patient" in clause (b)(1); inserted "to serve adults" and added exception in clause (b)(2); added clause (b)(3); redesignated former clause (b)(3) as clause (b)(4); inserted "or type of service received" in clause (b) (4); added references to sections 609.221 to 609.235 in clause (d)(1); and added designation for clause (e)(1) and added clause (e)(2).

In subd. 3, inserted "social services" and "or an employee of a rehabilitation facility certified by the commissioner of economic security for vocational rehabilitation" in the first sentence; added subd. 3A; in subd. 4, deleted the former second and third paragraphs; in subd. 10, substituted "may" for "the right to" in the second sentence and "situation in which" for "caretaker in whose care" in the fifth sentence of clause a; rewrote all except the first sentence of subd. 12; and in subd. 14, inserted "except home health agencies" in the first sentence of clause (a) and inserted reference to "clause (b)(3)" in the first sentence of clause (b).

1984 Amendment. Laws 1984, c. 640, § 32, directed the revisor of statutes to change references to temporary rules and hearing examiners to references to emergency rules and administrative law judges, respectively, throughout Minnesota Statutes 1984.

Laws 1984, c. 654, art. 5, § 58, instructed the revisor of statutes to change references to the commissioner or department of public welfare to references to the commissioner or department of human services throughout Minnesota Statutes 1984.

1985 Amendments. Laws 1985, c. 150, in subd. 2, in par. (a) deleted "a mental health program receiving funds pursuant to section 245.61" preceding "or a home health agency"; in par. (d) inserted "609.223, 609.23" in cl. (1), rewrote cl. (2), and added cls. (3) and (4) and in par. (e) added cl. (3).

In subd. 3a, added cl. (c); rewrote subd. 5 (for former text, see main volume); in subd. 9 added "and, if applicable, each licensing agency" at the end of the last sentence; in subd. 10, in cl. (b) substituted "each appropriate licensing agency" for "the appropriate licensing agency or agencies", and added cl. (c), cls. (1) to (4) in cl. (c) and the two paragraphs at the end of cl. (c); and added subd. 11a.

Prior to revision, par. (d)(2) in subd. 2 read:

"The intentional and nontherapeutic infliction of physical pain or injury, or any persistent course of conduct intended to produce mental or emotional distress."

Laws 1985, c. 293, added subd. 10a; and rewrote subd. 12, which prior thereto read:

"Each licensing agency shall maintain summary records of reports of suspected abuse or neglect and suspected violations of the requirements of this section with respect to facilities or persons licensed or credentialed by that agency. As part of these records, the agency shall prepare an investigation memorandum. The investigation memorandum shall be accessible to the public pursuant to section 13.03. It shall contain a complete review of the agency's investigation, including but not limited to the facility's name, if any, a statement of the nature of the suspected abuse or neglect or violation of the requirements of this section, pertinent information obtained from medical or other records reviewed, the investigator's name, a summary of the investigation's findings, and a statement of any determination made or action taken by the agency. The investigation memorandum shall be written in a manner which protects the identity of the reporter and of the vulnerable adult and may not contain the name or, to the extent possible, the identity of the alleged perpetrator or of those interviewed during the investigation. During the licensing agency's investigation, all data collected pursuant to this section shall be classified as investigative data pursuant to section 13.39.

After the licensing agency's investigation is complete, the data on individuals collected and maintained shall be private data on individuals. All data collected pursuant to this section shall be made available to prosecuting authorities and law enforcement officials, local welfare agencies, and licensing agencies investigating the alleged abuse or neglect. Notwithstanding any law to the contrary, the name of the reporter shall be disclosed only upon a finding by the court that the report was false and made in bad faith.

"Notwithstanding the provisions of section 138.163:

"(1) All data maintained by licensing agencies, treatment facilities, or other public agencies which relate to reports which, upon investigation, the licensing agency finds to be false may be destroyed two years after the finding was made;

"(2) All data maintained by licensing agencies, treatment facilities, or other public agencies which relate to reports which, upon investigation, the licensing agency finds to be unsubstantiated may be destroyed four years after the finding was made;

"(3) All data maintained by licensing agencies, treatment facilities, or other public agencies which relate to reports which, upon investigation, the licensing agency finds to be substantiated may be destroyed seven years after the finding was made."

1986 Amendment. Laws 1986, c. 444, § 1, removed gender specific references applicable to human beings throughout Minn. Stats by adopting by reference proposed amendments for such revision prepared by the revisor of statutes pursuant to Laws 1984. c. 480. § 21. and certified and filed with the secretary of state on Jan. 24, 1986. Section 3 of Laws 1986, c. 444, provides that the amendments "do not change the substance of the statutes amended."

Administrative Code References

Protective services, vulnerable adults, see Mn. Rules pt. 9555 7100 et seq.

Notes of Decisions

Defenses, liability in tort for failure to report 2

Liability in tort for failure to report, in general 1

Scope, liability in tort for failure to report 3

1. Liability in tort for failure to report—In general

For hospital to be absolutely liable under the Vulnerable Adult Act [M.S.A. § 626.557] for failure to report employee's sexual abuse of 19-year-old female patient admitted for severe depression, it was not required to be shown that patient was unable to protect herself from type of abuse received. Thelen By and Through Thelen v. St. Cloud Hosp., App.1985, 879 N.W.2d 189.

The Vulnerable Adult Act [M.S.A. § 626.557] imposes absolute liability for damages caused by failure to report abuse of vulnerable adults; affirmative defenses of contributory negligence and assumption of risk are not available. Thelen By and Through Thelen v. St. Cloud Hosp., App 1985, 879 N.W.2d 189.

2. —— Defenses, liability in tort for failure to report

The Vulnerable Adult Act [M.S.A. § 626.557] did not preclude causation defenses in action against hospital for failure to report employee's sexual abuse of 19-year-old female patient admitted for severe depression; a showing that hospital violated the statute was per se evidence of negligence but, to prevail, plaintiff was required to show that failure to report the sexual abuse caused damage. Thelen By and Through Thelen v. St. Cloud Hosp., App.1985, 879 N.W.2d 189

3. —— Scope, liability in tort for failure to report

Hospital's liability under the Vulnerable Adult Act [M.S.A. § 626.557] for failure to report employee's sexual abuse of 19-year-old female patient did not extend beyond damage caused by failure to report to cover all damages caused by the abuse. Thelen By and Through Thelen v. St. Cloud Hosp., App.1985, 879 N.W.2d 189.

BIBLIOGRAPHY & RESOURCES

The following bibliography does not purport to be an
exhaustive list. It does, however, contain the titles of some
publications that may be of interest to anyone wishing to
learn more about advocacy or may provide useful information to
anyone engaged in advocacy, either for themselves or others.

Abrams, Philip, Sheila Abrams, Robin Humphrey and Ray Smith.
Action for Care: A Review of Good Neighbour Schemes in
England. Berkhamsted Herts, England: The Volunteer
Centre, 1981.

American Bar Association Commission on Legal Problems of the
Elderly and the National Citizens' Coalition for Nursing
Home Reform. Enforcing Nursing Home Residents' Rights:
A New Role for the Private Bar. Washington, D.C.: May
1982.

Anand, Raj. "Involuntary Civil Committment in Ontario:
The Need to Curtail the Abuses of Psychiatry."
Canadian Bar Review 57, 250.

Appelbaum, P. "The Rising Tide of Patients' Rights
Advocacy." Law and Psychiatry 39, No. I (1986), 9-10.

Apolloni, Tony. "Effective Advocacy: How to be a Winner."
The Exceptional Parent. (February, 1985), 14-19.

Atkinson, S., M.F. Madill, D. Solberg and T. Turner. "Mental
Health Advocacy: Paradigom or Panacea?" Canada's Mental
Health 33, No. 3 (1985), 3-7.

Baker, David. Essential Duties, Reasonable Accommodation and
Constructive Discrimination: The Evolution of Human
Rights Protections for the Handicapped in Ontario.
Prepared for the Law Society of Upper Canada Human
Rights Program. Toronto, Ontario, June 24, 1983.

-----------. The Need for Updated Guardianship Legislation.
Outline of a Speech delivered to the Ontario
Psychogeriatric Association. Toronto, Ontario: October
18, 1982.

Baker, Michael. Manual for Personal Representatives.
Wellesley, MA: Organization for Services in the Public
Interest, Inc. 1976.

----------. A Report on the Personal Representative Service
System Demonstration Project in Harrisburg,
Pennsylvania. Newton Centre, MA: Organization for
Services in the Public Interest, Inc., 1979.

Baucom, Linda. Citizen Advocacy: How to Make it Happen. Luddock, TX: Research and Training Centre in Mental Retardation, 1980.

Baucom, Linda and Gerrard J. Bensberg. Advocacy Systems for Persons with Developmental Disabilities. Luddock, TX: Research and Training Centre in Mental Retardation, 1977.

Biklen, Douglas. Let Our Children Go: An Organization Manual for Advocates and Parents. Syracuse, NY: Human Policy Press, 1974.

Boyd, Neil. "Ontario's Treatment of the 'Criminally Insane' and the Potentially Dangerous: The Questionable Wisdom of Procedural Reform." Canadian Journal of Criminology 22, (1980), 151.

Bradley, V. Further Explorations of Advocacy Models for the Mentally Disabled. Human Services Research Institute. NIMH, 1982.

Brown, A.S. "Grassroots Advocacy for the Elderly in Small Rural Communities." The Gerontologist 25, No. 4 (1985), 417-423.

Browning, Philip. Advancing your Citizenship: Essays on Consumer Involvement of the Handicapped. OREG: University of Oregon, 1980.

Bruck, Lilly. Access: The Guide to a Better Life for Disabled Americans. NY: Random House, 1978.

California Instruction Television Consortium. Advocacy Folio: Way To Go Series. Baltimore, MD: University Park Press, 1978.

Campbell, Michael, for the Metropolitan Toronto Association for the Mentally Retarded. Lobbying For People. Toronto, ONT: Policorp, 1979.

Canadian Hearing Society. Access to Legal Services for Deaf and Hard of Hearing People. Toronto, ONT: September, 1982.

Carpenter, Rodney. "The Consumer Movement." In Disabled Persons in Canada 29-37. Terrence P. McLaughlin, ed. Ottawa, ONT: Health and Welfare Canada, 1981.

Crosson, A., ed. Advocacy and the Developmentally Disabled. Monograph No. 9. College of Education, University of Oregon, 1977. (This monograph contains a helpful annotated bibliography with respect to literature on advocacy up to 1977.)

Day, Shelagh. "Rights and Advocacy." The Canadian Journal on Mental Retardation (Winter, 1985), 3-10.

DeBro, Diana. Learning to Live with Disability: A Guidebook for Families. Falls Church, VA: Institute for Information Studies, 1980.

Decker, John. Providing Advocacy Services for Mental Patients: An On-Site Demonstration. Washington, D.C.: American Bar Association Commission on the Mentally Disabled, September 1979.

Desjardins, Charlotte, et al. How To Get Services By Being Assertive. Chicago, IL: Co-ordinating Council for Handicapped Children, 1980.

----------. How to Organize Effective Parent and Advocacy Groups and Move Bureaucracies. Chicago, IL: Co-ordinating Council for Handicapped Children, 1980.

Dickman, Irving and Dr. S. Gordon. One Miracle At A Time. New York, NY: Simon and Schuster Inc., 1985.

Dickerson, Martha Ufford. "Mental Handicap and Parenting: Rights and Responsibilities of Full Citizenship." The Canadian Journal on Mental Retardation 35, No. 2 (Spring 1985), 40-43.

Dybwad, Rosemary F. International Directory of Mental Retardation Resources. Washington, DC: Government Affairs Office, National Association for Retarded Citizens, 1979.

Ehrlich, P. "Elderly Health Advocacy Group: An Integrative Planning Model of Elderly Consumers and Service Deliverers." The Gerontologist 23, No. 6 (1983), 569-572.

Ferguson, Dianne L. "Parent Advocacy Network." The Exceptional Parent (March 1984), 41-5.

Forest, Marsha and Judy Snow. "Joshua Committee: An Advocacy Model". Journal of Leisurability (Winter 1983), 20-3.

Francis, Ruth. "Update on Volunteerism - The Citizen Advocacy Program." Journal of Leisurability (Spring 1984).

Freddolino, P. and P. Appelbaum. "Rights Protection and Advocacy: The Need to do More with Less." Hospital and Community Psychiatry 35, no. 4 (1984), 319-320.

Fritz, D. "The Administration on Aging as an Advocate: Progress, Problems and Perspective." The Gerontologist 19 (1979), 141-150.

Gardner, Nancy E.S. The Self-Advocacy Workbook. KANS: Kansas
    Centre for Mental Retardation and Human Development, UAF, The
    University of Kansas, 1980. This workbook has a companion
    guide: An Advisors Guide for Self Advocacy, by J. Jeff
    Woodyard.

Gelfand, D.E. and K. Olsen. The Aging Network. NY: New York
    Springer Publishing Company, 1980.

Gorski, Robert. "Assertiveness: A Training Program For Disabled
    Ohioans." Disabled U.S.A. The President's Committee on
    Employment of Handicapped (November 18, 1984), 35.

Hallgren, Betty and Annette Norsman. Life, Liberty and the Pursuit
    of Happiness: A Self Advocacy Curriculum" Downsview, ONT:
    National Institute on Mental Retardation, 1977.

Heath, Dennis L., Valerie Schaaf and Larry W. Talkinton. People
    First: Evaluation Toward Self-Advocacy. Toronto, ONT:
    Canadian Association for the Mentally Retarded and National
    Institute for the Mentally Retarded, 1978.

Herr, Stanley. Advocacy. Philadelphia, PA: U.S. Department of
    Health, Education and Welfare, 1980.

----------. Advocacy: Under the Developmental Disabilities Act.
    Philadelphia, PA: U.S. Department of Health, Education,
    Welfare, 1982.

----------. Rights and Advocacy for Retarded People. Toronto,
    ONT: DC Health Company, 1983.

----------. From Rights to Realities: Advocacy By and For
    Retarded People in the 1980's . Washington, D.C.: U.S.
    Department of Health, Education, and Welfare, Publication No.
    (OHDS) 79-21026.

Heyman, George M. Advocates Guide to New York Education Laws for
    the Mentally Retarded and Other Developmental Disabilities.
    NY: N.Y. State Association for the Mentally Retarded, 1976.

Hill, Karen. Helping You Helps Me: A Guide Book For Self-Help
    Groups. Ottawa, ONT: Canadian Council on Social
    Development, 1983. This book is aimed at people who want to
    start new self-help groups or improve existing groups. The
    main chapters are "Getting Started" and "Maintaining
    Momentum".

Hoppe, Paul. "How to Organize Self-Help Groups in the School."
    The Exceptional Parent 9, no. 4 (August 1979), E22-E23.

235

Hutchison, Peggy, John Lord, Harvey Savage, Anne Schnarr. Listening: Building a Framework for Support. Canadian Mental Health Association, August 1985.

Human Interaction Research Institutee. National Directory of Mental Health Advocacy Programs. Los Angeles, CAL: 1982.

Inlander, Chrles V. and the staff of the Pennsylvania Fellowship Plan. Citizen Advocacy: A Co-ordinator's Handbook. Pennsylvania, PA: The Institute for Research and Development in Retardation Inc., 1975.

Intagliata, James. "Improving the Quality of Community Care for the Chronically Mentally Disabled: The Role of Case Management." Schizophrenia Bulletin 8 (1982), 655.

Jarvis, Terry and Tannis. You Are Not Alone. London, ONT: Terry P. Jarvis, 1985.

Kemp, D. "Resident Advocates: A Mechanism for Protecting the Rights of Institutionalized Mentally Retarded." Journal of Mental Health Administration 11, no. 2 (1984), 48-53.

Kopolow, L.E. and H. Bloom, eds. Mental Health Advocacy: An Emerging Force in Consumers' Rights. U.S. Department of Health, Education, and Welfare, National Institute of Mental Health, 1977.

Levine, Bonnie and Crystal Garrioch. Monitoring: Examining Quality of Life for People with Mental Retardation. Toronto, ONT: Ontario Press, April 1984.

Litwin, H., W. Kaye and A. Monk. "Conflicting Orientations to Patient Advocacy in Long Term Care." The Gerontologist 24, no. 3, 275-279.

Lourie, Norman V. "The Many Faces of Advocacy/Operational Advocacy: Objective and Obstacles." In Advocacy for Child Mental Health, 69-91. N. Berlin, ed. NY: Brunner/Mazel, Inc., 1975.

Meador, Karen. "What's Left After Rawley? The Future Of Advocacy in Special Education." The Exceptional Parent (February 1983), 59-64, 94-142.

Milner, N. "The Symbols and Means of Advocacy." International Journal of Law and Psychiatry, 8 (1986), 1-17.

M.J.S. "Please Test Our Son: The Role of Parents in the Assessment Process." The Exceptional Parent (February 1983), 49-54.

Monk, A. and L. Kaye. "Patient Advocacy Services in Long Term Care Facilities: Ethnic Perspectives." Journal of Long Term Care Administration 12, no. 1 (1984) 5-10.

Monsor, Ellen. Family Advocacy: A Manual for Action. NY: Family Services Association of America, 1973.

Mullins, L.C., J.I. Kosberg and E.J. McCarthy. Advocacy Organizations for Nursing Home Residents: Final Results of a National Survey. Presented at the 37th Annual Scientific Meeting of the Gerontology Society of America. San Antonio, Texas, November 1984.

National Centre for Law and The Handicapped. A Parent's Guide to Ensuring the Educational Rights of Children. Southbend, IND: 1978.

National Task Force for Community Living. Community Living with Dignity. Downsview, ONT: Canadian Association for the Mentally Retarded, 1983.

Netting, F.E. and H.N. Hinds. "Volunteer Advocates in Long Term Care: Local Implementation of a Federal Mandate." The Gerontologist 24, no. 1 (1984), 13-15.

Norley, Dolores B. "The Care and Feeding of Legislators". The Exceptional Parent 11, no. 3 (June 1981), 44-45.

O'Brien, John and Wolf Wolfensberger. Standards for Citizen Advocacy Program Evaluation (Cape). Toronto, ONT: The Canadian Association for the Mentally Retarded, Test edition, reviewed in 1981.

O'Brien, John. Learning from Citizen Advocacy. GA: Georgia Advocacy Office Inc., 1987.

Olsen, Nancy. Leader's Guide for Rights and Responsibilities. Toronto, ONT: National Institute on Mental Retardation, 1979.

Ontario Human Rights Commission. A Guide to the Human Rights Code, 1981. (no date given).

Ontario Office for Senior Citizens' Affairs. A New Agenda: Health and Social Services Strategies for Ontario's Seniors. Toronto, ONT: June 1986.

Paschall, N.C., A.J. Konick and S.A. Ostrander. "Institutional Advocacy: Impact One Year After Legislative Change." Administration in Mental Health 10, no. 1 (1982), 136-147.

Paul, James, Ron Wiegerink and G.R. Neufeld. Advocacy: A Role for D.D. Councils. NC: Developmental Disabilities/Technical Assistance System, University of North Carolina.

Paul, J.L., S. Rosenthal, J. Adams and A. Ramsbotham. Advocacy: Resources and Approaches. Chapel Hill, NC: Developmental Disabilities Technical Assistance System, 1976.

Paul, J.L., G.R. Neufeld and J.W. Pelosi. Child Advocacy Within the System. Syracuse, NY: Syracuse University Press, 1977.

Paul, J.L. and R. Gregory. Developing an Advocacy System for Children. Special Education Theory Into Practice, April 1976.

Perreira, Diane. Advocates' Training Manual for Protecting the Rights of the Developmentally Disabled. New York, NY: Protection and Advocacy System for Developmental Disabilities, Inc., 1977 and 1982.

Perske, R. A Process of Screening and Guidance for Citizen Advocates. Toronto, ONT: National Institute on Mental Retardation, 1973.

----------. Listen Please: A Special Issue of Mental Retardation. Downsview, ONT: Canadian Association for the Mentally Retarded, April 1979.

Pincus, Jane Kate and Peggy Nelson Wegman. Helping Ourselves Find Help in Ourselves and Our Children. Boston's Women's Health Book Collective. NY: Random House Publishing, 1978.

Powell, P.S. The Plan for the Protection and Advocacy System for Persons with Developmental Disabilities in Georgia. Developmental Disabilities Office, H.E.W. Region IV.

President's Committee on Mental Retardation. Mental Retardation and the Law. Washington, DC: U.S. Government Printing Office, 1980.

Public Education Program, Metropolitan Toronto Association fo the Mentally Retarded. Lobbying For People. Toronto, ONT: Political and Corporate Relations - no date given.

Regan, John. "When Nursing Home Patients Complain: The Ombudsman or Patient Advocate." Georgetown Law Journal 65, (1977), 691.

Research Training Center in Mental Retardation. Action Through Advocacy. TX: Texas Tech. University, 1980.

Rhoades, C.M., P.L. Browning and E.J. Thorin. "Self-Help Advocacy Movement: A Promising Peer Support System for People with Mental Disabilities." Rehabilitation Literature 47, nos. 1-2 (1986), 2-7.

Rosenberg, Howard, Dennis G. Tesolowski and Rochelle J. Stein. "Advocacy: Education's Professional Responsibility to Handicapped Citizens." Education and Training of the Mentally Retarded. Lancaster, PA: Lancaster Press, December 1983.

Ross, E. Clarke. Public Policy Issues Affecting Services to Persons with Disabilities: A 1980 Perspective. Washington, DC: United Cerebral Palsy Associations, Inc., Governmental Activities Office, 1980.

Rude, Carolyn. Action Through Advocacy - A Manual for Training Volunteers. TX: Texas Research and Training Centre in Mental Retardation, Texas Tech. University, 1980.

Rude, Carolyn, Pamela A. Aiken. Advocacy in Residential Program. Lubbock, TX: Research and Training Centre in Mental Retardation, Texas Tech University, 1982.

Savage, Harvey S. Justice for Some. Downsview, ONT: National Institute on Mental Retardation, 1983.

Schwartz, Steven J., et al. Protecting the Rights and Enhancing the Dignity of People with Disabilities: Standards for Effective Legal Advocacy. Northampton, MASS: May 1982.

Shevin, Mayer. "Meaningful Parental Involvement in Long Range Educational Planning for Disabled Children." Education and Training of the Mentally Retarded. Lancaster, PA: Lancaster Press, February 1983.

Snider, R. and M. Howell. "Rights of Persons in Long Term Care Facilities." Journal of American Geriatrics Society 34, no. 2 (1986), 176.

Sonnenschein, Phyllis. "Parents and Professionals: An Uneasy Relationship." The Council for Exceptional Children, 1981.

Systems Research and Development Corporation. Review of Federal Regulations and Legislation Affecting Programs and Services to Persons With Developmental Disabilities. Research Triangle Park, NC: Author, 1979.

Turner, T., M.F. Madill and D. Solberg. "Patient Advocacy: The Ontario Experience." International Journal of Law and Psychiatry, 7 (1984), 329-350.

Weiner, John. "Judy Snow." In Not One Of The Crowd, 94-104.
    Toronto, ONT: Educational Communications Authority, 1981.

Wice, Betsy and Happy Fernandez. "Meeting the Bureaucracy Face to
    Face: Parent Power in the Philadelphia Schools." The
    Exceptional Parent (September 1985), 14-22.

Williams, Paul and Bonnie Shoultz. We Can Speak for Ourselves.
    London, ONT: Souvenir Press, 1982.

Wolfensberger, Wolf. A Balanced Multi-Component Advocacy/Protection
    Schema. Canadian Association for the Mentally Retarded, 1977.

----------. Citizen Advocacy Leadership Training Workshop.
    Downsview, ONT: National Institute for the Mentally Retarded,
    1970.

----------. Citizen Advocacy for the Handicapped, Impaired and
    Disadvantaged. An Overview. Washington, DC: Superintendent of
    Documents, U.S. Government Printing Office, 1972.

----------. Reflections on the Status of Citizen Advocacy.
    Downsview, ONT: National Institute on Mental Retardation and
    the Georgia Advocacy Office Inc., 1983.

----------. Voluntary Associations on Behalf of Societally Devalued
    and/or Handicapped People. Toronto, ONT: National Institute on
    Mental Retardation, 1984.

Wolfensberger, Wolf and Helen Zauha. Citizen Advocacy and Protective
    Services for the Impaired and Handicapped. Toronto, ONT:
    Macdonald-Downie, Ltd., for National Institute on Mental
    Retardation, 1973.

----------. "We Fill Two Advocacy Roles for a Foster Child", In
    Citizen Advocacy and Protective Services for the Handicapped,
    243-44. Downsview, ONT: National Institute on Mental
    Retardation, 1973.

Wolfensberger, Wolf and Bridget Moylan Brown. "Youth Advocacy." In
    Citizen Advocacy. Downsview, ONT: National Institute on Mental
    Retardation, 1973.

Woodyard, J. Jeff. An Advisor's Guidebook for Self-Advocacy.
    Lawrence, KANS: University of Kansas Press, 1980.

Worrell, Bill. "People First: A Perspective." The Canadian Journal
    on Mental Retaration 35, no. 3 (Summer, 1985), 37-42.

Zauha, Helen. Implementation of Citizen Advocacy to Date. Downsview, ONT: National Institute on Mental Retardation.

Zauha, H. and W. Wolfensberger. Funding, Governance and Safeguards of Citizen Advocacy Services. Toronto, ONT: National Institute on Mental Retardation, 1973.

Ziegenfuss, J.T., J. Charette and M. Guenin. "The Patients Rights Representative Program: Design of an Ombudsman Service for Mental Patients." Psychiatric Quarterly 56, no. 1 (1984), 3-11.

Zischka, P.C. and I. Jones. "Volunteer Community Representatives as Ombudsmen for the Elderly in Long Term Care Facilities." The Gerontologist 24, no. 1 (1984), 9-12.

Zwarun, Suzanne. "Sterilization and the Retarded: Who Decides?" Chatelaine (March 1986), 57, 140-146.